THE COMPLETE Instant Pot® COLLECTION

PHOTOGRAPHY BY
ERIN SCOTT

weldonowen

CONTENTS

Instant Pot Max
www.InstantPot.com
Pressure Cook
Sauté/ Brown
Rice
Steam
Slow Cook
Soup/ Broth
Canning
Yogurt
Pre-Heat
Pressure
Temperature
Keep Warm
Venting
Delay
Cancel
Start

INTRODUCTION

The Instant Pot® first burst onto the cooking scene in 2009, and there's every indication it has serious staying power. The multifaceted countertop kitchen appliance is loved by hundreds of thousands of home cooks who use it to transform economical cuts of meat into melt-in-your-mouth perfection; create one-pot pasta dishes on busy weeknights; cook nourishing soups; and prepare healthy staples like homemade stocks, cooked beans, and tender whole grains. And the Instant Pot®'s flexible functionality means you can retire your pressure cooker, slow cooker, rice cooker, and yogurt maker—freeing up a lot of countertop real estate, and streamlining your cooking, in the process.

With every cooking method at your fingertips, you can pressure cook, sauté, steam, slow cook, sous vide, air fry, bake, roast, broil, and dehydrate—just attach the pressure cooking lid or the air fryer lid, select a program, and have breakfast, lunch, dinner, or dessert on the table in minutes. Whether you've been using your Instant Pot® or air fryer for a while or a novice at both pressure cooking and air frying, this book is for you.

Arguably best in the Instant Pot® are large chunks of meat like pork shoulder for mouthwatering chile carnitas (page 178) and whole chickens perfect for Waldorf chicken salad (page 107). Soups, such as chicken enchilada stew (page 89) and coconut fish curry (page 96), become intensely delicious when cooked under pressure. Even crispy snacks and sides like hush puppies (page 63) and spring rolls (page 56) get perfectly "fried" in the Instant Pot with a fraction of the oil used in traditional frying. Did we mention that the Instant Pot® can keep food safely warm, so everyone in the clan can enjoy a healthy, hot meal, no matter when they get to the table? Yes, the Instant Pot® really is indispensable!

With over 175 recipes and some knowledge of the appliance's basic functions, Instant Pot®-ing will become your favorite kitchen technique. So let's get cooking!

INSTANT POT® PRIMER

Welcome to the new world of fast, even, and flavorful cooking. The Instant Pot Duo Crisp® and the Instant Pot Air Fryer Lid® combine the power of pressure cooking and the ease of air frying into one countertop machine.

HOW DOES IT WORK?

In a nutshell, the Instant Pot® cuts cooking to a fraction of the time, making long-simmering dishes at record speed. When pressure cooking, the tightly sealed pot boils liquid quickly, then traps the steam and generates pressure. With this method, heat is evenly, deeply, and quickly distributed.

Like pressure cooking, air frying (using the Instant Pot Duo Crisp® or the stand-alone Instant Pot Air Fryer Lid®) helps you save time and cook healthy meals—The air fryer lid relies on very hot, fast-blowing air to cook and crisp food, similar to the way a convection oven works. You can use it to cook food from fresh or frozen, or to crisp up a dish after it's been cooked on a pressure-cooking setting. Compared to a full-size oven, the Air Fryer Lid is also a fast, easy, and energy-efficient way to reheat and recrisp leftovers.

The recipes in this book were developed and tested using the Duo Plus and Duo Crisp 6-Quart Instant Pot®. If you've just purchased an Instant Pot®, read the user manual first to get comfortable with your model's specific parts, buttons, settings, and indicator lights. Here are some key points to know before you start.

FUNCTIONS & SETTINGS

Both lids correspond to their own set of smart programs. With the pressure cooking lid, you can use the smart programs to sauté, pressure cook, slow cook, steam, and sous vide. With the air fryer lid, you can air fry, roast, bake, broil, and dehydrate.

Sauté: This function allows you to sear meat before pressure cooking or after sous vide cooking, simmer stock, reduce liquid, and more, similar to how you use a sauté pan on the stovetop. It has three modes: Less is ideal for cooking bacon or other foods that might stick; Normal is best for simmering, thickening, and reducing liquids; and More is handy for browning meat. The timer automatically sets for 30 minutes, but when you need it on for longer than that, press the Sauté button after it shuts off and continue cooking. Never put the locking lid on while using this function.

Pressure Cook: There are two levels for pressure cooking, Hi and Lo. Most recipes call for the Hi setting. The Lo setting can be used for delicate foods like fish or eggs. Press the Pressure Level key or Adjust key (depending on your model) to adjust pressure levels, and the + and - keys to change the cooking time.

Slow Cook: This is a non–pressure cooking program, where the Less, Normal, and High modes correspond to the low, medium, and high settings of temperature-controlled slow cookers. It works similarly to a traditional slow cooker, cooking food slowly with more liquid than required for pressure cooking. Use this function to prepare your favorite slow-cooker recipes.

Steam: For this program, always use the steam rack that came with the pot or a metal or silicone steam basket. The food can scorch if it's not raised off the bottom of the pot.

Sous Vide: Sous vide cooking brings vacuum-sealed food to a precise temperature and maintains that heat for a long period of time to achieve high-quality, consistently delicious results. To use this program, you'll need tongs, an instant-read thermometer, and airtight or vacuum-sealed food pouches. Refer to the pot's manual for specific sous vide cooking guidelines.

Keep Warm/Cancel: These buttons, sometimes combined into one, turn off any cooking program so that you can switch to another program or end the cooking. The Keep Warm setting holds the food at a safe temperature for up to 10 hours.

Delay Start: This feature allows you to delay the start of cooking, which is particularly handy if you want to soak dried beans before cooking them. Delay Start may be applied to the Pressure Cook, Slow Cook, and Steam smart programs. To set a Delay Start timer, select a smart program and adjust the settings as you like, then press Delay Start. You can set Delay Start for a minimum of 10 minutes to a maximum of 24 hours.

Time Display: The countdown timer indicates cooking and Delay Start time in hours and minutes (05:20 is 5 hours, 20 minutes). The timer counts up while in Keep Warm.

Temperature/Pressure Display: The pressure cooking lid display indicates Lo (Low) or Hi (High) pressure or temperature level. For the sous vide smart program, the display specifies temperature in °F (Fahrenheit) or °C (Celsius). The air fryer lid indicates temperature in °F or °C.

PRESSURE RELEASE

On most 6-quart (6-L) models compatible with the air fryer lid, the steam release valve has two positions—Venting and Sealing. The pot can come up to pressure only when the lid is locked and the valve is set to Sealing. On the Duo Crisp, the steam release value is automatically set to sealing. As a safety precaution, you will not be able to open the lid unless the valve is switched to Venting (on the 6-quart/6-L models) or the Quick Release Button is pressed (on the Duo Crisp).

There are two main ways to release the pressure when the program ends:

Quick Release: Manually turn the valve to Venting or press the Quick Release Button as soon as the cooking program has ended. Use an oven mitt, wooden spoon, or kitchen tongs when moving the valve and do not put your face over or near the valve.

Natural Release: The pot will lose pressure on its own as it cools. The time needed for a natural pressure release varies depending on the volume of food and liquid in the pot and can be as quick as a few minutes or up to 30 minutes. Once the program has finished, the pot defaults to the Keep Warm setting and will remain there for up to 10 hours.

You can also combine the two releases, letting the pressure release naturally for a few minutes and then turning the valve to Venting or pressing the Quick Release Button to release any residual steam.

PRESSURE COOKING PRACTICALITIES

- Unlike a slow cooker, which allows liquids to evaporate and reduce during cooking, a pressure cooker is completely sealed and therefore loses no steam during cooking. To come up to pressure, the pot needs enough steam buildup, which is created from the amount of liquid in the recipe.
- Be sure to respect the fill line: to leave room for the steam buildup, the inner pot should never be more than two-thirds full.
- The steam release valve might feel a bit wobbly when switching between Venting and Sealing.
- The program timer will not start until the machine has come up to pressure.
- All of the pressure needs to be released before you can remove the lid from the pot.

AIR FRYING PROGRAMS

Air Fry: The most common air frying program, this setting produces food with a crispy exterior, such as French fries, chicken wings, potatoes, breaded cutlets, meatballs, fish and seafood, tofu, doughnuts, fritters, and more.

Roast: The Roast setting is best for large cuts of meat.

Broil: Using direct, top-down heating, Broil yields juicy chicken and beef dishes. You can place foods for broiling either in the air fryer basket or on the broil/dehydrating tray, which brings them closer to the pot's heating element.

Bake: This setting is ideal for cakes, quick breads, brownies, and cookies. If baking in the multilevel air fryer basket, line the interior with parchment paper for recipes involving loose batter. (You can also purchase air fryer liners, which have tiny holes to help the air circulate.) If using a baking dish, place the rack on the bottom of the inner pot, then place the dish on the rack in the inner pot. Leave about 1 inch (2.5 cm) of space around all sides of the dish to allow heat to circulate evenly.

Dehydrate: This program applies low heat over a long period of time to safely dry out foods. Use it for preparing fruit leather, jerky, and dried fruits and vegetables.

MAKE IT A MEAL: POT-IN-POT Cooking

In Instant Pot® parlance, pot-in-pot cooking refers to a main dish, such as chicken or pork chops, cooking directly in the Instant Pot®, while a side dish—rice, sweet potatoes, or polenta—cooks in a steamer basket or in a small baking dish or pan set on a tall trivet above the main dish.

Two tools are useful for this technique:

- Oven-safe baking dish 6–7 inches (15–18 cm) in diameter, or a round metal pan 7 inches (18 cm) in diameter, with a 6-cup (1.4-L) capacity, that fits into the inner pot.
- Metal trivet with tall (2-inch/5-cm) feet

Baking dishes and tall trivets are inexpensive and easy to find online and in kitchenware stores. Just search for "Instant Pot® baking dish" and "Instant Pot® tall trivet" and you'll find lots of options.

TOOLS OF THE TRADE

The Instant Pot® is an incredible appliance all by itself, but a few additional items are used in the recipes in this book to expand its possibilities.

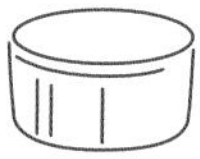

1½-quart (1.5-L) round oven-safe baking dish for frittatas and more "baked" dishes

Wire-mesh or silicone steaming basket for eggs and vegetables

Sturdy kitchen tongs for browning meat, transferring ingredients from the pot, and safely lifting a baking dish out of the pot

Standard blender or immersion blender for pureeing soups and baby food

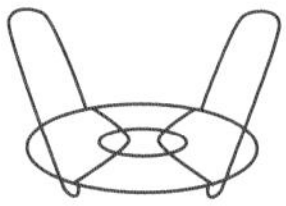

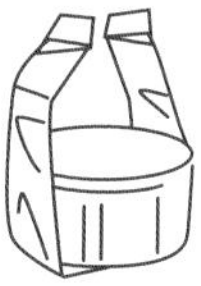

Steam rack with handles to raise and lower pans and dishes, as well as for cooking eggs (Note: If your model does not have handles, create a sling by folding a long piece of aluminum foil into thirds so it can rest underneath the steam rack and extend up the sides like handles.)

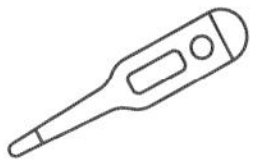

Digital instant-read thermometer for checking meat doneness

TIPS FOR INSTANT POT® SUCCESS

KEEP YOUR POT CLEAN

Just like your stove and pans, your Instant Pot® must be cleaned. After every use, wash the inner pot, detach and wash the condensation cup on the back of the device, the sealing ring, and the lid. Clean the recessed edge of the pot with a rolled-up paper towel dipped in hot soapy water.

GET THE POT HOT

To sauté and brown, it's best to add the oil to the pot and let it get hot (it will shimmer) before adding ingredients. The LCD screen will eventually display "hot," but the oil is usually ready for sautéing your ingredients before this.

DON'T OVERCROWD WHEN BROWNING MEAT

The objective of browning is to create a flavorful base for sauces and broths by caramelizing the natural sugars in meat. If you add too much meat to the pot, it will begin to steam instead of brown. In this book, you'll often be instructed to brown just a handful of the meat; this is sufficient to create loads of flavor and skips the tedium of browning every last bit of meat, saving lots of time.

ADJUST COOK TIME TO ALTITUDES

If you are cooking at 3,000 feet and are using the pressure cooking programs on your Instant Pot®, you will need to increase the cook times by 5 percent. For every 1,000 feet above 3,000, increase the cook times by an additional 5 percent, so that cook times would increase by 10 percent at 4,000 feet, 15 percent at 5,000 feet, and so on.

DEGLAZE

The Instant Pot® will display a "burn" notice and interrupt the cooking cycle if the sensors detect ingredients are burning or sticking on the bottom of the pot. To avoid this, make sure to deglaze and scrape up any browned bits from the bottom of the pot after sautéing or browning, and follow the recipe to add the correct amount of stock, water, or other liquid.

DON'T DROWN THE DISH

In most cases, ½–1 cup (120–240 ml) of liquid is enough to bring the Instant Pot® up to pressure. Keep in mind that lots of ingredients contribute moisture as they cook—a 2-lb (1-kg) chuck roast will add up to 2½ cups (600 ml) of liquid, and broccoli is about 90% water. Follow the rigorously tested recipes in this book and you'll never have to give it another thought.

STAND BY

The Instant Pot® is great because once the food is in the pot, you can safely leave it unattended. That said, it's wise to hang around until the appliance has fully come up to pressure, especially if you're riffing on a new recipe or are inexperienced with pressure cooking. Once the cook time starts to count down on the screen, you can let the Instant Pot® do its thing and go about your busy day.

THICKEN AT THE END

Because the Instant Pot® cooks food in a sealed system, sauces won't reduce as they would in stove-top recipes. Adding thickeners like cornstarch or flour at the start of pressure cooking can cause clumping and settling, and you may get the dreaded "burn" notice. It's best to thicken sauces and gravies right before serving. You can also thicken a sauce by simmering it on the Sauté function with the lid off.

AIR FRYING HOW-TOS

Some recipes in this book "fry" a variety of foods with a fraction of the oil used in traditional frying and offer creative ways for using the high-powered convection technology to cook a selection of unexpected dishes. These guidelines will help you master air frying in no time.

The Instant Pot Duo Crisp + Air Fryer® all-in-one machine and the stand-alone Instant Pot Air Fryer Lid® use rapid air circulation to crisp or cook food, giving your meals all the rich, crispy flavor of deep-frying, with little or no oil. There are a couple of ways to use the air fryer lid:

- Give your dish a crunchy, golden finish after cooking with the Pressure Cook, Slow Cook, Steam, or Sous Vide smart programs.
- Cook your dish entirely using the air fryer lid with the Air Fry, Roast, Bake, or Broil smart programs.
- Give the food room to breathe and don't overcrowd. For most recipes, place the ingredients in a single layer in the air fryer basket, making sure there is space for the hot air to circulate. If everything doesn't fit in one layer, cook in batches, as for chicken cutlets and meatballs.
- Some baked recipes call for a ceramic dish or baking pan set on the steam rack instead of in the air fryer basket. Any oven-safe cookware can be used in the inner pot.
- After lifting the air fryer lid off the cooker base, always place it on the protection pad provided. Do not rest the lid on a countertop or on its power cord. To store your air fryer lid, flip the protective pad over so the grooved side faces up. Align the back of the air fryer lid with OPEN on the protective pad, then turn the air fryer lid clockwise to the lock position.
- Depending on the smart program, the air fryer lid may beep partway through to remind you to turn the food. If you don't lift the lid, the air fryer will continue cooking at the selected temperature until the designated time is up. The recipes in this book indicate whether you should flip or rotate the food or cook it undisturbed.
- An air fryer works similarly to a powerful convection oven. To adapt an existing recipe from a conventional oven, a rule of thumb is to decrease the temperature by 25°F (-4°C) and reduce the cooking time by 25 percent.
- Invest in an instant-read meat thermometer to ensure food is cooked safely and doesn't dry out. Since cuts of meat vary, a thermometer is the only way to guarantee it is cooked correctly and not overdone.

TYPES OF OIL

Cooking oil sprays are available in many types, including canola, vegetable, olive, coconut, and avocado oil. The most commonly used sprays in this book are canola and olive oil. Just as with other cooking methods, these oils stand up well to high temperatures. Opt for canola oil spray when you want a neutral-flavored oil to blend in with food and use olive oil to enhance the flavors. You can use store-bought oil sprays or make your own with a spray bottle or aerosol mister. Unless otherwise noted in a recipe, be generous with oil sprays. The oil acts as a barrier between the fast-circulating hot air and your food, so it not only helps to create a golden brown color and crispy texture on the outside, but also keeps food moist inside.

Fried Banana Egg Rolls
(page 259)

BREAKFAST

Cinnamon French Toast with Mixed Berries

Buttery brioche or challah provide the perfect pillowy texture for a lush breakfast studded with fresh berries (cinnamon-twist challah will take this dish to the next level). You can prepare it the night before, let it set in the fridge overnight, and cook it in the morning for an effortless brunch.

SERVES 6

Unsalted butter, for greasing

3 large eggs

½ cup (120 ml) heavy cream

½ cup (120 ml) milk

⅓ cup (70 g) granulated sugar

½ teaspoon ground cinnamon

1½ teaspoons pure vanilla extract

¼ teaspoon kosher salt

½ teaspoon finely grated lemon zest

¾ lb (340 g) brioche or challah bread, cut into 2-inch (5-cm) cubes

1 cup (140 g) mixed berries, such as blueberries, blackberries, and raspberries

2 cups (475 ml) water

Confectioners' sugar, for serving (optional)

Grease a 1½-qt (1.5-L) round ceramic baking dish with butter.

In a medium bowl, whisk together the eggs, cream, milk, granulated sugar, cinnamon, vanilla, salt, and lemon zest. Arrange one layer of bread cubes on the bottom of the prepared baking dish so they nestle in snugly. Scatter half the berries on top, followed by a second layer of bread cubes and berries. Pour the egg mixture over the top and press lightly to help it absorb into the bread. Cover with aluminum foil and refrigerate for at least 1 hour or up to overnight.

Pour the water into the Instant Pot® and place the baking dish on the steam rack. Using the handles, lower the baking dish and steam rack into the pot. Lock the lid in place and turn the valve to Sealing. Press the Pressure Cook button and set the cook time for 30 minutes at high pressure.

Let the steam release naturally for 15 minutes, then turn the valve to Venting to quick-release any residual steam. Carefully remove the lid and, using the steam rack handles, lift out the baking dish. Let the French toast cool slightly, then dust with confectioners' sugar, if using. Spoon it onto individual plates and serve warm.

BONUS STEP *After removing it from the pot, sprinkle the French toast with 1 tablespoon of turbinado sugar and bake in a preheated 400°F (200°C) oven for 10 minutes. The crispy top will complement the gooey center, creating the perfect texture contrast in every bite.*

Yogurt Parfaits

The Instant Pot® is the secret weapon for making yogurt at home, creating creamy, full-fat yogurt that is significantly less tangy than store-bought varieties. Layered with your favorite seeds, nuts, and fruit, the almost sweet-tasting yogurt takes on a decidedly treat-like appeal.

SERVES 4

8 cups (2 L) whole milk

2 tablespoons plain yogurt

FOR SERVING

Sunflower seeds, pepitas, toasted sliced almonds, chopped pecans, granola, puffed quinoa, and/or toasted coconut flakes

Fresh or dried stone fruit, fresh or dried berries

Pour the milk into the Instant Pot®. Lock the lid in place and turn the valve to Sealing. Press the Yogurt button until the screen says "Boil" and cook until the milk reaches 180°F (82°C), about 25 minutes. Have ready an ice-water bath in the sink. Carefully remove the lid and check the milk temperature with an instant-read thermometer. If it is not 180°F (82°C), press the Cancel button to reset the program, then select Sauté and heat until the milk temperature reaches 180°F (82°C). Transfer the inner pot to the ice-water bath, then stir the milk until it cools to 110°F (43°C), about 10 minutes. Transfer 1 cup (240 ml) of the milk to a small bowl, whisk in the yogurt until smooth, then return the milk-yogurt mixture to the pot. Whisk until blended.

Return the inner pot to the Instant Pot® housing. Lock the lid in place; the valve can be turned to Sealing or Venting. Press the Cancel button to reset the program, then press the Yogurt button and set the cook time for 10 hours. When the yogurt is ready (the screen will read "Yogt"), carefully remove the lid, use pot holders to lift out the inner pot, cover it with plastic wrap, and refrigerate until the yogurt sets, about 4 hours. Do not stir at this point.

When the yogurt is set, line a large fine-mesh sieve with 4 layers of cheesecloth, place the sieve over a bowl, spoon the yogurt into the sieve, and refrigerate for 2 hours to drain.

To serve, spoon some of the yogurt into the bottom of 4 medium-size glasses or jars. Top with a layer of seeds, nuts, and/or grains, followed by a layer of fruit. Repeat to fill all glasses.

Steel-Cut Oats with Three Toppings

Authentic steel-cut oatmeal has never been easier—no soaking or stirring required! Mix and match toppings as you like, or create savory breakfast oats by adding Soft-Boiled Eggs (page 263), sautéed greens, and grated Parmesan cheese on top.

MAKES ABOUT 4 CUPS (1 L) • SERVES 4

1 cup (185 g) steel-cut oats

1 cup (240 ml) milk of your choice (dairy, nut, coconut)

2 cups (475 ml) water

FOR BANANA-CINNAMON TOPPING

1 banana, sliced and tossed with 1 tablespoon sugar and 1 teaspoon cinnamon

FOR CHOCOLATE TOPPING

½ cup (3 oz/85 g) semisweet chocolate chips or shavings, plus cocoa powder for dusting

FOR APPLE-MAPLE-PECAN TOPPING

1 apple, cut into ¼-inch (6-mm) slices; ½ cup (60 g) chopped pecans; 2 tablespoons maple syrup, for drizzling

Combine the oats, milk, and water in the Instant Pot® and stir to mix well. Lock the lid in place and turn the valve to Sealing. Press the Pressure Cook button and set the cook time for 10 minutes at high pressure.

Let the steam release naturally for about 12 minutes, then turn the valve to Venting to quick-release any residual steam. Carefully remove the lid. Stir to combine the oats with any remaining liquid. To serve, spoon the oatmeal into individual bowls and top as desired.

Egg Cups with Spinach & Sun-Dried Tomatoes

These individual egg cups are the perfect size for a breakfast on the go. You can add any of your favorite vegetables in place of the spinach and sun-dried tomatoes used here, as long as you cook any heartier veggie such as broccoli or kale in advance. For a lighter alternative, sub in egg whites for half of the eggs.

SERVES 4

Nonstick cooking spray

8 eggs

1 cup (60 g) chopped spinach

¼ cup (25 g) sun-dried tomatoes, chopped

¼ cup (40 g) crumbled goat cheese

1 tablespoon chopped chives

Kosher salt and freshly ground black pepper

2 cups (475 ml) water

Grease four 6-oz (180-ml) mason jars or ramekins with nonstick cooking spray.

In a medium bowl, whisk the eggs. Stir in the spinach, tomatoes, goat cheese, chives, ½ teaspoon salt, and ¼ teaspoon pepper. Pour the egg mixture into the prepared jars, dividing it evenly. Cover each with aluminum foil.

Pour the water into the Instant Pot® and place the mason jars on the steam rack. Using the handles, lower the jars and steam rack into the pot. Lock the lid in place and turn the valve to Sealing. Press the Pressure Cook button and set the cook time for 5 minutes at low pressure.

When the eggs have finished cooking, turn the valve to Venting to quick-release the steam. Carefully remove the lid and, using the steam rack handles, lift out the jars.

Serve warm, or seal with the mason jar lids (or plastic wrap) and store in the refrigerator for up to 3 days.

Potato, Prosciutto & White Cheddar Frittata

Think of this flavor-packed frittata as a super creamy quiche without all the fuss. Naturally gluten-free without a crust, it's a crowd-pleasing brunch or lunch dish paired with fresh greens (and don't forget the mimosas!).

SERVES 6

2 tablespoons unsalted butter, plus more for greasing

8 large eggs

¾ cup (180 ml) whole milk

Kosher salt and freshly ground black pepper

1 large shallot, sliced

1 medium russet potato, peeled and cut into ½-inch (12-mm) cubes

3 oz (90 g) prosciutto, chopped

1 cup (115 g) shredded white Cheddar cheese

2 cups (475 ml) water

Grease a 1½-qt (1.5-L) round ceramic baking dish with butter. In a large bowl, whisk together the eggs, milk, ¼ teaspoon salt, and ¼ teaspoon pepper. Set aside.

Select Sauté on the Instant Pot® and heat the 2 tablespoons butter. Add the shallot and cook until just softened, 1 minute. Add the potatoes and ¼ teaspoon salt and cook, stirring occasionally with a wooden spoon and scraping up any browned bits, until the potatoes have started to soften and brown in some spots, about 4 minutes. Add the prosciutto and cook for 1 minute.

Press the Cancel button to reset the program. Transfer the potato mixture to the egg mixture and stir to combine. Fold in the cheese. Pour into the prepared baking dish. Cover with aluminum foil.

Pour the water into the Instant Pot® and place the baking dish on the steam rack. Using the handles, lower the baking dish and steam rack into the pot. Lock the lid in place and turn the valve to Sealing. Press the Pressure Cook button and set the cook time for 17 minutes at high pressure.

Let the steam release naturally for 15 minutes, then turn the valve to Venting to quick-release any residual steam. Carefully remove the lid and, using the steam rack handles, lift out the baking dish. Let the frittata cool slightly before cutting it into wedges and serving. Alternatively, remove the entire frittata from the baking dish by sliding a butter knife along the edges to loosen it. Place a plate on top of the baking dish, invert it, and shake gently to loosen the frittata onto the plate. Using a spatula, flip the frittata right-side-up onto the plate. Cut into wedges and serve.

For a meatless meal, you can skip the prosciutto and adjust the salt to ½ teaspoon during the sauté step.

If you prefer firmer yolks, adjust the cooking time to 2 minutes at low pressure, or more for completely set centers.

Baked Eggs with Creamy Spinach & Ham

This easy all-in-one breakfast is the perfect companion to a thick slice of toasted sourdough or country bread. You can skip the ham, or try it with Canadian bacon or crispy pancetta instead.

SERVES 4

4 tablespoons (½ stick/60 g) unsalted butter

1 tablespoon chopped shallot

4 oz (115 g) sliced ham, cut into ½-inch (12-mm) pieces

1 lb (450 g) baby spinach

⅓ cup (75 ml) heavy cream

Kosher salt and freshly ground black pepper

4 large eggs

FOR SERVING

Chopped fresh flat-leaf parsley (optional); crusty bread

Select Sauté on the Instant Pot® and heat 2 tablespoons of the butter. Add the shallot and cook, stirring occasionally, until just softened, about 1 minute. Add the ham and cook, stirring occasionally, for 2 minutes. Add the remaining butter and the spinach and cook until the spinach is wilted, about 5 minutes. Add the cream and ½ teaspoon salt and cook until most of the liquid has been reduced, about 15 minutes. Add ¼ teaspoon pepper and taste, adjusting seasoning as desired.

Press the Cancel button to reset the program. Make four wells in the spinach and carefully crack one egg into each well. Lock the lid in place and turn the valve to Sealing. Press the Pressure Cook button and set the cook time for 1 minute at low pressure.

Turn the valve to Venting to quick-release the steam. When the steam stops, carefully remove the lid. Transfer each egg on a bed of spinach to a plate, top with parsley, if using, and more pepper, and serve with a slice of crusty bread.

Quinoa & Egg Breakfast Bowl

This warm, flavorful, and protein-packed grain bowl cooks in minutes, making it a powerful breakfast or midday meal. Prepare the toppings while the quinoa is in the pot, then arrange them over the bowls when it is ready.

SERVES 4

1 cup (180 g) quinoa (red, white, or mixed), rinsed

1¼ cups (300 ml) water

½ teaspoon salt

FOR SERVING

4 soft- or hard-boiled eggs (page 263)

Cherry tomatoes, halved

Sliced avocado

Black sesame seeds or "everything but the bagel" seasoning

Flaked sea salt and freshly ground black pepper

Put the quinoa, water, and salt in the Instant Pot®. Stir to combine.

Lock the lid in place and turn the valve to Sealing. Press the Pressure Cook button and set the cook time for 1 minute at high pressure.

Let the steam release naturally for 10 minutes, then turn the valve to Venting to quick-release any residual steam. Carefully remove the lid and fluff the quinoa with a fork.

To serve, divide the quinoa evenly among 4 bowls and place one egg on top of each bowl. Top the quinoa with the tomatoes, avocado, and seeds, sprinkle with salt and pepper, and serve right away.

Green Veggie Frittata

Kale, zucchini, and a trio of green herbs contribute fresh flavor to this hearty breakfast. Cut the frittata into wedges to serve as part of a weekend brunch, reserving any leftovers for easy grab-and-go breakfasts through the week.

SERVES 6

Unsalted butter or cooking spray, for greasing

8 large eggs

¾ cup (180 ml) whole milk

Kosher salt and freshly ground black pepper

1 tablespoon canola or avocado oil

1 large shallot, sliced

4 oz (115 g) kale, chopped

2 cups (475 ml) plus 3 tablespoons water

1 zucchini, thinly sliced

1 tablespoon chopped fresh flat-leaf parsley

1 tablespoon chopped fresh dill

1 tablespoon minced fresh chives

1 cup (120 g) shredded mozzarella cheese

Grease a 1½-qt (1.5-L) round ceramic baking dish with butter or cooking spray. In a large bowl, whisk together the eggs, milk, ½ teaspoon salt, and ¼ teaspoon pepper. Set aside.

Select Sauté on the Instant Pot® and heat the oil. Add the shallot and cook until just softened, 1 minute. Add the kale, ¼ teaspoon salt, and 2 tablespoons of the water and cook, stirring occasionally with a wooden spoon and scraping up any browned bits, until the kale has started to soften and brown in some spots, about 3 minutes. Add the zucchini and 1 tablespoon water and cook for 3 minutes more.

Press the Cancel button to reset the program. Transfer the vegetable mixture to the egg mixture and stir to combine. Fold in the herbs and cheese. Pour into the prepared baking dish. Cover with aluminum foil.

Pour the 2 cups (475 ml) water into the Instant Pot® and place the baking dish on the steam rack. Using the handles, lower the baking dish and steam rack into the pot. Lock the lid in place and turn the valve to Sealing. Press the Pressure Cook button and set the cook time for 17 minutes at high pressure.

Let the steam release naturally for 10 minutes, then turn the valve to Venting to quick-release any residual steam. Carefully remove the lid and, using the steam rack handles, lift out the baking dish. Let the frittata cool slightly before cutting it into wedges and serving. Alternatively, remove the entire frittata from the baking dish by sliding a butter knife along the edges to loosen it. Place a plate on top of the baking dish, invert it, and shake gently to loosen the frittata onto the plate. Using a spatula, flip the frittata right-side up onto the plate. Cut into wedges and serve.

Zucchini Bread

Cooking with steam heat and adding coconut oil to the batter results in an evenly moist cake with just the right amount of sweetness. Source a 6-cup (1.5-L) Bundt pan online, or try a 7-inch (18-cm) springform pan in a pinch.

SERVES 6–8

Nonstick cooking spray

1½ cups (6½ oz/175 g) all-purpose flour

2 teaspoons baking powder

1 teaspoon baking soda

1½ teaspoons cinnamon

½ teaspoon nutmeg

½ teaspoon salt

2 eggs

½ cup (120 ml) coconut oil, melted and cooled

1 cup (215 g) firmly packed brown sugar

1 teaspoon vanilla extract

2 medium zucchini, grated, excess water drained on a paper towel (about 2 cups/225 g grated)

2 cups (475 ml) water

Grease a 6-cup (1.5-L) Bundt pan with nonstick cooking spray.

In a small bowl, whisk together the flour, baking powder, baking soda, cinnamon, nutmeg, and salt. In a medium bowl, whisk together the eggs, coconut oil, brown sugar, and vanilla. Fold in the zucchini using a rubber spatula. Gently fold the flour mixture into the egg mixture, being careful not to overmix the batter. Pour into the prepared pan and cover with aluminum foil.

Pour the water into the Instant Pot® and place the Bundt pan on the steam rack. Using the handles, lower the pan and steam rack into the pot. Lock the lid in place and turn the valve to Sealing. Press the Pressure Cook button and set the cook time for 35 minutes at high pressure.

Let the steam release naturally for 10 minutes, then turn the valve to Venting to quick-release any residual steam. Carefully remove the lid and, using the steam rack handles, lift out the Bundt pan. Let the bread cool slightly before using an offset spatula to gently loosen the edges and remove it from the pan.

Cut into slices and serve.

Maple-Walnut Banana Bread

If your bananas aren't ripe, tuck them into a paper bag, add an apple, and close the top loosely. This combo increases the production of ethylene gas—the invisible gas that promotes ripening—so your bananas will be ready in a day or two.

SERVES 8–10

½ cup (4 oz/120 g) unsalted butter, at room temperature

½ cup (100 g) firmly packed light brown sugar

2 large eggs, whisked

2 teaspoons vanilla paste or vanilla extract

½ cup (110 ml) maple syrup

3 ripe bananas, peeled and mashed

¼ cup (60 ml) buttermilk

2 cups (9 oz/240 g) all-purpose flour

1 teaspoon baking soda

1 teaspoon baking powder

1 teaspoon ground cinnamon

2 teaspoons kosher salt

¾ cup (90 g) chopped walnuts

1½ cups (350 ml) water

Lightly spray a 6-inch (15-cm) springform pan with nonstick cooking spray. In a stand mixer fitted with the paddle attachment, beat together the butter and sugar on medium speed until smooth and light. On low speed, add the eggs and vanilla and beat until incorporated. Then beat in ¼ cup (55 ml) of the maple syrup, the bananas, and buttermilk until blended.

In a bowl, whisk together the flour, baking soda, baking powder, cinnamon, and salt. With the mixer on low speed, gradually pour the flour mixture into the butter mixture, beating just until fully incorporated. Fold in the walnuts. Transfer to the prepared pan and smooth the top. Cover the pan with aluminum foil, crimping the edges.

Pour the water into the Instant Pot®. Place the springform pan on the steam rack. Using the rack handles, lower the pan into the pot. Lock the lid in place and turn the valve to Sealing. Press the Pressure Cook button and set the cook time for 55 minutes at high pressure.

Let the steam release naturally for 15 minutes, then turn the valve to Venting to quick-release any residual steam. Carefully remove the lid and transfer the springform pan to a cooling rack. Remove the foil and let the bread cool in the pan for about 5 minutes.

To serve, remove the pan sides and brush the remaining ¼ cup (55 ml) maple syrup on the warm bread. Serve warm or at room temperature.

Savory French Toast

Layered with sautéed asparagus and mushrooms then covered with a rich, herb-infused egg mixture, cubes of bread take on a dense, almost custard-like, texture.

SERVES 4–6

Unsalted butter or cooking spray, for greasing

3 large eggs

2 cups (475 ml) whole milk

2 tablespoons chopped fresh chives

1 tablespoon chopped fresh basil

1 teaspoon freshly grated lemon zest

¼ teaspoon freshly grated nutmeg

Kosher salt and freshly ground black pepper

1 tablespoon canola or avocado oil

6 oz (180 g) asparagus, cut into 1-inch (2.5-cm) pieces

6 oz (180 g) cremini or white button mushrooms, sliced

1 teaspoon chopped fresh thyme leaves

8 oz (250 g) day-old baguette or country bread, cut into 1-inch (2.5-cm) cubes

2 cups (475 ml) water

Freshly grated Parmesan cheese (optional)

Grease a 1½-qt (1.5-L) ceramic baking dish with butter or cooking spray.

In a medium bowl, whisk together the eggs, milk, chives, basil, lemon zest, nutmeg, ¼ teaspoon salt, and ¼ teaspoon pepper. Set aside.

Select Sauté on the Instant Pot® and heat the oil. Add the asparagus, mushrooms, thyme, and ½ teaspoon salt and cook until the asparagus stems are bright green and the mushrooms begin to turn golden brown, about 5 minutes. Transfer to a plate. Press Cancel to reset the program.

Arrange one-third of the bread cubes in a single layer in the prepared baking dish. Layer half of the vegetable mixture on top. Place another third of the bread cubes in another layer on top, followed by the remaining vegetable mixture. Layer the remaining bread cubes on top and pour the egg mixture over all, pressing down gently so that the bread absorbs the liquid. Cover with aluminum foil and refrigerate for at least 1 hour or up to overnight.

Pour the water into the Instant Pot® and place the baking dish on the steam rack. Using the handles, lower the dish and steam rack into the pot. Lock the lid in place and turn the valve to Sealing. Press the Pressure Cook button and set the cook time for 30 minutes at high pressure.

Let the steam release naturally for 15 minutes, then turn the valve to Venting to quick-release any residual steam. Carefully remove the lid and, using the steam rack handles, lift out the dish. Transfer to a cooling rack, remove the foil, and let cool slightly. Cut into wedges and serve.

BONUS STEP *After removing it from the pot, sprinkle the savory French toast with Parmesan cheese and bake in a preheated 400°F (200°C) oven until golden brown, 8–10 minutes.*

Broccoli & Everything Bagel Strata

This lovely bread-and-egg casserole, which features savory "everything" bagels, Cheddar, and broccoli, is equally at home on the breakfast and the dinner table. It's vegetarian, but feel free to add a bit of cooked Italian sausage, diced ham, or crumbled bacon if you'd like.

SERVES 4–6

3 "everything" bagels (¾ lb/340 g), cut into ¼-inch (6-mm) pieces

8 oz (225 g) broccoli crowns, finely chopped

2 green onions, chopped

6 large eggs

1¼ cups (300 ml) half-and-half or whole milk

1½ teaspoons finely grated lemon zest

½ teaspoon ground nutmeg

Kosher salt and black pepper

½ cup (60 g) grated Cheddar cheese

Spray a 7-inch (18-cm) round metal pan with a 6-cup (1.4-L) capacity thoroughly with nonstick cooking spray. Spray a 12-inch (30-cm) length of aluminum foil with cooking spray.

In a large bowl, toss together the bagels, broccoli, and green onions and transfer to the prepared baking dish. In a medium bowl, whisk together the eggs, half-and-half, lemon zest, nutmeg, ¾ teaspoon salt, and a few grinds of pepper. Gradually pour the egg mixture over the bagel mixture, pressing down with a spatula so the bagels will absorb the eggs. Sprinkle with the cheese. Cover the dish tightly with the prepared foil, sprayed-side down.

Pour 2 cups (475 ml) water into the Instant Pot®. Place a trivet with tall (2-inch/5-cm) feet in the pot and place the dish on the trivet.

Lock the lid in place and turn the valve to Sealing. Press the Pressure Cook button and set the cook time for 15 minutes at high pressure.

When the cooking time is up, let the steam release naturally for 15 minutes, then turn the valve to Venting to quick-release any residual steam. Carefully remove the lid.

Blot the top of the foil with a paper towel to absorb excess moisture. Using tongs, transfer the dish to a heatproof surface. Remove the foil, cut the strata into wedges, and serve.

Jam-Filled Brioche Doughnuts

Jelly doughnuts, a highly coveted treat among the assorted-doughnut box, get a makeover that turns them into an everyday treat. Allow time for the dough to rest overnight and then proof once more the next day.

SERVES 6

1¼ teaspoons active dry yeast

3 tablespoons water

1 large egg, lightly beaten

1½ cups (6½ oz/185 g) bread flour

3 tablespoons sugar

1 teaspoon kosher salt

Grated zest of ½ lemon

4 tablespoons (2 oz/60 g) unsalted butter, cut into 4 pieces, at room temperature, plus 2 tablespoons unsalted butter, melted

1 cup (10 oz/285 g) Strawberry Jam (page 275 or store-bought)

Confectioners' sugar, for dusting

In a large bowl, stir together the yeast, water, and egg. In a medium bowl, whisk together the flour, sugar, salt, and lemon zest. Add the flour mixture to the yeast mixture and use your fingers or a bowl scraper to mix until combined; it will be messy and sticky. Transfer the mixture to a work surface and knead until it starts to come together and feel like dough, 5–8 minutes. (Alternatively, mix the dough in the bowl of a stand mixer fitted with the paddle attachment for 4 minutes.)

Add the room-temperature butter to the dough, 1 tablespoon at a time, kneading after each addition until incorporated. Continue to knead the dough until glossy, smooth, and very elastic when stretched, 5–8 minutes longer. (If using a stand mixer, mix for 5 minutes.) Return the dough to the bowl, cover with plastic wrap, and let the dough rise in a warm spot until doubled in size, about 1 hour. Knock back the dough (give it a good punch), cover the bowl again, and refrigerate overnight or up to 1 day.

Line a rimmed baking sheet with parchment paper. Divide the dough into 6 equal pieces. Working with 1 piece at a time, place it on a work surface. Make a claw shape with your hand and place your palm loosely on top of the dough, then move your fingers in a circular motion around the dough to gently shape into a smooth ball. Transfer to the prepared baking sheet. Repeat with the remaining pieces of dough. Cover the baking sheet with plastic wrap and let stand in a warm spot until the balls are slightly springy when gently poked with your finger, 45 minutes–1 hour.

Homemade strawberry jam (page 275) is the perfect filling, but any flavor of homemade or store-bought jam will taste great in these pillowy doughnuts, which can double as sandwich buns (minus the jam).

Coat the Instant Pot® air fryer basket with canola oil spray. Working in batches, arrange a single layer of doughnuts in the basket (about 3), making sure they don't touch. Coat the top of the doughnuts with canola oil spray. Insert the basket into the pot and attach the air fryer lid. Press the Air Fry button and set the cook time for 5 minutes at 375°F (190°C), then press Start. Bake undisturbed.

When the cooking time is up, use tongs or a non-metal spatula to carefully transfer the doughnuts to a plate. Immediately brush the top of the doughnuts with some of the melted butter. Repeat to bake the remaining batches.

Use a small, sharp knife to poke a deep, wide hole on one side of each doughnut, being careful not to poke through the other side. Fit a large pastry bag with a round tip. Fill the bag with the jam, leaving at least 2 inches (5 cm) at the top of the bag unfilled, and twist the top of the bag closed. To fill the doughnuts, insert the tip of the pastry bag into the hole, and pipe the jam until it reaches the top of the hole. (Alternatively, use a small espresso spoon or a ½-teaspoon measure to fill the doughnuts with jam.) Dust the top of the doughnuts with confectioners' sugar and serve.

VARIATION

Brioche Sandwich Buns: *Prepare the dough as directed but divide it into 4 equal pieces instead of 6. Bake 2 doughnuts at a time for 7 minutes, brushing them with melted butter immediately after baking. Cut in half crosswise and use as buns for Crispy Fried Chicken Sandwiches (page 121), Juicy Turkey Burgers (page 138), or Cheese-Stuffed Beef Burgers (page 161). (You may need to double or triple the bun recipe depending on the number of servings.)*

Cardamom Coffee Cake

Cardamom brings a sweet, slightly piney, delicate flavor to this easy-to-like brunch cake. To give it a bright citrusy note, add 1 teaspoon grated orange zest to the filling and 1 tablespoon grated orange zest to the cake batter.

SERVES 8

FOR THE FILLING

3 tablespoons light brown sugar

1½ teaspoons ground cinnamon

½ teaspoon ground cardamom

¼ teaspoon kosher salt

FOR THE TOPPING

¼ cup (1 oz/30 g) plus 1 tablespoon all-purpose flour

¼ cup (60 g) light brown sugar

½ teaspoon ground cinnamon

¼ teaspoon ground cardamom

2 tablespoons unsalted butter, melted

FOR THE CAKE

2 cups (9 oz/240 g) all-purpose flour

2 teaspoons baking powder

½ teaspoon baking soda

1 teaspoon kosher salt

½ cup (4 oz/120 g) unsalted butter, melted and cooled

½ cup (4 oz/120 g) granulated sugar

1 large egg

1 teaspoon vanilla extract

⅔ cup (160 ml) whole milk

1½ (350 ml) cups water

To make the filling, in a small bowl, stir together the brown sugar, cinnamon, cardamom, and salt.

To make the topping, in a small bowl, stir together the flour, brown sugar, cinnamon, and cardamom. Stir in the butter until a crumbly, evenly moistened mixture forms.

To make the cake, spray a 7-inch (18-cm) springform pan with nonstick cooking spray. In a bowl, whisk together the flour, baking powder, baking soda, and salt. In a large bowl, whisk together the butter, sugar, egg, and vanilla until smooth. Add the flour mixture to the butter mixture in two batches alternately with the milk, beginning and ending with the flour mixture and stirring just until mixed after each addition. Transfer half of the batter to the prepared pan and spread into an even layer. It will be thick and difficult to spread. Sprinkle evenly with the filling mixture, then top with the remaining batter, again spreading it evenly. Sprinkle the topping evenly over the surface. Cover the pan with aluminum foil, crimping the edges.

Pour the water into the Instant Pot®. Place the springform pan on the steam rack. Using the rack handles, lower the pan into the pot. Lock the lid in place and turn the valve to Sealing. Press the Pressure Cook button and set the cook time for 65 minutes at high pressure.

Let the steam release naturally for 10 minutes, then turn the valve to Venting to quick-release any residual steam. Carefully remove the lid and transfer the springform pan to a cooling rack. Remove the foil and let the cake cool for 10 minutes.

To serve, remove the pan sides, cut into wedges, and serve warm.

Mini Chocolate-Filled Scones

These fluffy, chocolate-filled bites boast an almost biscuit-like texture that makes them quite addictive. Little hands can help make, shape, and fill the dough with chocolate chunks. Include a slice of banana inside, too, if you like.

MAKES ABOUT 12 SCONES

1¾ cups (7½ oz/210 g) all-purpose flour

2 teaspoons baking powder

½ teaspoon kosher salt

2 large eggs

⅓ cup (70 g) granulated sugar

⅓ cup (80 ml) whole milk

2 tablespoons unsalted butter, melted and cooled

2 oz (60 g) dark or milk chocolate, cut into 12 large chunks

1 teaspoon water

In a large bowl, whisk together the flour, baking powder, and salt. In a medium bowl, whisk together 1 egg and the sugar until thick and creamy. Whisk in the milk and melted butter until combined. Add the egg mixture to the flour mixture and mix with a rubber spatula until just blended.

Line a rimmed baking sheet with parchment paper and coat the parchment with canola oil spray. Use a tablespoon measure, a small ice cream scoop about 1½ inches (4 cm) in diameter, or a melon baller to scoop a rounded tablespoon of the dough, then press a piece of chocolate into the center. Shape the dough into a ball, enclosing the chocolate completely. Roll the ball in the palm of your hands until smooth. (The balls should be 1½–2 inches/4–5 cm in diameter.) Place the balls on the prepared baking sheet.

Coat the Instant Pot® air fryer basket with canola oil spray. In a small bowl, whisk together the remaining egg and the water. Working in batches, brush the top of the balls with some of the egg mixture and arrange a single layer of balls in the basket, making sure they don't touch. Insert the basket into the pot and attach the air fryer lid. Press the Air Fry button and set the cook time for 7 minutes at 350°F (180°C), then press Start. Bake undisturbed.

When the cooking time is up, use tongs or a non-metal spatula to carefully transfer the scones to a plate. Repeat to bake the remaining batches.

VARIATION

Mini Chocolate-Banana Filled Scones: *Cut 1 banana into thin slices and add a slice to the center of each dough ball along with the piece of chocolate. (It's okay if the banana bends a little when shaping the dough into balls.) Bake the scones as directed above.*

Apple Fritters

The sweet, nutty, and creamy brown butter glaze that's poured over these hot apple goodies is hard to resist. Here, a large, retractable ice cream scoop, plus air fryer liners or parchment paper will help streamline the cooking process.

MAKES ABOUT 10

1¾ cups (7½ oz/210 g) all-purpose flour

1 tablespoon baking powder

½ teaspoon kosher salt

1¼ cups (300 ml) whole milk

2 cups (8 oz/225 g) peeled, cored, and diced sweet apples (about 2), such as Pink Lady, Honeycrisp, Braeburn, or Jonagold

2 tablespoons granulated sugar

¼ teaspoon ground cinnamon

FOR THE BROWN BUTTER GLAZE

4 tablespoons (2 oz/60 g) unsalted butter

1 cup (3½ oz/100 g) confectioners' sugar

2 tablespoons whole milk, plus more as needed

½ teaspoon pure vanilla extract

In a large bowl, whisk together the flour, baking powder, and salt. Stir in the milk with a rubber spatula or wooden spoon until just combined. In a medium bowl, toss together the apples, granulated sugar, and cinnamon until well coated. Fold the apples into the batter.

Line the Instant Pot® air fryer basket with an air fryer liner or parchment paper cut to fit. Working in batches, use a large ice cream scoop about 2 inches (5 cm) in diameter or a tablespoon measure to scoop equal-size portions of the batter, each about 3 tablespoons, onto the liner or parchment, spacing the fritters at least ½ inch (12 mm) apart. Coat the fritters with canola oil spray. Insert the basket into the pot and attach the air fryer lid. Press the Air Fry button and set the cook time for 12 minutes at 390°F (199°C), then press Start. Bake undisturbed.

Meanwhile, make the brown butter glaze: In a small saucepan over medium-high heat, melt the butter. Continue cooking the butter until it is light brown and starting to foam, swirling the pan occasionally. Watch the butter carefully at the end to prevent it from burning. Remove from the heat and let cool slightly. (There will be small, brown specks in the butter.) Place the confectioners' sugar in a small bowl or glass measuring cup. Add the melted butter, milk, and vanilla and whisk to combine. The glaze should be thick but pourable. If needed, add more milk 1 teaspoon at a time until it reaches the desired consistency. (Since it will be poured over the hot fritters, it will liquefy quickly.)

When the cooking time is up, use tongs to carefully transfer the fritters to a plate. Pour the glaze over the top to coat the fritters completely. Repeat to bake and glaze the remaining batches. Serve warm.

SNACKS & SIDES

Homemade Hummus

Making your own hummus from dried chickpeas that don't even need to be soaked is a thing of beauty—and deliciousness. For a sophisticated presentation, choose vegetables in similar colors and a variety of shapes and textures for your crudité platter. A purple palette, including cauliflower, endive, and radishes, contrasts nicely with the orange hue of the hummus.

MAKES ABOUT 3 CUPS (225 G)

1 cup (7 oz/200 g) dried chickpeas

4 cups (1 L) water

Kosher salt

2 cloves garlic, chopped

Juice of 1 lemon

¼ cup (60 ml) tahini

¼ teaspoon ground cumin

2 teaspoons smoked paprika

¼ cup (60 ml) olive oil, plus more for serving

Red pepper flakes, for serving (optional)

FOR SERVING (OPTIONAL)

Pita bread or pita chips and/or crudités such as cauliflower florets, radishes, endive, daikon, bell peppers, carrots, cucumber, and cherry tomatoes

Combine chickpeas, water, and 1 teaspoon salt in the Instant Pot®. Lock the lid in place and turn the valve to Sealing. Press the Beans/Chili button and set the cook time for 40 minutes at high pressure.

Let the steam release naturally, or for at least 15 minutes, before turning the valve to Venting to quick-release any residual steam. Carefully remove the lid and ladle 1 cup (240 ml) of the cooking liquid into a measuring cup. Drain the chickpeas in a colander set in the sink. Transfer the chickpeas to a blender or food processor. Add the garlic, lemon juice, tahini, cumin, 1 teaspoon of the smoked paprika, 1 teaspoon salt, and ½ cup (120 ml) of the reserved cooking liquid. Blend until almost smooth, adding more cooking liquid and scraping down the sides of the blender as needed. With the blender running, add the olive oil through the pour spout in a slow, steady stream until incorporated, about 2 minutes. Taste and add more salt if needed.

Transfer the hummus to a serving bowl, sprinkle with the remaining paprika and red pepper flakes, if using, drizzle with oil, and serve with pita and/or crudités.

Pipe the yolk mixture decoratively into the egg white shells, or spoon in the yolks for a simpler approach.

Sriracha Deviled Eggs with Spicy Bread Crumbs

Vinegary, garlicky Sriracha chile sauce brightens the filling for these easy stuffed eggs. Cooling the eggs in an ice bath after steaming shrinks the egg interior from the shell, making it especially easy to remove.

MAKES 24

1 cup (240 ml) water

12 large eggs

½ cup (120 ml) mayonnaise

5 teaspoons Sriracha sauce

2 teaspoons Dijon mustard

1 teaspoon white wine vinegar

Kosher salt and freshly ground pepper

Finely chopped fresh flat-leaf parsley, for garnish

FOR THE BREAD CRUMBS

2 tablespoons olive oil

1½ cups (5 oz/150 g) fresh or fine dried bread crumbs

½ teaspoon granulated garlic

½ teaspoon sweet paprika

Pinch of cayenne pepper

2 teaspoons chopped fresh flat-leaf parsley

Pour the water into the Instant Pot® and place the steam rack on the pot bottom. Carefully arrange the eggs on the rack, stacking them on top of one another if necessary. Lock the lid in place and turn the valve to Sealing. Press the Egg button and cook on high, or press the Manual/Pressure button and set the cook time for 8 minutes at high pressure.

While the eggs are cooking, prepare an ice bath. When the eggs are ready, let the steam release naturally for 5 minutes, then turn the valve to Venting to release any residual steam. Carefully remove the lid and transfer the eggs to the ice bath. When the eggs are cool enough to handle, lift them from the water. Crack the egg shells, remove, and discard.

While the eggs are cooling, make the bread crumbs. In a frying pan over medium heat, warm the oil. Add the bread crumbs, garlic, paprika, cayenne, and parsley and cook, stirring constantly, until the crumbs are well toasted, about 3 minutes. Remove from the heat and let cool.

Cut each egg in half lengthwise. Use a spoon to scoop the yolks into a bowl. Set the egg white halves, hollow side up, on a serving platter and set aside. Add the mayonnaise, Sriracha sauce, mustard, and vinegar to the yolks and whisk until no lumps remain. Season with salt and pepper.

Spoon the yolk mixture into a pastry bag fitted with a large star tip and pipe about 1 heaping tablespoon into each egg white half. Top with some bread crumbs and a sprinkle of parsley and serve.

Kale Artichoke Dip

Old-fashioned hot artichoke dip gets an update and a big dose of nutrients with the addition of kale. Assemble this party classic up to a few hours in advance, then slip it under the broiler just before your guests arrive.

SERVES 6–8

3 tablespoons olive oil

1 yellow onion, finely chopped

2 cloves garlic, minced

1 can (14 oz) artichoke hearts, drained and roughly chopped

1 large bunch kale, stemmed and roughly chopped

1 package (8 oz) cream cheese

½ cup (120 ml) mayonnaise

½ cup (115 g) sour cream

¾ cup (90 g) grated Parmesan cheese

1¼ cups (150 g) shredded mozzarella cheese

1½ teaspoons Worcestershire sauce

½ teaspoon cayenne pepper

Salt and freshly ground black pepper

Crostini or fresh baguette slices, for serving

Select Sauté on the Instant Pot® and warm the oil. Add the onion and cook, stirring occasionally, until softened, about 3 minutes. Add the garlic and cook, stirring, for 1 minute. Add the artichokes and kale and cook, stirring, until the kale is just wilted and the artichokes have released their liquid, about 7 minutes. Add the cream cheese, mayonnaise, sour cream, ½ cup (60 g) of the Parmesan, and 1 cup (120 g) of the mozzarella and stir to combine. The mixture will not be completely smooth; do not overmix. Add the Worcestershire sauce and cayenne, season with salt and pepper, and stir briefly.

Lock the lid in place and turn the valve to Sealing. Press the Keep Warm/Cancel button to reset the program, then press the Manual/Pressure Cook button and set the time for 10 minutes at high pressure. While the dip cooks, set a rack in the upper third of the oven and preheat the broiler.

Let the steam release naturally for 3 minutes, then turn the valve to Venting to release any residual steam. Carefully remove the lid, give the mixture a stir, and transfer it to a broiler-safe baking dish. Top evenly with the remaining ¼ cup (30 g) each of Parmesan and mozzarella.

Broil until the cheeses are bubbling and lightly browned, about 3 minutes. Serve the hot dip with crostini.

Long, thin slices of crisp crostini make an efficient tool for scooping up this creamy, cheese-topped dip. Pita or tortilla chips work well too.

Crispy Chickpeas

Re-creating this addictive snack in the air fryer is easy: Pressure cook dried beans, then fry them in a blend of paprika, cumin, and cayenne. Both steps take some time, but it's all hands-off cooking so you can relax and mix up some cocktails while you wait.

SERVES 4

1 cup (7 oz/200 g) dried chickpeas, rinsed and picked over

4 cups (950 ml) water

1 teaspoon canola oil

Kosher salt

1 tablespoon olive oil

1 teaspoon paprika

½ teaspoon ground cumin

Pinch of cayenne pepper

Combine the chickpeas, water, canola oil, and 1 teaspoon salt in the Instant Pot®. Lock the pressure-cooking lid in place and turn the valve to Sealing. Press the Pressure Cook button and set the cook time for 35 minutes at high pressure, then press Start.

When the cooking time is up, let the steam release naturally for 10 minutes, then press the Quick Release Button or turn the valve to Venting to quick-release any residual steam. Carefully remove the lid and drain the chickpeas in a colander set in the sink. Press the Cancel button to reset the program.

In a large bowl, toss together the chickpeas, olive oil, paprika, cumin, cayenne, and ½ teaspoon salt. Add the chickpeas to the Instant Pot® air fryer basket. Insert the basket into the pot and attach the air fryer lid. Press the Air Fry button and set the cook time for 25 minutes at 390°F (199°C), then press Start. Gently toss the chickpeas when prompted.

When the cooking time is up, if the chickpeas aren't crispy enough, add more cooking time in 2-minute intervals until the chickpeas are cooked to the desired crispness. Carefully remove the basket from the pot and pour the chickpeas into a bowl. Taste and adjust the seasoning with salt and serve.

NOTE *To save time, you can use 1 can (15 oz) of cooked chickpeas instead. Drain and rinse the chickpeas, dry well with paper towels, then toss with the olive oil and seasonings. Add to the air fryer basket, setting the cook time for 18–20 minutes at 375°F (190°C).*

Eggplant & Olive Dip

Caramelizing eggplant in a little olive oil on Sauté mode before pressure cooking it creates a slightly smoky flavor that pairs well with tangy olives and lemon juice. Serve this Middle Eastern–inspired spread with toasted pita triangles or baguette slices and a sprinkling of pomegranate seeds.

SERVES 4–6

2 lb (1 kg) eggplant

5 tablespoons (75 ml) olive oil, plus more as needed

Kosher salt and freshly ground black pepper

2 cups (475 ml) water

4 unpeeled cloves garlic

⅓ cup (75 ml) fresh lemon juice

½ cup (60 g) pitted Kalamata olives, chopped, plus more for garnish

3 tablespoons chopped fresh flat-leaf parsley, plus more for garnish

Pomegranate seeds, for garnish (optional)

4–6 pita bread rounds, toasted and cut into wedges, for serving

Using a vegetable peeler, peel the eggplant in alternating stripes of skin and no skin, then cut into large chunks.

Select Sauté on the Instant Pot® and heat the oil. Working in batches, add the eggplant and cook, turning the pieces occasionally with tongs, until beginning to smoke slightly and caramelize, about 4 minutes. Transfer to a plate as browned. Add more oil between batches if needed. Return the eggplant to the pot and season generously with salt and pepper.

Pour the water into the Instant Pot® and add the garlic. Lock the lid in place and turn the valve to Sealing. Press the Pressure Cook button and set the time for 3 minutes at high pressure.

Turn the valve to Venting to quick-release the steam. When the steam stops, carefully remove the lid. Remove the garlic cloves and squeeze the garlic flesh into a food processor. Transfer the eggplant to the processor. Add the lemon juice, olives, and parsley and process until smooth, about 2 minutes. Transfer the eggplant dip to a serving bowl and let cool to room temperature.

Drizzle the dip with olive oil and garnish with olives, parsley, and pomegranate seeds, if using. Serve the pita toasts alongside.

TIP *For a chunkier texture, transfer the cooked eggplant and garlic flesh to a large bowl and mash with a large whisk or potato masher, then stir in the remaining ingredients.*

Mozzarella Sticks with Marinara Sauce

This simple recipe has three crucial steps—double-dipping the sticks in egg and bread crumbs, freezing the sticks before frying, and cooking for exactly 4 minutes (any longer and the cheese will ooze out into a gooey mess). Resist the urge to dig right in—letting the sticks rest for 1 minute allows the heat from the breading to transfer into the cheese, creating a delightful stringy center.

SERVES 4

2 large eggs

1 tablespoon water

¾ cup (2½ oz/75 g) dried plain or Italian bread crumbs

2 tablespoons freshly grated Parmesan cheese, plus more for serving

Kosher salt

1 block (225 g) mozzarella cheese, preferably whole milk, or 8 mozzarella sticks

Marinara Sauce (page 265), for serving

To cut the block of cheese, using a sharp knife, slice into rectangles about 3 inches (7.5 cm) long, 1 inch (2.5 cm) wide, and ½ inch (12 mm) thick. If using mozzarella sticks, cut the sticks in half horizontally.

In a medium bowl, whisk together the eggs and water. In a large bowl or on a plate, stir together the bread crumbs, Parmesan, and ½ teaspoon salt.

Line a rimmed baking sheet with parchment paper. Working with a few sticks at a time, dip the mozzarella in the egg mixture, letting the excess drip off, then dredge in the bread crumb mixture, turning to coat well and pressing gently to adhere. Dip the mozzarella in the egg mixture again, then dredge again in the bread crumbs. Place the coated mozzarella on the prepared baking sheet as you go. Cover the baking sheet tightly with plastic wrap and freeze for at least 2 hours or up to 2 days.

Coat the Instant Pot® air fryer basket with canola oil spray. Working in batches, coat the mozzarella sticks generously with olive oil spray and arrange a single layer of sticks in the basket, making sure they don't touch. Return the remaining mozzarella to the freezer. Insert the basket into the pot and attach the air fryer lid. Press the Air Fry button and set the cook time for 4 minutes at 375°F (190°C), then press Start. Cook undisturbed.

When the cooking time is up, use tongs to carefully transfer the mozzarella sticks to a plate (the cheese will be very soft). Sprinkle with Parmesan and let rest for at least 1 minute. Repeat to cook the remaining batches. Serve with marinara sauce alongside for dipping.

Spring Rolls with Nuoc Cham

A sweet, sour, salty, savory, and spicy dipping sauce, nuoc cham is the perfect partner for crispy spring rolls filled with a rich blend of ground pork, shiitake mushrooms, cabbage, and carrots. Experiment with the filling ingredients to

SERVES 4

1 tablespoon canola oil

1 shallot, minced

2 cloves garlic, minced

Kosher salt and freshly ground black pepper

½ lb (225 g) ground pork

1 tablespoon soy sauce

1½ cups (4½ oz/130 g) chopped napa cabbage

½ cup (1¾ oz/50 g) shredded carrots

2 oz (60 g) fresh shiitake mushrooms or rehydrated dried shiitake mushrooms, stemmed and caps diced

2 teaspoons fish sauce

2 teaspoons sugar

10 (8-inch/20-cm) square frozen spring roll wrappers, made with wheat flour, thawed

2 tablespoons toasted sesame oil

Select Sauté on the Instant Pot®, press Start, and heat the oil. Add the shallot, garlic, and ¼ teaspoon pepper and cook, stirring occasionally, until fragrant, about 1 minute. Add the ground pork and 1 teaspoon of the soy sauce and cook, breaking up the meat with a wooden spoon and stirring occasionally, until the pork has started to release some fat, 2–3 minutes. Add the cabbage, carrots, mushrooms, fish sauce, sugar, the remaining 2 teaspoons soy sauce, and ½ teaspoon salt and cook, stirring occasionally, until the cabbage has wilted and the pork is cooked through, 3–4 minutes. Press the Cancel button to reset the program.

Transfer the pork mixture to a paper towel–lined plate. Wipe out or rinse the pot.

Fill a small bowl with cool water. Working with 1 spring roll wrapper at a time, place it on a work surface positioned in a diamond shape (cover the other wrappers with a damp cloth so they won't dry out). Spread ¼ cup of the pork filling in a horizontal line on the lower third of the wrapper, leaving at least a ½-inch (12-mm) border around the filling. Dip your finger in the bowl of water and moisten the edges of the wrapper. Fold the bottom corner over the filling, encasing it. Fold in the left and right corners toward the center and roll the wrapper away from you into a tight cylinder. Transfer to a plate. Repeat with the remaining wrappers and filling.

suit your taste, but be sure to remove any excess moisture with paper towels so the wrappers won't get soggy. Purchase frozen spring roll wrappers made with wheat, not the rice wrappers used for summer rolls and fresh spring rolls.

FOR THE NUOC CHAM

½ cup (120 ml) warm water

3 tablespoons fresh lime juice, plus more as needed

2 tablespoons sugar, plus more as needed

2 teaspoons rice vinegar

3 tablespoons fish sauce

1 or 2 red Thai or small serrano chiles, seeded, if desired, and thinly sliced

1 clove garlic, minced

Insert the air fryer basket into the Instant Pot®. Working in batches, brush the spring rolls generously with the sesame oil and arrange a single layer of rolls in the Instant Pot® air fryer basket, making sure they don't touch. Insert the basket into the pot and attach the air fryer lid. Press the Air Fry button and set the cook time for 8 minutes at 400°F (200°C), then press Start. Cook undisturbed.

Meanwhile, make the nuoc cham: In a small bowl, stir together the warm water, lime juice, sugar, and vinegar. Add the fish sauce, chiles, and garlic and stir to combine. Taste and adjust the seasoning with lime juice and sugar if needed.

When the cooking time is up, the spring rolls should be light golden brown and slightly darker golden brown on the ends. If a darker color is desired, cook for 2 minutes longer. Use tongs to carefully transfer the spring rolls to a plate. Repeat to cook the remaining batches. Serve with the nuoc cham alongside for dipping.

Crab Rangoon

If fresh wonton wrappers aren't available for this retro appetizer, you can find them frozen in the freezer section of Asian markets or large grocery stores—just be sure to thaw the wrappers before working with them.

SERVES 4

3 oz (90 g) cooked crabmeat, preferably lump

2 oz (60 g) cream cheese, at room temperature

2 tablespoons chopped green onions, white and pale green parts

1½ teaspoons Worcestershire sauce

16 square wonton wrappers, preferably made with egg (see note)

Thai sweet chili sauce or duck sauce, for serving

In a medium bowl, stir together the crabmeat, cream cheese, green onions, and Worcestershire sauce.

Line a rimmed baking sheet with parchment paper. Fill a small bowl with cool water. Working with 1 wonton wrapper at a time, place it on a work surface. Place a heaping 1 teaspoon of the crab filling in the center of the wrapper. Dip your finger in the bowl of water and moisten the edges of the wrapper. Bring the opposite corners of the wrapper up to meet each other and gently pinch them together. Bring the two remaining corners of the wrapper up to meet the other corners and gently pinch all four corners together, removing any air pockets, and seal the wrapper into an X shape. Transfer to the prepared baking sheet. Repeat with the remaining wrappers and filling.

Working in batches, coat the wontons on all sides with canola oil spray and arrange a single layer of wontons in the Instant Pot® air fryer basket, making sure they don't touch. Insert the basket into the pot and attach the air fryer lid. Press the Air Fry button and set the cook time for 8 minutes at 340°F (171°C), then press Start. Cook undisturbed.

When the cooking time is up, if the wontons are not golden brown and crisp, add more cooking time in 2-minute intervals until wontons are cooked to desired crispness. Use tongs to carefully transfer the wontons to a plate. Repeat to cook the remaining batches. Serve with chili sauce or duck sauce alongside for dipping.

NOTE *Wonton wrappers made with egg work best for this recipe. If using wrappers not made with egg, add more cooking time, if needed, until the wontons are golden and crisp. The top edges will be slightly darker than the rest of the wontons. If using very thin egg wrappers, use ½ teaspoon filling per wrapper and cook at 300°F (150°C) for 10–12 minutes.*

Buffalo Cauliflower Bites

An excellent vegetarian option for game days, cauliflower can stand up to high heat and hot sauce just as well as chicken. Cut florets into similar sizes so they cook evenly, and leave a flat surface on one side to help the egg mixture and breading adhere.

SERVES 4–6

¼ cup (2 oz/60 g) ketchup

¼ cup (60 ml) hot pepper sauce, such as Frank's RedHot cayenne pepper sauce

2 large egg whites

Kosher salt and freshly ground black pepper

2 cups (7 oz/200 g) panko bread crumbs

1 head cauliflower, cut into large florets

Blue Cheese Dip (page 62), for serving

In a large bowl, whisk together the ketchup, hot pepper sauce, egg whites, 1 teaspoon salt, and ¼ teaspoon black pepper. Place the bread crumbs in a medium bowl or on a large plate.

Line a rimmed baking sheet with parchment paper. Working in batches, toss the cauliflower florets in the ketchup mixture to coat. Transfer to the bread crumbs and toss to coat completely. Place the coated cauliflower on the prepared baking sheet as you go. Repeat to coat the remaining florets.

Coat the Instant Pot® air fryer basket with canola oil spray. Working in batches, spray the cauliflower florets with oil spray and arrange a single layer of florets in the basket, making sure they touch as little as possible. Insert the basket into the pot and attach the air fryer lid. Press the Air Fry button and set the cook time for 20 minutes at 325°F (165°C), then press Start. Gently toss the cauliflower when prompted, then coat the cauliflower again.

When the cooking time is up, use tongs to carefully transfer the cauliflower to a bowl, or remove the basket from the pot and carefully pour the cauliflower into a bowl. Repeat to cook the remaining batches. Serve hot with blue cheese dip alongside.

Wings Four Ways

Air frying chicken wings couldn't be easier, no matter what flavor sauce is your favorite. Simply coat the wings with a little canola oil and air fry, then toss the warm wings with the sauce after cooking. Make a few batches for your next party so you can try all of the sauces featured here.

SERVES 4–6

2 lb (1 kg) chicken wings

1 tablespoon canola oil

Sauces of choice (recipes, page 62)

In a large bowl, toss together the chicken wings and oil.

Coat the Instant Pot® air fryer basket with canola oil spray and add the wings, stacking them to leave as much space as possible between them. Insert the basket into the pot and attach the air fryer lid. Press the Air Fry button and set the cook time for 25 minutes at 400°F (200°C), then press Start. Rotate and flip the wings when prompted.

Meanwhile, make the sauce(s) of your choice. (Sauce measurements will cover a full 2-pound recipe of wings. If using multiple sauces for one batch of wings, you'll only need to use a portion of each sauce, not the full amount.)

When the cooking time is up, use tongs to carefully transfer the wings to a clean large bowl. Toss the wings with the sauce to coat well. If using multiple sauces, divide the wings among multiple bowls and toss the desired amount of sauce with each bowl of wings. (If making BBQ wings, use only as much sauce as needed, ½–1 cup (120–240 ml), depending on the desired texture.) Serve right away.

MAKES 1½ CUPS (300 G)

BLUE CHEESE DIP

In a small bowl, stir together the sour cream, blue cheese, garlic, ¼ teaspoon salt, and a few grindings of pepper. Taste and adjust the seasoning with salt and pepper.

1 cup (225 g) sour cream

½ cup (70 g) crumbled blue cheese

2 cloves garlic, minced or grated

Kosher salt and freshly ground black pepper

MAKES ½ CUP (135 ML)

BUFFALO SAUCE

In a small saucepan over medium heat, melt the butter. Add the garlic and cook, stirring frequently, until fragrant, about 2 minutes. Add the hot pepper sauce and vinegar and stir to combine. Remove from the heat. After coating the wings with the sauce, serve the blue cheese dip alongside (recipe above).

4 tablespoons (2 oz/60 g) unsalted butter

3 cloves garlic, minced

¼ cup (60 ml) hot pepper sauce, such as Frank's RedHot cayenne pepper sauce

1 teaspoon distilled white vinegar

MAKES ABOUT 1 CUP (160 ML)

SESAME SAUCE

In a small saucepan over medium heat, stir together the soy sauce, hoisin sauce, sesame oil, honey, vinegar, and garlic. Bring to a gentle simmer and cook, stirring occasionally, until the sauce is reduced by one-fourth, about 8 minutes. If the sauce begins to simmer too vigorously, reduce the heat to medium-low. Remove from the heat. After coating the wings with the sauce, sprinkle with the green onions and sesame seeds.

3 tablespoons soy sauce

3 tablespoons hoisin sauce

3 tablespoons toasted sesame oil

3 tablespoons honey

1 tablespoon rice vinegar

1 clove garlic, grated

2 green onions, white and pale green parts, thinly sliced

1 tablespoon toasted sesame seeds

MAKES ABOUT 1 CUP (320 ML)

SPICY HONEY SAUCE

In a small saucepan over medium heat, stir together the honey, Sriracha, soy sauce, butter, and lime juice. Bring to a boil, then reduce the heat to medium-low and simmer until the sauce has thickened slightly, 2–3 minutes. Remove from the heat.

½ cup (180 g) honey

¼ cup (60 ml) Sriracha or other hot sauce

3 tablespoons soy sauce

2 tablespoons unsalted butter

Juice of 1 lime

Hush Puppies

These bite-size treats made from cornmeal batter are right at home alongside your favorite fried seafood. They're best eaten fresh from the fryer, so prepare these last on your menu—you can mix the batter a few hours ahead and refrigerate until ready to use.

MAKES ABOUT 18

1 cup (4½ oz/130 g) cornmeal

¾ cup (3 oz/90 g) all-purpose flour

1 tablespoon sugar

1½ teaspoons baking powder

Kosher salt

Pinch of cayenne pepper (optional)

1 cup (240 ml) full-fat buttermilk or ¾ cup (180 ml) low-fat buttermilk

1 large egg

1 green onion, white parts and pale green parts, finely chopped

½ cup (3 oz/90 g) fresh corn kernels (from about 1 ear) or frozen corn kernels

In a medium bowl, whisk together the cornmeal, flour, sugar, baking powder, 1½ teaspoons salt, and the cayenne (if using). In a small bowl or glass measuring cup, whisk together the buttermilk, egg, and green onion. Add the buttermilk mixture to the cornmeal mixture and stir with a rubber spatula until combined. Fold in the corn.

Line the Instant Pot® air fryer basket with an air fryer liner or parchment paper cut to fit. Working in batches, use a small ice cream scoop about 1½ inches (4 cm) in diameter or a tablespoon measure to drop the batter onto the liner or parchment, leaving about ½ inch (12 mm) between the rounds. Coat them generously with canola oil spray. Insert the basket into the pot and attach the air fryer lid. Press the Air Fry button and set the cook time for 9 minutes at 400°F (200°C), then press Start. Coat the rounds again with oil when prompted to flip, but don't flip them.

When the cooking time is up, use tongs to carefully transfer the hush puppies to a plate. Repeat to cook the remaining batches, then serve.

Blistered Shishito Peppers

When shishito peppers are in season, there's no simpler or better starter to a meal than peppers seared in hot olive oil and sprinkled with salt. Now this summer treat is even easier, with no frying pan required. If you're feeding a crowd, cook in batches of about ½ lb (225 g) peppers at a time so they'll have enough room in the basket to blister.

SERVES 2

6–8 oz (170–225 g) shishito peppers

2 teaspoons olive oil

Kosher salt

Flaky sea salt

In a bowl, toss together the shishito peppers, oil, and ¼ teaspoon kosher salt.

Coat the Instant Pot® air fryer basket with canola oil spray and add the peppers. Insert the basket into the pot and attach the air fryer lid. Press the Air Fry button and set the cook time for 6 minutes at 400°F (200°C), then press Start. Toss the peppers when prompted.

When the cooking time is up, use tongs to carefully transfer the peppers to a bowl, or remove the basket from the pot and carefully pour the peppers into a bowl. Sprinkle with flaky sea salt and serve.

Awesome Onion Rings

If you're skeptical about how well onion rings can adapt to an air fryer, this recipe will win you over. Plain dried bread crumbs are the secret to producing the proper texture, and dipping the onions twice in an egg batter helps the breading stay on during cooking.

SERVES 2–4

3 large eggs

1 tablespoon mayonnaise

½ cup (2 oz/60 g) all-purpose flour

¾ cup (2¾ oz/75 g) plain dried bread crumbs

1 teaspoon smoked paprika

Kosher salt and freshly ground black pepper

1 large yellow or sweet onion, cut into ½-inch (12-mm) rings and separated

In a medium bowl, whisk together the eggs and mayonnaise. Place the flour in a small bowl. In another medium bowl, stir together the bread crumbs, paprika, 1 teaspoon salt, and a few grindings of pepper.

Line a rimmed baking sheet with parchment paper. Working with 1 onion ring at a time, dip the ring in the egg mixture, letting the excess drip off, then dredge in the flour, shaking off the excess. Dip the ring in the egg mixture again, then dredge in the bread crumb mixture, pressing gently to adhere to both the outside and inside of the ring. Place the coated onion rings on the prepared baking sheet as you go.

Working in batches, coat the onion rings well with canola oil spray and arrange a single layer of rings in the Instant Pot® air fryer basket, making sure they don't touch. Insert the basket into the pot and attach the air fryer lid. Press the Air Fry button and set the cook time for 8 minutes at 350°F (180°C), then press Start. Flip the rings when prompted.

When the cooking time is up, if the rings aren't completely golden and crisp, cook for 2 minutes longer. Use tongs to carefully transfer the onion rings to a bowl. Repeat to cook the remaining batches, then serve.

Fried Pickle Spears

This country-fair staple is now achievable at home with a simple beer batter and seasoned panko bread crumbs. Taste your pickles for saltiness since they vary from brand to brand. If they are on the saltier side, skip the salt in the bread crumb mixture.

SERVES 2–4

6 small dill pickles

¼ cup (1 oz/30 g) cornstarch

½ cup (2 oz/60 g) all-purpose flour

½ teaspoon baking powder

Kosher salt

¼ cup (60 ml) plus 2 tablespoons dark beer

5 tablespoons (75 ml) water

1½ cups (5¼ oz/150 g) panko bread crumbs

1 teaspoon paprika

Spicy Mayo (page 121), for serving (optional)

Cut the pickles lengthwise into thick spears and pat thoroughly dry with paper towels.

Spread the cornstarch on a plate. In a bowl, whisk together the flour, baking powder, and ½ teaspoon salt. Add the beer and water and whisk to combine; the batter should be thick but pourable. On another plate, stir together the bread crumbs, paprika, and 1 teaspoon salt, then transfer half the mixture to a small bowl and set aside.

Line a rimmed baking sheet with parchment paper. Working with a few spears at a time, coat the pickles in the cornstarch, shaking off the excess, then dip in the batter, letting the excess drip off. Dredge in the bread crumb mixture on the plate, turning to coat well and pressing gently to adhere. Place the coated pickles on the prepared baking sheet as you go. When the bread crumb mixture starts to become soggy, add the reserved mixture to the plate.

Working in batches, coat the pickles generously with canola oil spray and arrange a single layer of spears in the Instant Pot® air fryer basket, making sure they don't touch. Insert the basket into the pot and attach the air fryer lid. Press the Air Fry button and set the cook time for 8 minutes at 375°F (190°C), then press Start. Turn the spears when prompted, coating both sides again with oil.

When the cooking time is up, if the pickles are not deep golden brown and crisp, cook for 2 minutes longer. Use tongs to carefully transfer the pickles to a plate. Repeat to cook the remaining batches. Serve with spicy mayo alongside, if desired.

Mexican Corn on the Cob

Often referred to as elote, this dish is irresistible when corn reaches its peak in summer. You'll need a few plates or trays to keep the multistep process organized, but the corn assembly line will be well worth it in the end. Serve with Crispy Fried Chicken Sandwiches (page 121) for the perfect outdoor picnic.

SERVES 4

4 ears of yellow corn, shucked

2 tablespoons unsalted butter, melted

½ teaspoon chipotle chile powder, plus more for serving

Kosher salt and freshly ground black pepper

¼ cup (60 ml) mayonnaise

¼ cup (60 g) sour cream

½ cup (70 g) Cotija cheese or queso fresco, crumbled

¼ cup (15 g) chopped fresh cilantro

1 lime, cut into wedges

Place the corn on a large plate or rimmed baking sheet and brush the ears with the melted butter. In a small bowl, stir together the chipotle chile powder, ¼ teaspoon salt, and a generous pinch of pepper. Sprinkle the spice mixture over the corn, rolling the ears to coat evenly.

Coat the Instant Pot® air fryer basket with canola oil spray and add 2 ears of corn. Insert the basket into the pot and attach the air fryer lid. Press the Air Fry button and set the cook time for 12 minutes at 400°F (200°C), then press Start. Rotate the corn when prompted.

Meanwhile, in a small bowl, stir together the mayonnaise, sour cream, and ½ teaspoon salt. Place half of the cheese on a large plate. Set aside.

When the cooking time is up, use tongs to carefully transfer the corn to a clean plate or rimmed baking sheet. Brush the corn with some of the sour cream mixture and let rest for 1 minute, allowing the mixture to be absorbed. Brush the corn again with more sour cream mixture, reserving about half for the remaining corn, then roll in the cheese to coat evenly. Sprinkle with chile powder and half of the cilantro.

Repeat to cook the remaining corn. Transfer the remaining cheese to the plate and coat the corn with the remaining sour cream mixture, cheese, chile powder, and cilantro. Serve with lime wedges alongside.

Crispy Brussels Sprouts with Honey-Lime Glaze

Oven-roasted brussels sprouts are often avoided (except on Thanksgiving, of course), because they seem to require more work than they should—and end up a soft, steamy mess without a lot of flavor. Thankfully, the solution is effortless: Plump, firm, and crunchy, these air-fried sprouts boast an incredible texture with a delectable spicy-sweet finish.

SERVES 2–4

1 lb (450 g) brussels sprouts, trimmed and halved lengthwise (quartered if very large)

1 tablespoon olive oil

¼ teaspoon red pepper flakes

Kosher salt

2 tablespoons honey

Juice of 1 lime

In a large bowl, toss together the brussels sprouts, oil, red pepper flakes, and ¼ teaspoon salt.

Coat the Instant Pot® air fryer basket with canola oil spray and add the brussels sprouts. Insert the basket into the pot and attach the air fryer lid. Press the Air Fry button and set the cook time for 20 minutes at 350°F (180°C), then press Start. Toss the brussels sprouts when prompted.

Meanwhile, in a small bowl, stir together the honey, lime juice, and a generous pinch of salt. Set aside.

When the cooking time is up, use tongs to carefully transfer the brussels sprouts to a bowl, or remove the basket from the pot and carefully pour the brussels sprouts into a bowl. Drizzle with the honey-lime glaze, toss gently to coat (it's okay if some crispy outer leaves fall off in the process), and serve.

Spicy Sweet Potato Wedges

Sweet potatoes are a fabulous superfood, but getting them to cook up crispy can be challenging. This is where air frying really shines, creating beautifully crisp skins and tender, sweet centers. We toss the potatoes with a simple blend of garlic powder, smoked paprika, salt, and pepper to pack a serious flavor punch.

SERVES 2–4

1 large or 2 medium sweet potatoes (about 1 lb/450 g total), trimmed

1 teaspoon garlic powder

1 teaspoon smoked paprika

Kosher salt and freshly ground black pepper

1½ tablespoons olive oil

Using a sharp knife, cut the sweet potatoes into wedges about ½ inch (12 mm) thick and 3 inches (7.5 cm) long.

In a small bowl, stir together the garlic powder, paprika, ½ teaspoon salt, and ¼ teaspoon pepper. In a large bowl, toss together the sweet potatoes and oil. Sprinkle with the spice mixture and toss to coat.

Coat the Instant Pot® air fryer basket with canola oil spray and add half of the sweet potatoes. Insert the basket into the pot and attach the air fryer lid. Press the Air Fry button and set the cook time for 15 minutes at 400°F (200°C), then press Start. Toss the potatoes when prompted.

When the cooking time is up, use tongs to carefully transfer the potatoes to a bowl, or remove the basket from the pot and carefully pour the potatoes into a bowl. Repeat to cook the remaining batches, then serve.

Spiced Green Beans

A wonderful pantry staple, Old Bay seasoning doesn't get enough credit for its versatility and power-packed punch of flavor, spicing up more than just seafood. A sprinkle here transforms ordinary green beans into everyone's new favorite side dish—and a dash of Old Bay tossed with hot potato wedges (page 72) would be awesome, too.

SERVES 2–4

1 lb (450 g) green beans, trimmed

1 teaspoon olive oil

½ teaspoon Old Bay seasoning

In a large bowl, toss together the green beans, oil, and Old Bay seasoning.

Coat the Instant Pot® air fryer basket with canola oil spray and add the beans. Insert the basket into the pot and attach the air fryer lid. Press the Broil button and set the cook time for 12 minutes at 400°F (200°C), then press Start. Toss the beans when prompted.

When the cooking time is up, use tongs to carefully transfer the beans to a bowl, or remove the basket from the pot and carefully pour the beans into a bowl.

SOUPS & SALADS

Rainbow Minestrone

This everything-but-the-kitchen-sink soup is flavorful, colorful, and versatile. Use other vegetables in season, if you like, cooking hearty ones under pressure and adding more delicate ones to the hot liquid after the pressure is released.

SERVES 6

Select Sauté on the Instant Pot® and melt the butter. Add the onion and cook, stirring occasionally, until softened and translucent, about 5 minutes. Add the carrots and celery and cook, stirring occasionally, until they start to soften, about 3 minutes. Add the garlic and cook, stirring, until fragrant, about 1 minute. Add the potatoes, tomatoes, stock, water, beans, oregano, Parmesan rind (if using), 1½ teaspoons salt, and ¼ teaspoon pepper and stir to mix. Press the Cancel button to reset the program.

Lock the lid in place and turn the valve to Sealing. Press the Pressure Cook button and set the cook time for 30 minutes at high pressure.

Let the steam release naturally for 15 minutes, then turn the valve to Venting to quick-release any residual steam. Press the Cancel button to reset the program. Carefully remove the lid.

Add the pasta and stir to combine. Lock the lid in place and turn the valve to Sealing. Press the Pressure Cook button and set the cook time for 2 minutes at high pressure.

Turn the valve to Venting to quick-release the steam. Carefully remove the lid and discard the cheese rind. Immediately add the kale and zucchini and stir to mix. The kale will wilt and the zucchini will soften in 3–5 minutes. Taste and adjust the seasoning if needed.

Ladle the soup into bowls and top with cheese and basil.

2 tablespoons unsalted butter

1 yellow onion, chopped

2 carrots, peeled, halved lengthwise, and cut into half-moons ¼ inch (6 mm) thick

2 ribs celery, sliced

2 cloves garlic, minced

½ lb (225 g) small waxy potatoes in assorted colors, halved

1 can (15 oz/425 g) diced tomatoes and their juice

4 cups (950 ml) chicken stock (page 270 or store-bought)

4 cups (950 ml) water

1 cup (200 g) dried white beans, picked over and rinsed

3 fresh oregano sprigs

1 large piece Parmesan cheese rind (optional)

1 cup (100 g) dried ditalini, tubetti, macaroni, or other small pasta

1 bunch kale or other hearty green, stemmed and coarsely chopped

½ lb (225 g) summer squash, cut into small cubes

FOR SERVING

Freshly grated Parmesan cheese, fresh basil leaves

Five-Spice Beef with Udon Noodles & Bok Choy

Economical beef cuts like blade and flat-iron become fork-tender when cooked under pressure. Shichimi togarashi, a Japanese seven-spice seasoning blend, makes a flavorful garnish.

SERVES 4–6

2 small or 1 large shallot, minced (about 3 tablespoons)

2-inch (5-cm) piece fresh ginger, peeled and minced (about 1 tablespoon)

½ teaspoon Chinese five-spice powder

4 cups (950 ml) beef stock (page 272 or store-bought)

2 cups (475 ml) water

2 lb (1 kg) boneless beef blade, flat-iron, or beef chuck steak, cut into slices against the grain ¼ inch (6 mm) thick

Kosher salt

4 heads baby bok choy, trimmed and quartered lengthwise

1 package (about 10 oz/285 g) dried udon noodles

1 teaspoon sugar

FOR SERVING

Minced green onions, shichimi togarashi (optional)

Combine the shallot, ginger, five-spice powder, stock, water, beef, and 2 teaspoons salt in the Instant Pot® and stir to mix.

Lock the lid in place and turn the valve to Sealing. Press the Pressure Cook button and set the cook time for 30 minutes at high pressure.

Let the steam release naturally for 15 minutes, then turn the valve to Venting to quick-release any residual steam. Carefully remove the lid. Using tongs, transfer the beef to a plate. Carefully pour the broth through a fine-mesh sieve set over a heatproof bowl. Return the strained broth to the pot. Press the Cancel button to reset the program.

Press the Sauté button twice to select More mode. Add the bok choy and noodles and cook until just tender, about 5 minutes. (If you don't plan to eat the all of the soup in one sitting, cook the noodles separately according to the package directions and add them in individual portions so they don't get mushy.) Stir in the sugar and taste and adjust the seasoning if needed.

Ladle the soup into bowls and top with green onions. Sprinkle with shichimi togarashi, if desired.

Pork & Vegetable Ramen

Customize this homey noodle soup with your choice of toppings. Fresh ramen, which can be found in the refrigerated section of well-stocked grocery stores or Asian markets, will taste best, but dried noodles are a respectable substitute.

SERVES 6

2 lb (1 kg) boneless pork shoulder, cut into 3 equal pieces

Kosher salt

1 tablespoon canola oil

1 yellow onion, chopped

6 cloves garlic, chopped

2-inch (5-cm) piece fresh ginger, peeled and chopped

8 cups (2 L) chicken stock (page 270 or store-bought)

1 leek, white and pale green parts only, halved lengthwise, rinsed well, and sliced

¼ lb (115 g) cremini or white button mushrooms, brushed clean and sliced

1½ lb (680 g) fresh or dried ramen noodles

1 tablespoon soy sauce, plus more if needed

FOR SERVING

Baby bok choy, sliced napa cabbage, sliced fresh shiitake mushrooms, peeled and halved soft-boiled eggs, sliced green onions, sesame seeds, and/or roasted nori seaweed strips, plus toasted sesame and/or chile oil

Pat the pork dry with paper towels. Season generously all over with salt. Select Sauté on the Instant Pot® and heat the oil. Working in batches, add the pork and brown evenly on all sides, about 5 minutes per side. As each batch is done, transfer it to a plate. Grasp a paper towel with tongs and wipe out all but 2 tablespoons of fat from the pot.

Add the onion to the pot and cook, stirring occasionally and scraping up any browned bits, until softened, about 3 minutes. Add the garlic and ginger and cook, stirring, until fragrant, about 1 minute. Add 1 cup (240 ml) of the stock and cook for 1 minute. Press the Cancel button to reset the program.

Add the leek, mushrooms, and remaining 7 cups (1.7 L) stock and stir to mix. Return the pork to the pot. Lock the lid in place and turn the valve to Sealing. Press the Pressure Cook button and set the cook time for 45 minutes at high pressure.

Meanwhile, cook the noodles according to the package directions and set aside.

Let the steam release naturally for 20 minutes, then turn the valve to Venting to quick-release any residual steam. Carefully remove the lid. Transfer the pork to a plate, let cool slightly, then shred into bite-size pieces with two forks. Strain the broth through a fine-mesh sieve set over a heatproof bowl. Discard the solids, reserving the mushroom slices if desired. Skim off the fat from the surface of the broth. Add the soy sauce, then taste and add more soy if needed.

Divide the noodles among 6 bowls and ladle the broth over the noodles. Add the pork and toppings.

Texas Beef Chili

Texas-style chili has no beans. It's traditionally a long-simmered dish made with beef stew meat (such as chuck) and a combo of chile peppers and spices. For the most authentic taste, use ground chiles rather than preblended chile powder (see Tip below).

SERVES 4–6

3 lb (1.5 kg) beef chuck, cut into 1-inch (2.5-cm) cubes

Kosher salt

3 tablespoons canola oil

1 yellow onion, chopped

2 cloves garlic, minced

3 tablespoons ancho chile powder, homemade or store-bought

1 tablespoon sweet paprika

2 teaspoons ground cumin

1 teaspoon dried oregano

1½ cups (375 ml) water

½ cup (120 ml) tomato paste

FOR SERVING

Sour cream, grated Cheddar cheese, and/or sliced green onions

Pat the meat dry with paper towels and season it lightly all over with salt.

Select Sauté on the Instant Pot® and heat 2 tablespoons of the oil. Working in batches, brown the meat evenly, about 8 minutes total. Transfer to a plate as browned. Add the remaining 1 tablespoon oil and the onion and cook until softened, about 3 minutes. Add the garlic and cook until fragrant, about 1 minute. Stir in the chile powder, paprika, cumin, and oregano. Pour in the water, then stir in the tomato paste until blended. Return the meat and any accumulated juices to the pot, then stir to coat the meat with sauce. Press the Cancel button to reset the program.

Lock the lid in place and turn the valve to Sealing. Press the Pressure Cook button and set the cook time for 15 minutes at high pressure.

Let the steam release naturally. Carefully remove the lid and let the chili stand for 5 minutes to settle the flavors.

Ladle the chili into bowls and top each portion with sour cream, cheese, and/or green onions, as desired. Serve right away.

TIP *You can make your own ancho chile powder by lightly toasting dried ancho chiles in a dry frying pan over low heat on the stove for a few minutes. When the chiles are cool enough to handle, remove the stems and tear the chiles into pieces. Put the pieces into a spice grinder, clean coffee grinder, or small food processor, and blend until ground.*

Turkey Meatball & Farro

A cozy cauldron of meatballs is the perfect comfort food. Farro pairs deliciously with the meatballs, adding heft and a mild earthy flavor. Ground dark-meat chicken can be substituted for the turkey.

SERVES 6

FOR THE MEATBALLS

1 lb (450 g) ground turkey

2 cloves garlic, minced or grated

¼ cup (1 oz/25 g) panko bread crumbs

2 tablespoons freshly grated Parmesan cheese

1 egg, lightly beaten

1 tablespoon tomato paste

1 teaspoon dried oregano

Kosher salt and freshly ground black pepper

2 tablespoons olive oil

1 yellow onion, chopped

2 cloves garlic, minced

2 tablespoons tomato paste

1 cup (200 g) pearled farro

6 cups (1.4 L) chicken stock (page 270 or store-bought)

1 large bunch Swiss chard, stemmed and chopped

FOR SERVING

Freshly grated Parmesan cheese

To make the meatballs, in a bowl, combine the turkey, garlic, panko, cheese, egg, tomato paste, oregano, 1 teaspoon salt, and ¼ teaspoon pepper. Using your hands or a wooden spoon, mix gently just until all the ingredients are evenly distributed. Be careful not to overmix, or the meatballs will be tough. To shape each meatball, scoop up a heaping teaspoon of the turkey mixture and, using lightly dampened hands, roll it into a ball between your palms. As the meatballs are shaped, set them aside on a large plate. You should have about 30 meatballs.

Select Sauté on the Instant Pot® and heat the oil. Add the onion and cook, stirring occasionally, until softened, about 5 minutes. Add the garlic and cook, stirring, until fragrant, about 1 minute. Add the tomato paste, 1 teaspoon salt, and ¼ teaspoon pepper and cook, stirring, for about 1 minute to blend well. Press the Cancel button to reset the program.

Add the farro, stock, and meatballs to the pot and stir gently to mix. Lock the lid in place and turn the valve to Sealing. Press the Pressure Cook button and set the cook time for 15 minutes at high pressure.

Let the steam release naturally for 10 minutes before turning the valve to Venting to quick-release any residual steam. Carefully remove the lid. Immediately add the chard and stir to mix. The chard will wilt in the hot liquid in about 3 minutes. Taste and adjust the seasoning as needed.

Ladle the soup into bowls and sprinkle with cheese.

Farro is an ancient Italian wheat variety that provides nutrients and fiber, as well as a pleasing chewy texture, to this wholesome soup.

Posole Rojo with Pork

The toppings and tortillas are as essential to this centuries-old Mexican soup as the pork, hominy, and spices. Choose a selection of pretty bowls, fill them with the suggested toppings, and set them out on a big platter or tray.

SERVES 6

2 lb (1 kg) boneless thick-cut pork chops (about 4), excess fat trimmed

Kosher salt and freshly ground black pepper

2 tablespoons canola or avocado oil

1 large yellow onion, chopped

8 cloves garlic, minced

2 tablespoons tomato paste

2 tablespoons chili powder

1½ teaspoons dried oregano, preferably Mexican

½ teaspoon dried thyme

4 cups (950 ml) chicken stock (page 270 or store-bought)

1 cup (240 ml) water

1 can (25 oz/710 g) hominy, rinsed and drained

FOR SERVING

Shredded green cabbage, thinly sliced radishes and jalapeño chiles, diced onions (red, yellow, or white), sour cream, fresh cilantro leaves, charred corn tortillas, lime wedges

Pat the pork dry with paper towels. Season the pork generously with salt and pepper.

Select Sauté on the Instant Pot® and heat 1 tablespoon of the oil. Working in batches, add the pork and brown evenly on both sides, about 3 minutes per side. As each batch is ready, transfer to a plate.

Add the remaining 1 tablespoon oil and the onion to the pot and cook, stirring occasionally with a wooden spoon and scraping up any browned bits, until softened, about 3 minutes. Add the garlic and cook, stirring, until fragrant, about 1 minute. Add the tomato paste, chili powder, oregano, thyme, and 2 tablespoons of the stock and cook, stirring occasionally, for 1 minute. Press the Cancel button to reset the program.

Add the remaining stock, the water, and the hominy and stir to mix. Return the pork and any accumulated juices to the pot. Lock the lid in place and turn the valve to Sealing. Press the Pressure Cook button and set the cook time for 30 minutes at high pressure.

Let the steam release naturally for 20 minutes, then turn the valve to Venting to quick-release any residual steam. Carefully remove the lid. Using tongs, transfer the pork to a plate. Let the pork sit until cool enough to handle. Then, using two forks, shred it into bite-size pieces. Return the pork to the pot and stir in 1 teaspoon salt. Taste and adjust the seasoning with salt and pepper as needed.

Ladle the soup into bowls and top with cabbage, radishes, onion, sour cream, and/or cilantro. Serve with tortillas and lime wedges alongside.

Italian Wedding Soup

The origin of the name for this southern Italian soup comes from the "marriage" of flavors between the meat and greens. Traditionally simmered on the stove top for hours, this version cooks to perfection under pressure.

SERVES 6

FOR THE MEATBALLS

1 lb (450 g) ground pork

2 cloves garlic, minced or grated

¼ cup (1 oz/25 g) panko bread crumbs

2 tablespoons freshly grated Parmesan cheese, plus more for serving

1 egg, lightly beaten

1 tablespoon tomato paste

1 teaspoon dried oregano

Kosher salt and freshly ground black pepper

6 cups (1.4 L) chicken stock (page 270 or store-bought)

3 large carrots, peeled and chopped

1 rib celery, sliced

1 lb (450 g) kale, escarole, or other sturdy leafy green, stemmed and chopped

1 cup (225 g) acini di pepe pasta ("peppercorns" shape)

To make the meatballs, in a bowl, combine the pork, garlic, bread crumbs, cheese, egg, tomato paste, oregano, 1 teaspoon salt, and ¼ teaspoon pepper. Using your hands or a wooden spoon, mix gently just until all the ingredients are evenly distributed. Be careful not to overmix, or the meatballs will be tough. To shape each meatball, scoop up a heaping teaspoon of the turkey mixture and, using lightly dampened hands, roll it into a ball between your palms. As the meatballs are shaped, set them aside on a large plate. You should have about 30 meatballs.

Combine the stock, carrots, celery, meatballs, 1 teaspoon salt, and ¼ teaspoon pepper in the Instant Pot®. Lock the lid in place and turn the valve to Sealing. Press the Pressure Cook button and set the cook time for 15 minutes at high pressure.

Let the steam release naturally for 10 minutes, then turn the valve to Venting to quick-release any residual steam. Carefully remove the lid. Press the Cancel button to reset the program.

Press the Sauté button and bring the broth to a simmer. Add the kale and pasta and cook until the pasta starts to soften and kale is wilted, about 4 minutes. (The pasta will continue to soften as it sits in the hot broth.) Taste and adjust the seasoning if needed.

Ladle the soup into bowl and top with Parmesan cheese and pepper.

Chicken Enchilada Stew

You can feed a crowd on a weeknight with this easy-to-assemble soup. Load it up with the toppings suggested here—kids will love to choose their own—or add other favorites, such as sour cream, diced jalapeños, and salsa. To keep the culinary theme going, serve dulce de leche ice cream for dessert.

SERVES 6–8

1 yellow onion, chopped

2 cans (15 oz/425 g each) diced fire-roasted tomatoes and their juice

2 cans (4 oz/115 g each) diced green chiles and their juice

1 cup (200 g) dried black beans, picked over and rinsed

4 cups (950 ml) chicken stock (page 270 or store-bought)

2 tablespoons chili powder

2 teaspoons ground cumin

Kosher salt

2½ lb (1.1 kg) boneless, skinless chicken thighs

Grated zest and juice of 1 lime

FOR SERVING

Shredded Cheddar and/or Monterey Jack cheese, chopped fresh cilantro, diced jalapeño chile, sour cream, tortilla chips, lime wedges

Combine the onion, tomatoes, chiles, beans, stock, chili powder, cumin, and 1½ teaspoons salt in the Instant Pot® and stir to mix. Nestle the chicken pieces into the stock mixture.

Lock the lid in place and turn the valve to Sealing. Press the Pressure Cook button and set the cook time for 20 minutes at high pressure.

Let the steam release naturally for 10 minutes, then turn the valve to Venting to quick-release any residual steam. Using two forks, shred the chicken into bite-size pieces. Add the lime zest and half of the lime juice. Taste and adjust the seasoning with more lime juice and salt if needed.

Ladle the stew into bowls and layer with toppings as desired. Serve with lime wedges alongside.

Chicken Wild Rice

This creamy soup is a staple in Minnesota, where wild rice is the official state grain. Forget to thaw the chicken? You can use frozen thighs without adjusting the cooking time. Just keep in mind that the soup will take longer to come up to pressure.

SERVES 6

2 tablespoons unsalted butter

1 yellow onion, diced

2 carrots, peeled and diced

3 ribs celery, diced

½ lb (225 g) cremini mushrooms, brushed clean and sliced

6 cups (1.4 L) chicken stock (page 270 or store-bought)

1 cup (155 g) wild rice, rinsed

1 lb (450 g) boneless, skinless chicken thighs

2 bay leaves

Kosher salt and freshly ground black pepper

¼ cup (60 ml) heavy cream

½ teaspoon chopped fresh thyme leaves

Select Sauté on the Instant Pot® and melt the butter. Add the onion, carrots, and celery and cook, stirring occasionally, until softened, about 5 minutes. Add the mushrooms and cook, stirring occasionally, until softened, about 2 minutes. Add the stock, wild rice, chicken, bay leaves, 1½ teaspoons salt, and 1 teaspoon pepper and stir to mix. Press the Cancel button to reset the program.

Lock the lid in place and turn the valve to Sealing. Press the Pressure Cook button and set the cook time for 25 minutes at high pressure.

Let the pressure release naturally for 20 minutes, then turn the valve to Venting to quick-release any residual steam. Carefully remove the lid and discard the bay leaves. Using two forks, shred the chicken into bite-size pieces. Add the cream and thyme and stir to mix. Taste and adjust the seasoning as needed.

Ladle the soup into bowls and top with pepper.

Smoky Black Bean Soup with Tangy Crema

This robust yet simple-to-prepare soup comes together quickly when cooked under pressure. The beans simmer to perfection without presoaking, taking on the flavor of the herbs, spices, and smoky-flavored adobo sauce in the process.

SERVES 6

1 tablespoon canola or avocado oil

1 yellow onion, diced

1 red bell pepper, seeded and diced

1 jalapeño chile, seeded and minced

3 cloves garlic, minced

1 tablespoon adobo sauce from canned chipotle chiles

1 tablespoon ground cumin

1½ teaspoons smoked paprika

1 teaspoon dried oregano

Kosher salt and freshly ground black pepper

1 lb (450 g) dried black beans, picked over and rinsed

4 cups (1 L) vegetable stock (page 271 or store-bought)

FOR THE CREMA

1 cup (225 g) sour cream

¼ cup (7 g) chopped fresh cilantro, plus more for garnish

¼ cup (45 g) minced red onion

1 teaspoon grated lime zest

2 tablespoons fresh lime juice

Tortilla chips, for serving

Select Sauté on the Instant Pot® and heat the oil. Add the yellow onion and bell pepper and cook until softened, about 5 minutes. Add the jalapeño, garlic, adobo sauce, cumin, paprika, oregano, and 1 teaspoon salt and cook until fragrant, about 2 minutes. Add the beans and stock and stir to combine.

Lock the lid in place and turn the valve to Sealing. Press the Pressure Cook button and set the cook time for 45 minutes at high pressure.

While the soup cooks, make the crema. In a small bowl, combine the sour cream, cilantro, red onion, lime zest, 1 tablespoon of the lime juice, ½ teaspoon salt, and a few grindings of fresh pepper and stir to combine. Taste and adjust the seasoning as needed.

When the soup has finished cooking, let the steam release naturally for about 15 minutes, then turn the valve to Venting to quick-release any residual steam and carefully remove the lid. Stir the remaining 1 tablespoon lime juice and a few grindings of fresh pepper into the soup. Taste and adjust the seasoning as needed.

Ladle the soup into bowls and top each with a large spoonful of the crema, garnish with more cilantro, and serve with tortilla chips alongside.

Tom Kha Gai Soup

A robust blend of coconut milk, lemongrass, red chiles, Thai lime leaves, and galangal (a root in the ginger family) comes together for a delectable yet easy-to-make Thai soup. Bruising the lemongrass is key to unlocking its flavor.

SERVES 6

2 stalks lemongrass, tough outer leaves removed

1 lb (450 g) boneless, skinless chicken thighs

2-inch (5-cm) piece galangal or fresh ginger, peeled and thickly sliced

1 small onion, sliced

2–4 red Thai chiles (depending on heat desired), bruised

8 oz (250 g) white button mushrooms, quartered

8 Thai lime leaves

2 cans (13½ oz/400 ml each) full-fat coconut milk

1 cup (240 ml) chicken stock (page 270 or store-bought)

3 tablespoons fish sauce

1 tablespoon coconut sugar

Juice of 1 lime

FOR SERVING

Fresh cilantro sprigs, lime wedges

To bruise the lemongrass, use the flat side of your knife and firmly push down on the inner stalk until it splits open. Then cut the stalks into 3-inch (7.5-cm) pieces.

Combine all the ingredients except the coconut sugar, lime juice, and cilantro leaves in the Instant Pot®. Lock the lid in place and turn the valve to Sealing. Press the Soup button and set the cook time for 20 minutes at high pressure.

Let the steam release naturally, or for at least 15 minutes, before turning the valve to Venting to quick-release any residual steam. Carefully remove the lid and remove and discard the lime leaves, lemongrass, and galangal. Shred the chicken into bite-size pieces using two forks. Add the coconut sugar and lime juice and stir to combine.

To serve, ladle into bowls and top with cilantro, along with lime wedges.

Seek out lemongrass, Thai lime leaves, and Thai chiles, as they are all essential in creating the authentic flavors of this effortless soup.

Gumbo is a classic Louisiana recipe and testimony to the region's multicultural heritage.

Shrimp Gumbo

A roux is a mixture of equal parts flour and fat cooked together and used to thicken stews and sauces. To achieve the traditional flavor and texture of a gumbo, don't skip this step. Offer hot sauce to add at the table.

SERVES 6

1 tablespoon olive oil

1 lb (450 g) andouille sausages, cut into slices ½ inch (12 mm) thick

FOR THE ROUX

5 tablespoons canola oil

5 tablespoons all-purpose flour

1 yellow onion, chopped

1 red bell pepper, seeded and chopped

1 green bell pepper, seeded and chopped

3 cloves garlic, minced

5 cups (1.2 L) chicken stock (page 270 or store-bought)

1 can (15 oz/425 g) diced tomatoes and their juice

2 bay leaves

1 lb (450 g) okra, stemmed and cut into 1-inch (2.5-cm) pieces

1 cup (155 g) wild rice, rinsed

2 tablespoons Cajun Spice Rub (page 265)

Kosher salt and freshly ground black pepper

1 lb (450 g) shrimp, fresh or frozen, peeled and deveined

Select Sauté on the Instant Pot® and heat the olive oil. Add the sausages and cook, stirring occasionally, until browned, about 4 minutes. Using a slotted spoon, transfer the sausage slices to a plate. Grasp a paper towel with tongs and wipe out the pot.

To make the roux, heat the canola oil in the pot. Add the flour and cook, stirring constantly with a whisk or silicone spatula, until the mixture forms a dark brown paste, 15–20 minutes. (The roux can also be made in a saucepan over medium-high heat on the stove top and then transferred to the Instant Pot®.) Add the onion and bell peppers and cook, stirring often, until softened, about 4 minutes. Add the garlic and cook, stirring, until fragrant, about 1 minute. Gradually add the stock, stirring constantly with the spatula or a wooden spoon to prevent lumps from forming and to scrape up any browned bits. Press the Cancel button to reset the program.

Add the reserved sausages, the tomatoes, bay leaves, okra, rice, spice rub, 1 teaspoon salt, and ¼ teaspoon pepper and stir to mix. Lock the lid in place and turn the valve to Sealing. Press the Pressure Cook button and set the cook time for 20 minutes at high pressure.

Let the steam release naturally for 20 minutes, then turn the valve to Venting to quick-release any residual steam. Carefully remove the lid. Discard the bay leaves. Press the Cancel button to reset the program.

Press the Sauté button, add the shrimp, and cook until pink and opaque, 2–3 minutes for fresh or about 4 minutes for frozen. Taste and adjust the seasoning if needed.

Ladle the gumbo into bowls and serve.

Coconut Fish Curry

The province of Goa, on the west coast of India, boasts a tropical cuisine that draws on both the Portuguese and the Indian pantries. Not surprisingly, seafood turns up in many dishes, including simple coconut milk–based curries like this one.

SERVES 4

- 1-inch (2.5-cm) piece fresh ginger, peeled
- 8 cloves garlic
- ½ cup (120 ml) water
- 1 tablespoon coconut or canola oil
- 1 yellow onion, chopped
- 2 fresh red Thai chiles, sliced and then seeded (for less heat) if desired
- 2 teaspoons ground cumin
- 1 teaspoon ground turmeric
- 2 cans (13½ fl oz/400 ml) full-fat coconut milk
- 2 cups (480 ml) chicken or vegetable stock (pages 270–271 or store-bought)
- Kosher salt
- 1 red bell pepper, seeded and sliced
- 2 lb (1 kg) skinless firm white fish fillets, such as cod, halibut, or pollack, cut into 2-inch (5-cm) pieces

FOR SERVING

Steamed rice (page 266), optional; chopped fresh cilantro leaves

In a blender, combine the ginger, garlic, and water and blend until smooth.

Select Sauté on the Instant Pot® and heat the oil. Add the onion and cook, stirring occasionally, until softened, about 5 minutes. Add the ginger purée, chiles, cumin, and turmeric and cook, stirring, until well mixed, about 1 minute. Add the coconut milk, stock, and 1 teaspoon salt and stir to mix. Press the Cancel button to reset the program.

Lock the lid in place and turn the valve to Sealing. Press the Pressure Cook button and set the cook time for 10 minutes at high pressure.

Let the steam release naturally for 10 minutes, then turn the valve to Venting to quick-release any residual steam. Carefully remove the lid. Press the Cancel button to reset the program.

Press the Sauté button, add the bell pepper and fish, and cook until the pepper begins to soften and the fish is opaque when tested with a fork, about 5 minutes. Taste and adjust the seasoning with salt if needed.

Serve the curry in bowls, ladling it over rice, if using, and sprinkle with cilantro.

Ladle the soup over bowls of steamed white or brown rice for a more substantial meal.

Mediterranean Fish Stew

You can vary the fish you choose for this Mediterranean-inspired seafood dish, selecting what looks freshest at the market. Tilapia, halibut, cod, or a combination would be delicious in the tomato-based broth. A crusty loaf of bread makes for an excellent accompaniment.

SERVES 6

2 tablespoons olive oil

1 yellow onion, chopped

1 leek, halved lengthwise, rinsed well, and thinly sliced

½ fennel bulb, thinly sliced

4 cloves garlic, minced

1 can (28 oz/800 g) whole peeled tomatoes and their juice

2 cups (480 ml) fish stock (page 271) or bottled clam juice

2 cups (475 ml) water

1 bay leaf

2 pinches of saffron threads

¼ teaspoon red pepper flakes

1 teaspoon dried thyme

1 teaspoon grated orange zest

Kosher salt and freshly ground black pepper

1 lb (450 g) skinless white fish fillets (see note), cut into 2-inch (5-cm) pieces

1 lb (450 g) shrimp, fresh or frozen, peeled and deveined

FOR SERVING

Chopped fresh fennel fronds, chopped fresh flat-leaf parsley leaves, grilled crusty bread

Select Sauté on the Instant Pot® and heat the oil. Add the onion, leek, and fennel and cook, stirring occasionally, until softened, about 5 minutes. Add the garlic and tomatoes, breaking up the tomatoes with a wooden spoon. Cook, stirring occasionally, until combined, about 3 minutes. Add the stock, water, bay leaf, saffron, red pepper flakes, thyme, orange zest, 1 teaspoon salt, and ½ teaspoon black pepper and bring to a simmer, stirring occasionally. Press the Cancel button to reset the program.

Lock the lid in place and turn the valve to Sealing. Press the Pressure Cook button and set the cook time for 20 minutes at high pressure.

Let the steam release naturally, or for at least 15 minutes before turning the valve to Venting to quick-release any residual steam. Carefully remove the lid and discard the bay leaf. Press the Cancel button to reset the program.

Press the Sauté button, add the fish, and cook until opaque when tested with a fork, about 3 minutes. Add the shrimp and cook until they turn pink and opaque, 2–3 minutes for fresh or about 4 minutes for frozen. Taste and adjust the seasoning as needed.

Ladle the stew into bowls and top with fennel fronds, parsley, and pepper. Serve with bread alongside.

New England Clam Chowder

In this easy breezy chowder, clam juice and canned chopped clams save time and work in the kitchen. For a thicker base, add a roux of flour and butter to the soup after pressure cooking and before adding the milk and cream (see note below). Oyster crackers are a traditional accompaniment.

SERVES 6

2 slices thick-cut bacon chopped

1 yellow onion, chopped

2 ribs celery, sliced

3 fresh thyme sprigs, or ¼ teaspoon dried thyme

1 lb (450 g) russet potatoes (about 2 large), peeled and cut into 1-inch (2.5-cm) cubes

2 cans (6½ oz/185 g each) chopped clam meat, drained, with juice reserved

1 bottle (8 fl oz/240 ml) clam juice

2 cups (475 ml) water

Kosher salt and freshly ground black pepper

1½ cups (350 ml) whole milk

1 cup (240 ml) heavy cream

Pinch of cayenne pepper (optional)

FOR SERVING

Chopped fresh flat-leaf parsley, oyster crackers

Select Sauté on the Instant Pot® three times to select Less mode and add the bacon. Cook, stirring occasionally, until browned and most of the fat is rendered, about 5 minutes. Using a slotted spoon, transfer the bacon to a paper towel–lined plate. Add the onion and celery and cook, stirring occasionally and scraping up any browned bits, until softened, about 5 minutes. Add the thyme, potatoes, reserved clam juice, bottled clam juice, water, and 1 teaspoon salt and stir to mix. Press the Cancel button to reset the program.

Lock the lid in place and turn the valve to Sealing. Press the Pressure Cook button and set the cook time for 7 minutes at high pressure.

Let the steam release naturally for 15 minutes, then turn the valve to Venting to quick-release any residual steam. Carefully remove the lid and remove and discard the thyme sprigs, if used. Press the Cancel button to reset the program.

Press the Sauté button and bring the broth to a simmer. Add the milk and cream, stir to mix, and simmer until thoroughly combined and hot, about 3 minutes. Add the clam meat and cook until heated through, about 1 minute. Add the cayenne, if using, then taste and adjust the seasoning if needed.

Ladle the soup into bowls and top with parsley and the reserved bacon. Serve with oyster crackers alongside.

NOTE *To make a roux, heat 3 tablespoons butter in a small saucepan over medium-high heat. Add 3 tablespoons all-purpose flour and cook, stirring constantly, until a dark brown paste is formed, 15–20 minutes.*

Tomato-Fennel Broth with Mussels

This broth, rich with fennel, garlic, white wine, and tomatoes, creates a simple yet satisfying base for nearly any type of seafood. Try peeled and deveined shrimp or 2-inch (5-cm) chunks of firm white fish in place of the mussels.

SERVES 4–6

1 tablespoon olive oil

1 tablespoon unsalted butter

2 fennel bulbs, stalks and fronds removed, sliced (reserve fronds for serving)

2 shallots, minced

6 cloves garlic, sliced

½ cup (120 ml) dry white wine

1 can (28 oz/800 g) whole tomatoes and their juice

3 cups (700 ml) chicken, vegetable, or fish stock (pages 270–271 or store-bought)

3 fresh oregano sprigs

1 bay leaf

Kosher salt and freshly ground black pepper

2 lb (1 kg) mussels, scrubbed and debearded

FOR THE PARSLEY OIL

½ cup (30 g) minced fresh flat-leaf parsley

Grated zest and juice of 1 lemon

¼ cup (60 ml) extra-virgin olive oil

1 clove garlic, minced

Select Sauté on the Instant Pot® and heat the olive oil and butter. Add the fennel and shallots and cook, stirring occasionally, until softened, about 5 minutes. Add the garlic and cook, stirring, until fragrant, about 1 minute. Add the wine and cook until almost completely absorbed, about 2 minutes. Add the tomatoes, breaking them up with a wooden spoon, then add the stock, oregano, bay leaf, 2 teaspoons salt, and ½ teaspoon pepper and stir to mix. Press the Cancel button to reset the program.

Lock the lid in place and turn the valve to Sealing. Press the Pressure Cook button and set the cook time for 10 minutes at high pressure.

Meanwhile, make the parsley oil. In a small bowl or glass measuring jug, whisk together the parsley, lemon zest and juice, oil, garlic, 1 teaspoon salt, and ¼ teaspoon pepper, mixing well (or combine the ingredients in a small lidded jar and shake well). Taste and adjust the seasoning if needed. Set aside.

Let the steam release naturally for 10 minutes, then turn the valve to Venting to quick-release any residual steam. Carefully remove the lid. Discard the bay leaf. Press the Cancel button to reset the program.

Press the Sauté button and add the mussels, discarding any that do not close to the touch. Cook until the mussels open, about 5 minutes. Discard any mussels that failed to open. Taste and adjust the seasoning if needed.

Ladle the soup into bowls and drizzle with parsley oil.

Thai Butternut Squash & Tofu Soup with Peanut-Cilantro Relish

Thai curry paste and coconut milk marry beautifully with sweet butternut squash in this satisfying soup. Lime leaves are available in the produce section of some grocery stores or at Asian markets. Although optional here, they are worth seeking out, as they add a lime-and-floral flavor that makes his mouthwatering dish taste beautifully robust. Leftover lime leaves freeze well.

SERVES 4

FOR THE SOUP

2 tablespoons coconut oil or canola oil

1 yellow onion, chopped

1 red bell pepper, seeded and sliced

2 tablespoons vegetarian red curry paste (see Tip)

2 lb (1 kg) butternut squash, peeled, seeded, and cut into 1-inch (2.5-cm) cubes

1 can (13½ fl oz/400 ml) coconut milk

3 cups (700 ml) vegetable stock (page 271 or store-bought)

6 Thai lime leaves (optional)

FOR THE RELISH

½ cup (15 g) loosely packed fresh cilantro leaves

¼ cup (35 g) dry-roasted peanuts

1 small clove garlic, peeled

Zest of 1 lime

14 oz (400 g) firm tofu, cut into ½-inch (12-mm) cubes

Soy sauce or fish sauce

To make the soup, put the oil in the Instant Pot®, select Sauté, and adjust to More/High heat. Add the onion and bell pepper and cook, stirring frequently, until the vegetables are tender, about 5 minutes. Add the curry paste and cook, stirring constantly, until fragrant, about 15 seconds. Press the Cancel button.

Add the butternut squash, coconut milk, stock, and lime leaves (if using) to the pot and stir to combine.

Lock the lid in place and turn the valve to Sealing. Press the Pressure Cook button and set the cook time for 4 minutes at high pressure.

Meanwhile, make the relish: Mound the cilantro, peanuts, garlic, and lime zest on a cutting board. Chop until the cilantro and peanuts are broken down into confetti-size bits.

When the cooking time is up, turn the valve to Venting to quick-release the steam. Carefully remove the lid and remove the lime leaves and discard. Stir in the tofu and season to taste with soy sauce. Let stand for a few minutes to heat up the tofu.

Ladle the soup into bowls, top with the peanut-cilantro relish, and serve.

TIP *If you're serving vegetarians, be sure to check the curry paste label; some brands contain dried shrimp or fish sauce.*

Butternut Squash Curry Soup

Sweet and satisfying butternut squash cubes cook in an ever-so-slightly spicy coconut broth in just 4 minutes, making this the perfect weeknight choice when saving time is top of mind. Although this soup doesn't need anything more, steamed white or brown rice (page 266) and a few lime wedges for squeezing would be welcome alongside it.

SERVES 4

2 tablespoons canola or avocado oil

1 yellow onion, chopped

1 red bell pepper, seeded and sliced

3 tablespoons red curry paste

2 lb (1 kg) butternut squash, peeled, seeded, and cut into 1-inch (2.5-cm) cubes

1 can (13½ fl oz/400 ml) coconut milk

3 cups (700 ml) vegetable stock (page 271 or store-bought)

Kosher salt and freshly ground black pepper

Fresh basil leaves, preferably Thai, for serving

Select Sauté on the Instant Pot® and heat the oil. Add the onion and bell pepper and cook, stirring occasionally, until the vegetables start to soften, about 3 minutes. Add the curry paste and squash and stir until combined. Press the Cancel button to reset the program.

Add the coconut milk, stock, 1 teaspoon salt, and ¼ teaspoon pepper and stir to combine. Lock the lid in place and turn the valve to Sealing. Press the Pressure Cook button and set the cook time for 4 minutes at high pressure.

Turn the valve to Venting to quick-release the steam. Carefully remove the lid. Taste and adjust the seasoning if needed.

Ladle the soup into bowls and top with basil.

Asian Chicken Salad with Ginger Dressing

Fragrant ginger-marinated chicken pairs beautifully with wild rice, blood orange, and red cabbage in this colorful salad. Garnish with fresh cilantro leaves.

SERVES 4

FOR THE MARINADE

¼ cup (60 ml) tamari

2 teaspoons toasted sesame oil

2 teaspoons rice vinegar

2 tablespoons grated fresh ginger

1½ lb (680 g) boneless, skinless chicken breasts

1 tablespoon canola oil

½ cup (120 ml) chicken stock (page 270 or store-bought)

FOR THE DRESSING

2 tablespoons rice vinegar

1 tablespoon tamari

1 tablespoon brown sugar

2 tablespoons grated fresh ginger

¼ teaspoon freshly ground black pepper

¼ cup (60 ml) canola oil

FOR SERVING

Wild Rice (page 266)

4 cups (200 g) romaine lettuce, chopped

2 cups (200 g) shredded red cabbage

2 blood or navel oranges

½ cup (75 g) roasted peanuts

To make the marinade, in a small bowl or measuring cup, whisk together the tamari, sesame oil, vinegar, and ginger. Place the chicken breasts in a shallow pan or baking dish and pour the marinade over the top. Cover with plastic wrap and marinate in the refrigerator for at least 30 minutes and up to 2 hours, turning occasionally to coat.

Select Sauté on the Instant Pot® and heat the oil. Working in batches, add the chicken breasts, reserving the marinade, and brown evenly on both sides, 2–3 minutes per side. Add the stock and use a wooden spoon to scrape up any browned bits. Add the reserved marinade and stir to combine. Press the Cancel button to reset the program.

Lock the lid in place and turn the valve to Sealing. Press the Pressure Cook button and set the cook time for 6 minutes at high pressure.

Meanwhile, to make the dressing, put the vinegar, tamari, brown sugar, ginger, pepper, and canola oil in a blender or food processor and blend until smooth. Set aside.

When the chicken has finished cooking, let the steam release naturally for 5 minutes, before turning the valve to Venting to quick-release any residual steam.

Carefully remove the lid and use tongs to transfer the chicken to a plate. Let the meat cool slightly and then shred it with two forks.

Divide the rice, lettuce, cabbage, chicken, oranges, and peanuts evenly among 4 plates. Serve with dressing alongside.

Offer this chunky salad in appetizer portions (as here), or spoon it into butter lettuce cups for larger servings.

Waldorf Chicken Salad

Named for New York's Waldorf-Astoria Hotel, the Waldorf salad traditionally included only apples and celery bound by mayonnaise. Here, perfectly tender chicken adds to the classic mix.

SERVES 6

FOR THE CHICKEN

1 yellow onion, quartered

2 carrots, peeled and cut into 2-inch (5-cm) lengths

2 ribs celery, cut into 2-inch (5-cm) segments

4 cloves garlic, smashed

2 cups (475 ml) water

1 whole chicken, 4 lb (1.8 kg)

1 tablespoon kosher salt

½ tsp ground pepper

FOR THE SALAD

½ cup (120 ml) mayonnaise

2 tablespoons plain Greek yogurt

1 tablespoon fresh lemon juice

Kosher salt and freshly ground pepper

1 cup (115 g) diced apple

1 cup (140 g) seedless red grapes, halved

½ cup (70 g) finely diced celery

½ cup (70 g) thinly sliced fennel, plus fennel fronds for garnish

¾ cup (90 g) salted roasted cashews

1–2 heads Belgian endive, leaves separated

To cook the chicken, put the onion, carrots, celery, garlic, and water in the Instant Pot®, then place the steam rack on the pot bottom. Season the chicken inside and out with the salt and pepper and place it, breast side up, on the rack. Lock the lid in place and turn the valve to Sealing. Press the Manual/Pressure Cook button and set the cook time for 25 minutes at high pressure.

Let the steam release naturally for 20 minutes, then turn the valve to Venting to release any residual steam. Carefully remove the lid and transfer the chicken to a cutting board. When cool enough to handle, remove the meat, discarding the skin and bones. Cut enough meat into 1-inch (2.5 cm) cubes to measure 2 cups for the salad. Reserve the remaining meat for another use.

To make the salad, in a large bowl, whisk together the mayonnaise, yogurt, and lemon juice. Season with salt and pepper. Add the apple, grapes, celery, fennel, cashews, and cubed chicken and toss to coat evenly. Taste and adjust the seasoning with salt and pepper.

Arrange a bed of endive leaves on a serving platter and top with the salad. Garnish with fennel fronds and serve.

Zesty Wild Rice Salad

This blend of hearty rice, crunchy toppings, and a refreshing vinaigrette is wonderful as a main dish at an outdoor picnic or as a side dish paired with Cherry Cola Short Ribs (page 156) or Salmon Tacos with Crispy Slaw (page 211). Pack leftovers for lunch or a quick meal on the go.

SERVES 6

1½ cups (240 g) wild rice

4½ cups (1.1 L) water

Kosher salt and freshly ground black pepper

1 large red bell pepper, seeded and diced

2 green onions, thinly sliced

½ cup (80 g) pomegranate seeds

¾ cup (70 g) toasted sliced almonds

3 tablespoons apple cider vinegar

1½ teaspoons soy sauce

½ teaspoon peeled and grated fresh ginger

5 tablespoons (75 ml) olive oil

Rinse the rice in a sieve under cold running water until the water runs clear; shake the sieve to remove excess water.

In the Instant Pot®, combine the drained rice, water, and 1 teaspoon salt. Lock the lid in place and turn the valve to Sealing. Press the Pressure Cook button and set the cook time for 30 minutes at high pressure.

Let the steam release naturally for 10 minutes, then turn the valve to Venting to quick-release any residual steam. Carefully remove the lid. Fluff the rice with a fork.

In a large bowl, combine the rice, bell pepper, green onions, pomegranate seeds, and almonds. In a small bowl, whisk together the vinegar, soy sauce, and ginger. Slowly whisk in the oil to make a dressing. Season to taste with salt and pepper. Pour the dressing over the salad, mix well, and serve.

Quinoa, Lentil & Radicchio Salad

Enjoy this protein-packed salad at lunch for enough fuel to last through the day. Crumbled goat cheese contributes a mellow creaminess to the hearty bean-and-grain mix. Use the softest variety you can find so it blends in easily. If making the salad ahead, don't add the apple or dressing until just before serving.

SERVES 4

2 cups (370 g) cooked red, white, or mixed quinoa **(page 267)**

1 cup (200 g) black lentils, picked over and rinsed

2 cups (475 ml) water

Kosher salt and freshly ground black pepper

FOR THE DRESSING

¼ cup (60 ml) apple cider vinegar

2 tablespoons honey

⅓ cup (80 ml) olive oil

1 head radicchio, cored and sliced into strips

1 Pink Lady or other red-skinned apple, cored and thinly sliced

½ cup (80 g) crumbled goat cheese

Chopped fresh basil

Prepare the quinoa as directed.

Put the lentils, water, and ½ teaspoon salt in the Instant Pot®. Stir to combine. Lock the lid in place and turn the valve to Sealing. Press the Pressure Cook button and set the cook time for 10 minutes at high pressure.

Meanwhile, make the dressing. Combine the vinegar, honey, olive oil, and a pinch of salt in a small lidded jar. Close the lid and shake well until blended. Add more salt, if needed, and pepper to taste. Set aside.

When the lentils have finished cooking, let the steam release naturally for 10 minutes, then turn the valve to Venting to quick-release any residual steam. Carefully remove the lid.

To serve, divide the quinoa evenly among 4 plates or large bowls. Top the quinoa with a scoop of lentils (reserve any remaining lentils for another meal), radicchio, apple slices, goat cheese, and basil. Sprinkle with salt and a few grindings of black pepper. Drizzle some of the dressing on top and serve with the remaining dressing alongside.

Farro, Squash & Arugula Salad

These colorful grain bowls are packed full of fiber, nutrients, and a fresh mix of textures and flavors. For a quick and healthy lunch on the go, pack the salad into large jars or other airtight containers, storing the dressing in a separate container to toss in just before eating.

SERVES 4

2 cups (360 g) cooked farro (page 267)

1 cup (240 ml) water

1 large delicata squash (about 1 lb/450 g), halved and cut into pieces 1 inch (2.5 cm) wide

FOR THE DRESSING

¼ cup (60 ml) fresh orange juice

1 tablespoon fresh lemon juice

1 tablespoon champagne vinegar

½ cup (120 ml) olive oil

¼ teaspoon sugar

Kosher salt and freshly ground black pepper

2 cups (60 g) arugula

2 watermelon or other radishes, thinly sliced

¼ cup (40 g) pomegranate seeds

¼ cup (40 g) toasted pepitas (pumpkin seeds)

Wedge of Parmesan or pecorino romano cheese, for shaving

Prepare the farro as directed.

Pour the water into the Instant Pot®. Place the squash slices in a steamer basket or ovenproof bowl and set it on the steam rack. Using the handles, lower the steamer basket and steam rack into the pot. Lock the lid in place and turn the valve to Sealing. Press the Pressure Cook button and set the cook time for 4 minutes at high pressure.

Meanwhile, make the dressing. In a small lidded jar, combine the orange juice, lemon juice, vinegar, olive oil, sugar, and a pinch of salt. Close the lid and shake well until blended. Add more salt, if needed, and pepper to taste. Set aside.

When the squash has finished cooking, turn the valve to Venting to quick-release the steam. When the steam stops, carefully remove the lid and, using the steam rack handles, lift out the steamer basket.

To serve, divide the farro evenly among 4 plates or large bowls. Top the farro with squash, arugula, radish slices, pomegranate seeds, and pepitas. Use a vegetable peeler to shave large pieces of cheese on top. Sprinkle with salt and a few grindings of black pepper. Drizzle some of the dressing on top and serve with the remaining dressing alongside.

POULTRY

You can serve the potpie family-style in a large casserole dish covered with the crust, or parcel out individual potpies in gratin dishes or bowls, as shown.

Chicken Potpie with Puff Crust

There's no danger of a soggy crust with this easy and flavorful version of chicken potpie. The hearty filling is cooked in the Instant Pot® while you bake the flaky puff pastry crust separately.

SERVES 4–6

1 tablespoon olive oil

2 slices bacon

1 cup (115 g) chopped yellow onion

2 carrots, peeled and sliced

2 ribs celery, sliced

1 tablespoon chopped fresh thyme or 1 teaspoon dried thyme

1 teaspoon dried sage

¼ cup (60 ml) white wine

1½ lb (680 g) boneless, skinless chicken thighs, fat trimmed

1½ cups (350 ml) chicken stock (page 270 or store-bought)

1 red potato, diced

Kosher salt and black pepper

All-purpose flour, for dusting

1 sheet frozen puff pastry, thawed

1 cup (140 g) frozen peas, thawed

1½ teaspoons finely grated lemon zest

3 tablespoons cornstarch

3 tablespoons cold water

Put the oil in the Instant Pot®, select Sauté, and adjust to More/High heat. When the oil is hot, add the bacon and cook, turning occasionally, until crisp, about 5 minutes. Transfer the bacon to a cutting board and leave the drippings in the pot. Coarsely chop the bacon and set aside.

Add the onion, carrots, celery, thyme, and sage to the pot and cook, stirring frequently, until the onion is tender, about 4 minutes. Add the wine and simmer, stirring with a wooden spoon to scrape up any browned bits, until nearly evaporated, about 1 minute. Press the Cancel button.

Return the bacon to the pot and add the chicken, stock, potatoes, ½ teaspoon salt, and ¼ teaspoon pepper and stir to combine. Lock the lid in place and turn the valve to Sealing. Press the Pressure Cook button and set the cook time for 10 minutes at high pressure.

Meanwhile, preheat the oven to 400°F (200°C). On a lightly floured surface, unfold the puff pastry and roll out into a rectangle large enough to cover a 2-quart (1.9-L) casserole dish. Alternatively, unfold the pastry and cut it into 4–6 strips or rounds to cover individual gratin dishes or soup bowls with ½-inch (12-mm) overhang all around. Place the pastry on a baking sheet and prick all over with a fork. Bake until puffed and golden, about 15 minutes.

When the cooking time is up, turn the valve to Venting to quick-release the steam. Carefully remove the lid and use tongs or 2 forks to pull the chicken apart into bite-size pieces. Add the peas and lemon zest.

In a small bowl, stir together the cornstarch and cold water. Add to the pot, select Sauté, and adjust to Normal/Medium heat. Cook, stirring gently, until the sauce is thickened, about 2 minutes. Season to taste with salt and pepper. Spoon the filling into a casserole dish or individual gratin dishes, top with the puff pastry, and serve.

Chicken with Cider & Apples

Adding the apples to this comforting cold-weather dinner in two additions—with the chicken and just before serving—contributes flavor and chunky texture to the sweet-savory sauce. Serve over steamed rice or mashed potatoes.

SERVES 4–6

2½ lb (1.2 kg) bone-in, skin-on chicken thighs (about 6), excess fat trimmed

Kosher salt and freshly ground black pepper

1 tablespoon olive oil

3 shallots, sliced

2 cloves garlic, minced

1 cup (240 ml) apple cider

½ cup (120 ml) chicken stock (page 270 or store-bought)

2 tablespoons apple cider vinegar

2 Granny Smith apples, peeled, cored, and cut into wedges

1 sprig fresh rosemary leaves

½ tablespoon unsalted butter

Steamed rice (page 266), for serving

Pat the chicken dry with paper towels and season both sides generously with salt and pepper. Select Sauté on the Instant Pot® and heat the oil. Working in batches, cook the chicken, skin-side down, until nicely browned, about 5 minutes. Transfer to a plate. Add the shallots and cook until translucent and slightly soft, 3 minutes. Add the garlic and cook until fragrant, 1 minute. Add the cider, stock, and vinegar and stir to combine. Press the Cancel button to reset the program.

Return the chicken to the pot. Add half of the apples and the rosemary and stir to combine. Lock the lid in place and turn the valve to Sealing. Press the Pressure Cook button and set the cook time for 15 minutes at high pressure.

Let the steam release naturally, or for at least 10 minutes, before turning the valve to Venting to quick-release any residual steam.

Carefully remove the lid and use tongs to transfer the chicken to a plate. Press the Cancel button to reset the program. Press the Sauté button, add the butter and the remaining apples, and cook until the sauce is slightly reduced, about 3 minutes. (The sauce will continue to thicken as it cools.) Return the chicken to the pot and stir to coat.

Serve over rice, with sauce drizzled on top.

Substitute the bone-in chicken thighs for boneless, if you wish, and reduce the cooking time to 10 minutes.

Pulled Chicken Sandwiches with Kale & Cabbage Slaw

What could be better than a backyard barbecue where you don't need to fuss with the grill? The layered flavors of this homemade barbecue sauce enliven tender, juicy chicken that cooks in just 15 minutes. Top with a crunchy

SERVES 6–8

FOR THE SAUCE

½ cup (100 g) firmly packed light brown sugar

2 tablespoons cider vinegar

2 tablespoons tomato paste

1 tablespoon Dijon mustard

1 tablespoon Worcestershire sauce

1 teaspoon smoked paprika

1 teaspoon garlic powder

¼ teaspoon cayenne pepper

¼ teaspoon dry mustard

Kosher salt and freshly ground black pepper

⅓ cup (75 ml) chicken stock (page 270 or store-bought)

3 lb (1.5 kg) boneless, skinless chicken thighs

2 tablespoons canola oil

To make the sauce, in a small bowl, whisk together the brown sugar, cider vinegar, tomato paste, mustard, Worcestershire sauce, smoked paprika, garlic powder, cayenne, and dry mustard. Season with salt and black pepper, then whisk in the stock. Set the sauce aside.

Season the chicken with salt and black pepper. Select Sauté on the Instant Pot® and heat the oil. Working in batches, brown the chicken on both sides, 2–3 minutes per side. Transfer to a plate as browned. Press the Cancel button to reset the program.

Pour the sauce into the pot and add the chicken. Stir to coat. Lock the lid in place and turn the valve to Sealing. Press the Pressure Cook button and set the cook time for 15 minutes at high pressure.

Meanwhile, to make the slaw, in a large bowl, combine the cabbages, kale, and red onion. In a small bowl, whisk together the mayonnaise, mustard, and white wine vinegar and pour over the slaw. Sprinkle with the poppy seeds, season with salt and pepper, and toss to combine. Set aside.

kale-and-cabbage slaw and a buttery bun, and you've got the ideal party sandwich. You could swap the brioche buns for pretzel buns, or use a mini version of either to create sliders.

Let the steam release naturally, or for at least 15 minutes, before turning the valve to Venting to quick-release any residual steam. Carefully remove the lid and use tongs to transfer the chicken to a plate. Using two forks, shred the chicken. Press the Cancel button to reset the program.

Whisk the cornstarch slurry to recombine, and add it to the sauce in the pot. Press the Sauté button, and whisk occasionally until the sauce begins to simmer. Cook until thickened, about 3 minutes. Return the chicken to the pot and toss to coat.

Serve the chicken on the buns topped with the slaw.

TIP *Skip the bun and transform this sandwich into a bowl by serving the pulled chicken and slaw over steamed white or brown rice (page 266).*

FOR THE KALE & CABBAGE SLAW

1 cup (90 g) each thinly sliced napa and red cabbage

1 cup (90 g) thinly sliced kale leaves

¼ cup (45 g) minced red onion

¼ cup (60 ml) mayonnaise

2 teaspoons Dijon mustard

2 teaspoons white wine vinegar

1 tablespoon poppy seeds

Kosher salt and freshly ground black pepper

1 tablespoon cornstarch mixed with 1 tablespoon cold water

6–8 brioche buns (Jam-Filled Brioche Doughnuts, page 38), or pretzel buns, split and toasted

Crispy Fried Chicken Sandwiches

Crunchy, juicy, spicy, and satisfying, these crave-worthy sandwiches check all the boxes when it comes to healthier fried food. Rice flour provides a barrier between the extreme heat and tender chicken, helping to keep the meat moist inside and crispy outside. Add more hot sauce and/or cayenne pepper if you like it hot—the crunchy cabbage and cooling pickles balance the spicy richness of the sandwich.

SERVES 4–6

2 cups (10 oz/285 g) rice flour

1 tablespoon baking powder

Kosher salt and freshly ground black pepper

1 cup (240 ml) buttermilk, preferably full-fat

2 large eggs

½ teaspoon cayenne pepper

1 teaspoon hot pepper sauce (optional)

1–1½ lb (450–680 g) boneless, skinless chicken thighs (4–6)

FOR THE SPICY MAYO

¾ cup (180 ml) mayonnaise

1 tablespoon Sriracha or other hot sauce

Pinch of cayenne pepper

FOR SERVING

4–6 brioche buns (Jam-Filled Brioche Doughnuts, page 38 or store-bought)

Sliced bread and butter pickles, shredded red or green cabbage

In a medium bowl, whisk together the rice flour, baking powder, 2 teaspoons salt, and 1 teaspoon black pepper. In another medium bowl, whisk together the buttermilk, eggs, cayenne, and hot pepper sauce (if using).

Line a rimmed baking sheet with parchment paper. Pat the chicken dry with paper towels. Working with a few thighs at a time, coat the chicken in the rice flour mixture, shaking off the excess. Dip in the buttermilk mixture, letting the excess drip off. Transfer again to the flour mixture, turning to coat well and pressing gently to cover all the nooks and crannies. Place the coated chicken on the prepared baking sheet as you go.

Coat the Instant Pot® air fryer basket with canola oil spray. Working in batches, coat the chicken generously with olive oil spray and arrange a single layer of thighs in the basket, making sure they don't touch. Insert the basket into the pot and attach the air fryer lid. Press the Air Fry button and set the cook time for 14 minutes at 400°F (200°C), then press Start. Flip the chicken when prompted, coating both sides again with olive oil.

Meanwhile, make the spicy mayo: In a small bowl, stir together the mayonnaise, Sriracha, and cayenne. Set aside.

When the cooking time is up, use tongs to carefully transfer the chicken to a plate. Repeat to cook the remaining batches.

Spread a thin layer of the spicy mayo on the inside of the brioche buns. Top the bottom half of each bun with a piece of chicken, pickles, and shredded cabbage. Cover with the top of the buns and serve.

Chicken BLT

Wrapping chicken breasts in strips of bacon infuses the meat with flavor and also keeps it from drying out in the air fryer. Cut very thick chicken breasts in half horizontally or add more cooking time. Use country-style bread and toast it on the dehydrating tray just before assembling the sandwiches.

SERVES 2

2 boneless, skinless chicken breasts (each about 6 oz/170 g) (see note)

Kosher salt and freshly ground black pepper

4 slices bacon

4 slices thick country bread, such as sourdough

Regular or Spicy Mayo (Crispy Fried Chicken Sandwiches, page 121), for serving (optional)

2 large romaine lettuce leaves

4 thick tomato slices

Pat the chicken dry with paper towels. Season lightly with salt and pepper.

Wrap 2 bacon slices around each chicken breast, slightly overlapping the bacon so it covers as much surface area of the chicken as possible. Tuck the ends of the bacon underneath the slices so they stay in place when cooking. (Be sure the ends of both bacon slices are on the same side of the chicken so there is only 1 seam.)

Coat the Instant Pot® air fryer basket with canola oil spray. Place the chicken, seam-side down, in a single layer in the basket, making sure they don't touch. Insert the basket into the pot and attach the air fryer lid. Press the Air Fry button and set the cook time for 12 minutes at 400°F (200°C), then press Start. Cook undisturbed.

When the cooking time is up, insert an instant-read thermometer into the thickest part of the chicken; it should register 165°F (74°C). If the chicken is not fully cooked, add more cooking time in 2-minute intervals until the breasts are fully cooked. Use tongs to carefully transfer the chicken to a plate.

Place 2 bread slices on the dehydrating tray, insert the tray into the basket, and attach the air fryer lid. Press the Air Fry button and set the cook time for 2 minutes at 400°F (200°C), then press Start. When the cooking time is up, use tongs to transfer the bread to a plate. Repeat to toast the remaining bread slices.

For each sandwich, place 1 bread slice on a plate, spread evenly with mayo (if using), and place a chicken breast on the bread. Top with a lettuce leaf and 2 tomato slices, cover with another bread slice, and serve.

Buttermilk Fried Chicken

This cooking method for the air fryer incorporates incorporates many of the same classic fried chicken techniques, including an overnight soak in buttermilk, lots of fragrant spices, and a good dredge in a flour-cornstarch mixture. Coat the pieces well with canola oil spray, but there's no need to flip them during cooking.

SERVES 4–6

FOR THE SPICE MIXTURE

Freshly ground black pepper

1 tablespoon smoked paprika

1 tablespoon firmly packed light brown sugar

2 teaspoons granulated garlic

2 teaspoons dried oregano

½ teaspoon cayenne pepper

1 cup (240 ml) buttermilk, preferably full-fat

1 large egg

Kosher salt

3 lb (1.4 kg) bone-in, skin-on chicken thighs

1 cup (4 oz/115 g) all-purpose flour

¼ cup (1 oz/30 g) cornstarch

1 teaspoon baking powder

To make the spice mixture, in a small bowl, whisk together 2 tablespoons black pepper, the paprika, brown sugar, garlic, oregano, and cayenne.

In a large bowl, whisk together the buttermilk, egg, 1 tablespoon salt, and 2 tablespoons of the spice mixture (reserve the remaining spice mixture). Place the chicken in a large lock-top plastic bag, then pour the marinade into the bag. Seal the bag, massaging the marinade around the chicken. Refrigerate for at least 4 hours or up to overnight.

In a large bowl, whisk together the flour, cornstarch, baking powder, 2 teaspoons salt, and the reserved spice mixture.

Line a rimmed baking sheet with parchment paper. Working with 1 thigh at a time, remove the chicken from the marinade, letting the excess drip off, then coat in the flour mixture, shaking off the excess. Place the coated chicken on the prepared baking sheet as you go.

Coat the Instant Pot® air fryer basket with canola oil spray. Working in batches, coat the chicken generously with canola oil spray and arrange a single layer of thighs in the basket, making sure they don't touch. Insert the basket into the pot and attach the air fryer lid. Press the Air Fry button and set the cook time for 25 minutes at 400°F (200°C), then press Start. Cook undisturbed.

When the cooking time is up, insert an instant-read thermometer into the center of a thigh, away from the bone; it should register 175°F (80°C). If the chicken is not fully cooked, add more cooking time in 2-minute intervals. Repeat to cook the remaining batches, then serve.

Chicken Tacos with Avocado Spread

Spice-rubbed chicken thighs become fork-tender meat that is ideal for tacos. Spread a spoonful of citrusy avocado over each tortilla, then tuck in some of the chicken with a sprinkling of queso fresco and fresh cilantro for easy weeknight bites.

SERVES 6

1½ tablespoons ground cumin

2 teaspoons chili powder

Kosher salt and freshly ground black pepper

6 boneless, skinless chicken thighs (1½–2 lb/680 g–1 kg total)

2 tablespoons canola or avocado oil

½ cup (120 ml) chicken stock (page 270 or store-bought)

FOR THE AVOCADO SPREAD

2 ripe avocados, halved, pitted, and scooped from peel

2 teaspoons fresh lime juice

FOR SERVING

Pinto beans (page 268), optional; corn tortillas, crumbled queso fresco, fresh cilantro leaves

In a small bowl, mix the cumin, chili powder, and 1 teaspoon salt. Place the chicken in a shallow pan or on a plate and toss with the spice mixture to coat.

Select Sauté on the Instant Pot® and heat the oil. Working in batches, add the chicken thighs and brown evenly on both sides, about 5 minutes per side. Press the Cancel button to reset the program.

Add the stock, lock the lid in place, and turn the valve to Sealing. Press the Pressure Cook button and set the cook time for 10 minutes at high pressure.

Meanwhile, make the avocado spread. In a small bowl, mash the avocados with the lime juice and season with salt and pepper. Set aside.

When the chicken has finished cooking, let the steam release naturally for 10 minutes before turning the valve to Venting to quick-release any residual steam.

Carefully remove the lid and use tongs to transfer the chicken to a plate. When cool enough to handle, shred it with two forks.

To serve, spread a tortilla with avocado spread, add chicken, beans (if desired), queso fresco, and cilantro. Repeat with the remaining tortillas and serve right away.

Slip any remaining taco meat into a salad or soup for a nourishing snack.

Shredded Chicken Shawarma Wraps

A creamy tahini sauce balances the curry-infused marinade in this classic Middle Eastern dish. Serve the chicken in whole-wheat wraps with torn romaine, sliced tomatoes, and onion, or sideline the wraps and up the lettuce for a main dish salad.

SERVES 4

FOR THE MARINADE

- **2 tablespoons olive oil**
- **2 teaspoons curry powder**
- **1 teaspoon ground cumin**
- **2 cloves garlic, grated**
- **1 tablespoon fresh lemon juice**
- **Kosher salt and freshly ground black pepper**

- **2 lb (1 kg) boneless, skinless chicken thighs**
- **½ cup (120 ml) chicken stock (page 270 or store-bought)**

FOR THE TAHINI SAUCE

- **¾ cup (180 ml) Greek yogurt**
- **2 tablespoons tahini**
- **1 clove garlic, grated**
- **1 tablespoon chopped fresh cilantro**
- **1 tablespoon fresh lemon juice**

FOR SERVING

Whole-wheat wraps, romaine lettuce leaves, sliced tomatoes, thinly-sliced red onions (optional)

To make the marinade, in a measuring cup, combine the olive oil, curry powder, cumin, garlic, lemon juice, 1 teaspoon salt, and ⅛ teaspoon pepper and stir to combine. Place the chicken in a shallow pan or baking dish and pour the marinade over the top. Cover tightly with plastic wrap and marinate in the refrigerator for at least 30 minutes or up to overnight, turning occasionally to coat.

Select Sauté on the Instant Pot®. Working in batches, add the chicken and marinade and brown evenly on both sides, about 3 minutes per side. Transfer to a plate as browned. Press the Cancel button to reset the program.

Add the stock, lock the lid in place, and turn the valve to Sealing. Press the Pressure Cook button and set the cook time for 10 minutes at high pressure.

Meanwhile, make the tahini sauce. In a small bowl, combine the yogurt, tahini, garlic, cilantro, lemon juice, ½ teaspoon salt, and ½ teaspoon pepper. Taste and adjust the seasoning as desired.

When the chicken has finished cooking, let the steam release naturally for 10 minutes before turning the valve to Venting to quick-release any residual steam.

Carefully remove the lid and use tongs to transfer the chicken to a plate. When cool enough to handle, shred it with two forks.

To serve, spread a wrap with tahini sauce, add chicken, lettuce, tomato slices, and onion (if desired) and fold to close. Repeat with the remaining wraps and serve right away.

Chicken Taquitos

Fill these Mexican-inspired rollups with any of your favorite taco toppings—cheese and cilantro are just the beginning. Pico de Gallo is great for dipping, but any fresh salsa or guacamole would be a wonderful match as well. Use corn or flour tortillas—melted butter is the secret to holding them together and creating a crisp, golden crust.

SERVES 4–6

1½ tablespoons ground cumin

2 teaspoons chili powder

Kosher salt and freshly ground black pepper

6 boneless, skinless chicken thighs (1½–2 lb/680 g–1 kg total)

2 teaspoons canola oil

12 (6-inch/15-cm) corn or flour tortillas

2 cups (225 g) shredded Monterey jack or pepper jack cheese, or Mexican blend shredded cheese

1 lime, cut into wedges

¼ cup (15 g) chopped fresh cilantro

2 tablespoons unsalted butter, melted

Pico de Gallo (Veggie Tacos, page 220), for serving

In a small bowl, whisk together the cumin, chili powder, 1 teaspoon salt, and a few grindings of pepper.

Pat the chicken dry with paper towels and place in a bowl. Rub with the oil, then sprinkle with the spice mixture and toss to coat.

Coat the Instant Pot® air fryer basket with canola oil spray. Working in batches, arrange a single layer of thighs in the basket, making sure they don't touch. Insert the basket into the pot and attach the air fryer lid. Press the Broil button and set the cook time for 14 minutes at 400°F (200°C), then press Start. Flip the chicken when prompted.

When the cooking time is up, use tongs to carefully transfer the chicken to a cutting board. Shred or cut into strips.

Place a tortilla on a work surface and sprinkle a few tablespoons of the cheese in the center, leaving at least a 1-inch (2.5-cm) border all around the cheese. Top with chicken, lime juice, and cilantro. Roll the tortilla tightly, tucking in the filling. Brush the seam with a little melted butter to seal, then place it, seam-side down, on a plate. Repeat to roll the remaining taquitos.

Working in batches, brush the taquitos generously on both sides with the remaining melted butter, then place them, seam-side down, on the dehydrating tray. (It's okay if they touch; you should be able to fit 3 or 4 on the tray at one time.) Insert the tray into the air fryer basket and attach the air fryer lid. Press the Air Fry button and set the cook time for 5 minutes at 400°F (200°C), then press Start. Cook undisturbed.

Use tongs to carefully transfer the taquitos to a plate. Repeat to cook the remaining batches. Serve with pico de gallo alongside for dipping.

This kid-friendly comfort food gets a double dose of nutty Parmesan, which is used in the meatballs and also in the sauce.

Kid-O's Pasta & Turkey Meatballs

This homemade pasta-and-meatball recipe tastes reminiscent of the old-school canned version of your childhood, with a slightly sweet tomato sauce, tender mini pasta shapes, and little turkey meatballs. Your kids will love it, and the kid in you will, too.

SERVES 4

9 round buttery crackers, finely crushed (1 oz/30 g)

1½ tablespoons plain yogurt

1 large egg yolk

¾ lb (340 g) ground turkey (a mix of dark and white meat is best), or 90% lean ground beef

7 tablespoons (50 g) grated Parmesan cheese

½ teaspoon dried Italian seasoning

¼ teaspoon garlic powder

Kosher salt

1¼ cups (300 ml) chicken stock (page 270 or store-bought)

1 can (15 oz/425 g) tomato sauce

1 tablespoon sugar

6 oz (170 g) mini dried pasta, such as anelli, farfalle, ditalini, or penne (about 2 cups)

3 tablespoons unsalted butter, at room temperature

In a bowl, combine the crushed crackers, milk, and egg yolk and mash with a fork until the crackers are moistened. Add the turkey, 3 tablespoons of the Parmesan, the Italian seasoning, garlic powder, and ¼ teaspoon salt. Using your hands or a wooden spoon, stir gently to combine. Form into 26–30 meatballs, using a heaping teaspoon for each one. Refrigerate for 10 minutes.

In the Instant Pot®, whisk together the stock, tomato sauce, sugar, and ½ teaspoon salt. Add the pasta and stir to combine. Place the meatballs on top but don't stir.

Lock the lid in place and turn the valve to Sealing. Press the Pressure Cook button and set the cook time for 5 minutes at low pressure.

Let the steam release naturally for 5 minutes, then turn the valve to Venting to quick-release any residual steam. Carefully remove the lid. Using a rubber spatula, gently stir in the butter and the remaining ¼ cup Parmesan. Serve right away.

Coq au Vin Blanc

Coq au vin is a classic French dish in which chicken is slowly braised in red wine. Here, the famed dish is updated with white wine in place of the traditional red Burgundy and a last-minute addition of cream, mustard, and tarragon. Serve with mashed potatoes and a simple green salad.

SERVES 4–6

2 lb (1 kg) boneless, skinless chicken thighs

Kosher salt and freshly ground pepper

2 tablespoons extra-virgin olive oil

1 red onion, diced

¼ lb bacon, diced

3 cloves garlic, minced

6 oz (180 g) mushrooms, such as maitake or chanterelles, brushed clean and sliced

2 cups (480 ml) dry white wine

½ cup (120 ml) heavy cream

2 tablespoons Dijon mustard

¼ cup (7 g) lightly packed fresh tarragon leaves, roughly chopped

¼ cup (30 g) pine nuts, toasted

Season the chicken thighs on both sides with salt and pepper. Select Sauté on the Instant Pot® and warm the oil. In batches, sear the chicken until browned, about 4 minutes per side. Transfer the chicken to a plate. Add the onion and bacon to the pot and cook, stirring occasionally, until the onion is tender, about 3 minutes. Add the garlic and cook, stirring, until fragrant, about 1 minute. Add the mushrooms and cook, stirring occasionally, until tender, about 5 minutes more. Return the chicken to the pot and pour in the wine.

Lock the lid in place and turn the valve to Sealing. Press the Keep Warm/Cancel button to reset the program, then press the Manual/Pressure Cook button and set the cook time for 10 minutes at high pressure.

Turn the valve to Venting to manually release the steam. When the steam stops, carefully remove the lid and stir in the cream, mustard, and tarragon. Season with salt and pepper.

Transfer the chicken and sauce to a serving platter, top with the pine nuts, and serve.

Honey Chicken Cashew Un-Stir-Fry with Rice

This healthy Chinese takeout-style meal cooks sweet-and-tangy chicken and rice at the same time using the pot-in-pot method (see page 10). The veggies are added after the chicken and rice are done so you get perfectly cooked everything. The recipe is easily adaptable: swap in green beans or snow peas for the broccoli.

SERVES 4

1 tablespoon canola oil

1 tablespoon toasted sesame oil

1½ lb (680 g) boneless, skinless chicken breasts, cut into 1-inch (2.5-cm) pieces

Kosher salt and black pepper

1 cup (115 g) chopped yellow onion

3 cloves garlic, minced

3 tablespoons low-sodium soy sauce

2 tablespoons honey

2 tablespoons rice vinegar

1 teaspoon–1 tablespoon Sriracha

1½ cups (300 g) long-grain or short-grain (sushi) rice, rinsed and drained

3 cups (170 g) bite-size broccoli florets

1 red bell pepper, seeded and thinly sliced

2 tablespoons cornstarch

2 tablespoons cold water

1 cup (115 g) roasted cashews

Put the canola and sesame oils in the Instant Pot®, select Sauté, and adjust to Normal/Medium heat. When the oil is hot, add the chicken, ½ teaspoon salt, and ¼ teaspoon pepper and cook without stirring until the chicken is opaque white, about 2 minutes. Add the onion and garlic and cook, stirring frequently, until fragrant, about 45 seconds. Press the Cancel button.

In a small bowl, stir together the soy sauce, honey, vinegar, and Sriracha. Add to the pot and stir to combine. Place a trivet with tall (2-inch/5-cm) feet in the pot over the chicken mixture. In a 7-inch (18-cm) round metal pan with a 6-cup (1.4-L) capacity, stir together the rice and 1½ cups (350 ml) water. Cover tightly with aluminum foil and place on the trivet.

Lock the lid in place and turn the valve to Sealing. Press the Pressure Cook button and set the cook time for 5 minutes at high pressure.

When the cooking time is up, turn the valve to Venting to quick-release the steam. Carefully remove the lid and remove the pan and trivet. Keep the pan covered with foil.

Add the broccoli and bell pepper to the pot, select Sauté, and adjust to More/High heat. Place a regular pan lid on the pot, bring to a simmer, and cook until the vegetables are crisp-tender, about 3 minutes.

In a small bowl, stir together the cornstarch and the cold water. Add to the pot and cook until the sauce has thickened, about 1 minute. Serve the chicken, vegetables, and rice sprinkled with the cashews.

Chicken Adobo Quinoa Burrito Bowls

Flavorful Filipino-style chicken pairs beautifully with nutty quinoa, buttery corn, and earthy black beans for a tasty bowl. Everything is cooked in the Instant Pot® at the same time, so it makes a great weeknight dinner. Serve in bowls, or wrap up the ingredients in burrito-size flour tortillas with grated jack cheese for a handheld, do-ahead meal.

SERVES 4

¼ cup (60 ml) apple cider vinegar

2 tablespoons low-sodium soy sauce

1½ teaspoons firmly packed light brown sugar

1 tablespoon peeled and sliced fresh ginger

3 cloves garlic, chopped

1 lb (450 g) boneless, skinless chicken thighs

1 yellow onion, thinly sliced through root end

¾ cup (130 g) quinoa, rinsed and drained

¾ cup (180 ml) plus 1 tablespoon water

1 cup (170 g) canned black beans, rinsed and drained

½ cup (90 g) frozen corn, thawed

1 cup (240 ml) Pico de Gallo (Veggie Tacos, page 220)

1 avocado, pitted, peeled, and diced

In the Instant Pot®, whisk together the vinegar, soy sauce, brown sugar, ginger, and garlic. Add the chicken and onion and stir to coat with the sauce.

Place a trivet with tall (2-inch/5-cm) feet in the pot over the chicken mixture. In a 7-inch (18-cm) round metal pan with a 6-cup (1.4-L) capacity, stir together the quinoa and water. Place the beans and corn on top but don't stir. Cover tightly with aluminum foil and place on the trivet.

Lock the lid in place and turn the valve to Sealing. Press the Pressure Cook button and set the cook time for 12 minutes at high pressure.

When the cooking time is up, turn the valve to Venting to quick-release the steam. Carefully remove the lid and remove the pan and trivet.

Divide the quinoa, beans, and corn among 4 bowls. Top with the chicken, discarding the cooking liquid. Garnish with the pico de gallo and avocado and serve.

These nourishing, hearty bowls are easy to customize. Family members can choose their preferred toppings; try shredded Cheddar cheese, chopped fresh herbs, or diced steamed vegetables.

Chicken Tikka Masala

A mix of Indian spices, chicken, cauliflower, tomatoes, and cream creates a comforting and quick weeknight meal that comes together in minutes. Traditionally served over rice, it could also be used as a filling for a wrap or burrito, or served with a side of naan.

SERVES 4

2 tablespoons ghee or vegetable oil

1 yellow onion, diced

4 cloves garlic, minced

1-inch (2.5-cm) piece fresh ginger, peeled and grated

½ jalapeño chile, seeded and minced

1 cinnamon stick

1 teaspoon garam masala

1 teaspoon smoked paprika

1 teaspoon ground coriander

1 teaspoon ground turmeric

Kosher salt and freshly ground black pepper

2 lb (1 kg) boneless, skinless chicken thighs, cut into 2-inch (5-cm) cubes

1 can (14.5 oz/410 g) diced tomatoes with juice

2 cups (120 g) cauliflower florets

½ cup (120 ml) heavy cream or coconut milk

Steamed white or brown rice (page 266), for serving

Select Sauté on the Instant Pot® and melt the ghee. Add the onion and cook, stirring occasionally, until softened, about 3 minutes. Add the garlic, ginger, chile, cinnamon stick, garam masala, smoked paprika, coriander, turmeric, 1 teaspoon salt, and ¼ teaspoon pepper and cook, stirring, until fragrant, about 1 minute more. Add the chicken and cook, stirring occasionally, until cooked through, about 5 minutes. Stir in the tomatoes and cauliflower. Press the Cancel button to reset the program.

Lock the lid in place and turn the valve to Sealing. Press the Pressure Cook button and set the cook time for 10 minutes at high pressure.

Turn the valve to Venting to quick-release the steam. Carefully remove the lid, stir in the cream, and season with salt and pepper.

Spoon rice onto individual plates, top with the chicken, and serve.

Marinated Indian Chicken

For this recipe, which yields tender, juicy chicken breasts and vibrant curry flavors, be sure to use thick jarred Indian curry paste, not thinner simmer sauces. Look for the paste where Indian ingredients are sold in the grocery store and online. Serve with basmati rice or packaged garlic naan.

SERVES 4

½ cup (130 g) plain yogurt

3 tablespoons Indian curry paste (such as Patak's)

1 teaspoon ground turmeric

Kosher salt and black pepper

1½ lb (680 g) boneless, skinless chicken breasts, cut into 1½-inch (4-cm) pieces

1 tablespoon canola oil or ghee

1 yellow onion, thinly sliced through root end

3 cloves garlic, chopped

1 tablespoon minced peeled fresh ginger

½ cup (120 ml) chicken stock (page 270 or store-bought)

In a nonaluminum container or bowl, whisk together the yogurt, curry paste, turmeric, and ¼ teaspoon each salt and pepper. Add the chicken and toss to coat. Cover and refrigerate for at least 1 hour and up to 24 hours.

Put the oil in the Instant Pot®, select Sauté, and adjust to Normal/ Medium heat. When the oil is hot, add the onion and cook, stirring frequently, until beginning to brown, about 5 minutes. Add the garlic and ginger and cook until fragrant, about 30 seconds. Press the Cancel button. Add the chicken and marinade and the stock, and stir to combine.

Lock the lid in place and turn the valve to Sealing. Press the Pressure Cook button and set the cook time for 4 minutes at high pressure.

Let the steam release naturally for 10 minutes, then turn the valve to Venting to quick-release any remaining steam. Carefully remove the lid and serve the chicken with a few tablespoons of the cooking liquid spooned over the top.

TIP *If using boneless chicken thighs, increase the cook time to 10 minutes. Whole bone-in chicken (skin removed) can also be used. For bone-in chicken thighs, increase the cook time to 15 minutes. Cook bone-in chicken breasts for 7 minutes.*

In addition to Boston or butter lettuce, little gem or romaine leaves make great healthy bases for savory fillings.

Turkey Lettuce Wraps with Hoisin-Peanut Sauce

Tasty and thrifty, turkey thighs make a wonderful filling for lettuce wraps, served taco-style with a hoisin-peanut sauce for dipping. The recipe works equally well with bone-in chicken thighs; just reduce the cook time to 18 minutes.

SERVES 4

FOR THE TURKEY

2 tablespoons olive oil

2 bone-in turkey thighs (about 2 lb/1 kg)

Kosher salt and black pepper

3 dried shiitake mushrooms

¼ cup (60 ml) low-sodium soy sauce

2 tablespoons peeled and coarsely chopped fresh ginger

2 tablespoons rice vinegar

3 cloves garlic, chopped

FOR THE SAUCE

½ cup (120 ml) hot water

¼ cup (70 g) peanut butter

3 tablespoons hoisin sauce

1 tablespoon fresh lime juice

1 teaspoon Sriracha

½ cup (80 g) chopped water chestnuts

1 large carrot, peeled and julienned or shredded

3 green onions, chopped

1 head Boston lettuce, separated into individual leaves

To make the turkey, put the oil in the Instant Pot®, select Sauté, and adjust to More/High heat. Season the turkey all over with salt and pepper. When the oil is hot, brown the turkey on both sides, about 4 minutes per side. Transfer to a plate. Press the Cancel button.

Remove the inner pot, pour off the oil, and return the pot to the appliance. Add 2 tablespoons water, the mushrooms, soy sauce, ginger, vinegar, and garlic, stirring with a wooden spoon to scrape up any browned bits. Return the turkey to the pot.

Lock the lid in place and turn the valve to Sealing. Press the Pressure Cook button and set the cook time for 25 minutes at high pressure.

Meanwhile, make the hoisin-peanut sauce: In a small bowl, whisk together the hot water, peanut butter, hoisin sauce, lime juice, and Sriracha; set aside.

Let the steam release naturally for 10 minutes, then turn the valve to Venting to quick-release any residual steam. Carefully remove the lid and transfer the turkey and mushrooms to a cutting board. Cut the turkey and mushroom caps into bite-size pieces, discarding the skin, bones, and mushroom stems. In a medium bowl, stir together the turkey, mushrooms, water chestnuts, carrot, green onions, and ¼ cup (60 ml) of the cooking liquid.

Mound the turkey mixture in the lettuce leaves and serve with the hoisin-peanut sauce for drizzling or dipping.

Juicy Turkey Burgers

Steaming burgers in the Instant Pot® turns out juicy patties without all the greasy mess that panfrying produces. This turkey version is stuffed with Cheddar cheese for an extra-yummy burger with a surprise hidden inside. Complete the meal with waffle fries and a green salad.

SERVES 6

2 lb (1 kg) ground turkey (a mix of dark and white meat)

¼ cup (60 ml) plus 2 tablespoons mayonnaise

2 teaspoons Dijon or yellow mustard

¾ teaspoon seasoning salt

Six ¼-inch-thick (6.3-mm) pieces Cheddar cheese, each about 2 inches (5 cm) long by 1 inch (2.5 cm) wide

6 hamburger buns, toasted

6 lettuce leaves

FOR SERVING

Hamburger pickle slices, ketchup

In a large bowl, combine the turkey, mayonnaise, mustard, and seasoning salt and mix gently with your hands until well blended. Divide the meat into 6 even-size balls. Place one portion of the meat mixture in the palm of your hand and place a piece of cheese in the center. Form into a 4-inch (10-cm) patty, making sure the cheese is enclosed in the center of the meat. Wrap in aluminum foil. Repeat with the remaining meat and cheese to make a total of 6 foil-wrapped patties.

Pour ½ cup (120 ml) water into the Instant Pot®. Place a trivet with handles in the pot. Place the foil-wrapped patties on the trivet, layering them as needed.

Lock the lid in place and turn the valve to Sealing. Press the Pressure Cook button and set the cook time for 15 minutes at high pressure.

Turn the valve to Venting to quick-release the steam. Carefully remove the lid and transfer the burgers to a plate.

Carefully unwrap the burgers. Place them on the buns, top with the lettuce and pickles, and serve the ketchup on the side.

"Thanksgiving" Dinner

For this year-round riff on Thanksgiving dinner, you can save time by cooking the meat and stuffing together. The stuffing steams well, and quickly, but definitely benefits from baking for a few minutes in the oven at the end to give it a nice golden brown color and crunch (see Bonus Step).

SERVES 4

FOR THE STUFFING

2 tablespoons unsalted butter, plus more for greasing

¾ lb (340 g) dry white country bread, cut into 1-inch (2.5-cm) cubes

2 ribs celery, sliced

2 shallots, minced

Kosher salt and freshly ground black pepper

2 cloves garlic, minced

¼ cup (60 ml) white wine

2 large eggs, lightly beaten

¼ cup (7 g) chopped fresh flat-leaf parsley

3 cups (700 ml) chicken stock (page 270 or store-bought)

2 lb (1 kg) bone-in, skin-on turkey or chicken breasts

1 tablespoon canola oil

Crispy Brussels Sprouts with Honey-Lime Glaze (page 71)

To make the stuffing, preheat the oven to 425°F (220°C). Grease a 1½-qt (1.5-L) round ceramic baking dish with butter and set aside.

Place the bread cubes on a baking sheet and bake until crisp but not yet browned, 10–15 minutes. Remove from the oven and transfer to a large bowl.

Select Sauté on the Instant Pot® and melt the 2 tablespoons butter. Add the celery, shallots, ½ teaspoon salt, and ¼ teaspoon pepper and cook, stirring often, until softened, about 3 minutes. Add the garlic and cook until fragrant, about 1 minute. Add the wine and cook until almost all of it has evaporated, about 1 minute. Press the Cancel button to reset the program. Transfer the celery mixture to the bread cube bowl. Add the eggs, parsley, and ¼ teaspoon salt and toss to combine. Add 1 cup (240 ml) of the stock and toss to combine (there should be no liquid left at the bottom of the bowl). Transfer the stuffing to the prepared baking dish, and cover with aluminum foil.

Season the turkey with salt and pepper. Select Sauté on the Instant Pot® and heat the oil. Add the turkey and brown evenly on both sides, 6–8 minutes. Transfer to a plate. Add the remaining 2 cups (480 ml) of stock and bring to a simmer, stirring occasionally with a wooden spoon to scrape up any browned bits. Return the turkey to the pot, skin side up, and nestle it in so it fits in one layer. Press the Cancel button to reset the program.

Turkey breasts can be hard to find, but bone-in, skin-on chicken breasts work just as well for this recipe. If you have homemade turkey stock on hand, use that in place of the chicken stock. To truly make this a feast, serve it all with a big bowl of crispy Brussels sprouts.

Place the steam rack on top of the turkey, then place the baking dish on top of the steam rack. (Everything will fit snugly into the pot.) Lock the lid in place and turn the valve to Sealing. Press the Pressure Cook button and set the cook time for 12 minutes at high pressure.

Turn the valve to Venting to quick-release the steam. Remove the lid and, using the steam rack handles, lift out the baking dish. Transfer to a cooling rack, remove the foil, and let cool slightly.

Serve the turkey and stuffing right away, along with Brussels sprouts, if desired.

BONUS STEP *After removing it from the pot, bake the stuffing in a preheated 450°F (230°C) oven, uncovered, until golden brown, 10–12 minutes. The crispy top will complement the moist center, creating a perfect texture in every bite.*

TIP *If you'd like to cook more chicken at one time, or if your chicken breasts are too big to fit into one layer in the pot, you can cook the chicken and stuffing separately, each for 12 minutes at high pressure, ensuring that there are at least 2 cups (475 ml) of liquid in the pot for each round. Once the pot is hot, it comes up to pressure much quicker than when it is cold, so the second round of cooking will go quickly.*

BEEF

Be sure the meat fits in your air fryer basket before cooking.

Classic Sunday Roast

If you've had a "Sunday lunch" in England, you may remember beautifully cooked roast beef paired with crispy roast potatoes and horseradish cream sauce. Now you can create that traditional meal at home in the Instant Pot®. Drizzling the cooked roast with butter and honey might seem a little indulgent, but the creamy-sweet combo is a brilliant finish for the well-seasoned meat.

SERVES 4–6

1 tablespoon loosely packed fresh rosemary leaves

Kosher salt

1 teaspoon black or pink peppercorns

1 eye of round roast (2–3 lb/1–1.4 kg)

½–1 tablespoon olive oil

1–2 tablespoons unsalted butter

FOR THE HORSERADISH CREAM

⅓ cup (70 g) sour cream

1½ tablespoons prepared horseradish

Kosher salt

1 tablespoon honey

In a mortar with a pestle, or in a small bowl using the handle of a wooden spoon, grind together the rosemary, 1½ teaspoons salt, and the peppercorns. The mixture should be chunky. Pat the roast dry with paper towels. Rub the meat all over with ½–1 tablespoon oil (depending on the size of the roast) and sprinkle the seasoning on all sides.

Coat the Instant Pot® air fryer basket with canola oil spray. Place the roast in the center of the basket. Insert the basket into the pot and attach the air fryer lid. Press the Air Fry button and set the cook time for 16–18 minutes per pound of meat at 325°F (165°C) (start with the lower amount of time and add more time if needed), then press Start. Turn the meat when prompted.

Meanwhile, make the horseradish cream: In a small bowl, stir together the sour cream, horseradish, and ¼ teaspoon salt. Taste and adjust the seasoning with salt. Cover and refrigerate until ready to use.

When the cooking time is up, insert an instant-read thermometer into the center of the meat; it should register 130°–135°F (54°–57°C) for medium-rare and 135°–145°F (57°–63°C) for medium. If the roast is not cooked to the desired doneness, add more cooking time in 2-minute intervals. Use tongs to transfer the roast to a cutting board. Place 1–2 tablespoons butter on top (depending on the size of the roast) and let it melt. Drizzle with the honey, cover loosely with aluminum foil, and let rest for 15–20 minutes.

Serve with the horseradish cream alongside.

Barbacoa Tacos

Browning the beef at the beginning of cooking adds a crispy edge to this super-succulent meat, which then gets a sassy kick from the tangy sauce at the end. Inspired by the classic Caribbean-Mexican dish, the meat is then tucked into soft tortillas and topped with fresh lime juice, onion, and cilantro.

SERVES 6–8

3 lb (1.5 kg) boneless beef chuck, cut into 2-inch (5-cm) cubes

Kosher salt and freshly ground black pepper

1 tablespoon canola oil

1 yellow onion, chopped, plus more for serving (optional)

1 cup (240 ml) beef stock (page 272 or store-bought)

4 cloves garlic, minced

1 tablespoon ground cumin

1½ teaspoons chopped fresh oregano

4 chipotle chiles in adobo plus 2 tablespoons sauce

Juice of 1 lime

2 tablespoons firmly packed brown sugar

¼ teaspoon ground cloves

2 bay leaves

FOR SERVING

Warmed corn or flour tortillas, steamed white or brown rice (page 266), chopped fresh cilantro leaves, and lime wedges

Pat the beef cubes dry with a paper towel and season generously with salt and pepper.

Select Sauté on the Instant Pot® and heat the oil. Working in batches, brown the meat on all sides, about 8 minutes total. Transfer to a plate as browned. Add the onion and 2 tablespoons of the stock and cook, stirring occasionally with a wooden spoon and scraping up any browned bits, for 3 minutes. Add the garlic, cumin, and oregano and stir to combine, 1 minute. Press the Cancel button to reset the program.

Add the remaining stock, the chiles and their sauce, lime juice, sugar, cloves, bay leaves, 1 teaspoon salt, and ½ teaspoon pepper, and stir to combine. Return the beef and its juices to the pot, nestling it in snugly. Lock the lid in place and turn the valve to Sealing. Press the Pressure Cook button and set the cook time for 30 minutes at high pressure.

Let the steam release naturally, or for at least 15 minutes, before turning the valve to Venting to quick-release any residual steam. Carefully remove the lid and use tongs to transfer the beef pieces to a plate.

Press the Cancel button to reset the program and then select Sauté. Using tongs, transfer the beef to a large bowl and, using 2 forks, shred the beef. Bring the sauce to a simmer and cook until it thickens, about 10 minutes. Discard the bay leaves. Transfer to a bowl and use a spoon to skim the fat off the top. Transfer to a blender and blend at medium speed until smooth, about 3 minutes. Add the sauce to the beef and stir.

Serve in tortillas or over rice with cilantro and additional chopped onion, if using, with lime wedges alongside.

To quickly char tortillas, place them directly over a low flame on the stove and use kitchen tongs to carefully turn them over.

The peas are optional in this filling dish (in case you have any pea haters in the family). For a more intense curry flavor, add an additional tablespoon of the curry paste.

Indian Spiced Beef with Peas & Basmati Rice

This thrifty ground beef dish, called keema in India, is typically served with rice but is also delicious tucked inside squishy hamburger buns, sloppy joe–style. The usual long list of spices is streamlined here by swapping in thick Indian curry paste, available in jars where Indian ingredients are sold. Don't use diluted curry-flavored simmer sauces, as they're too thin for this recipe.

SERVES 4

- **1 tablespoon unsalted butter**
- **1 yellow onion, finely chopped**
- **1 lb (450 g) 90% lean ground beef or lamb**
- **1 tablespoon peeled and minced fresh ginger**
- **3 cloves garlic, chopped**
- **½ cup (100 g) drained canned diced plum tomatoes**
- **1½ cups (360 ml) chicken stock (page 270 or store-bought)**
- **2 tablespoons mild Indian curry paste (such as Patak's)**
- **1 cinnamon stick**
- **1¼ cups (245 g) basmati rice, rinsed and drained**
- **1 cup (140 g) frozen peas, thawed (optional)**
- **1½ teaspoons garam masala (Indian spice blend)**

Put the butter in the Instant Pot®, select Sauté, and adjust to More/High heat. When the butter is hot, add the onion and cook, stirring frequently, until beginning to brown, about 5 minutes. Add the ground beef, ginger, and garlic and cook, breaking up the meat into large 1-inch (2.5-cm) chunks with a spatula, until beginning to brown, about 5 minutes. (Keeping the meat in larger pieces will add texture to the dish.) Press the Cancel button. Add the tomatoes, ¼ cup (60 ml) of the stock, the curry paste, and cinnamon stick, stirring with a wooden spoon to scrape up any browned bits.

Place a trivet with tall (2-inch/5-cm) feet in the pot over the beef mixture. In a 7-inch (18-cm) round metal pan with a 6-cup (1.4-L) capacity, stir together the rice and the remaining 1¼ cups (300 ml) stock. Cover tightly with aluminum foil and place on the trivet.

Lock the lid in place and turn the valve to Sealing. Press the Pressure Cook button and set the cook time for 6 minutes at high pressure.

When the cooking time is up, let the steam release naturally for 5 minutes, then turn the valve to Venting to quick-release any residual steam. Carefully remove the lid and remove the pan and trivet. Fluff the rice with a fork.

Remove the cinnamon stick from the meat mixture and discard. Stir in the peas (if using) and garam masala, select Sauté, and adjust to More/High heat. Simmer until the peas are heated through, about 1 minute. Serve with the rice.

Beef Pitas with Red Onion & Tzatziki

The popular Greek gyro sandwich has been simplified here with no sacrifice to flavor. Ready all of the sandwich fixings while the beef cooks, including the cool, creamy yogurt-based tzatziki. If you're serving a crowd, a side of tabbouleh salad or Homemade Hummus (page 46) make excellent pairings.

SERVES 8

1½ lb (680 g) boneless beef chuck, thinly sliced

1 tablespoon kosher salt

Freshly ground pepper

1 yellow onion, thinly sliced

⅓ cup (80 ml) water

3 tablespoons olive oil

Juice of 1 lemon

2 teaspoons dried oregano

1 tablespoon garlic powder

FOR THE TZATZIKI

1 cup (250 g) plain Greek yogurt

½ cucumber, finely diced

1 clove garlic, minced

2 tablespoons finely chopped fresh dill

Juice of 1 lemon

Kosher salt and freshly ground pepper

FOR SERVING

8 pita breads

Small lettuce leaves, sliced tomatoes, thinly sliced red onion, chopped dill

Season the beef on both sides with the salt and pepper. Put the beef and onion into the Instant Pot®. In a small bowl, whisk together the water, oil, lemon juice, oregano, and garlic powder, then add to the pot. Lock the lid in place and turn the valve to Sealing. Press the Manual/Pressure Cook button. Set the cook time for 30 minutes at high pressure.

While the beef cooks, make the tzatziki: In a small bowl, whisk together yogurt, cucumber, garlic, dill, and lemon juice. Season to taste with salt and pepper. Set aside until ready to serve.

Let the steam release naturally for about 15 minutes, then turn the valve to Venting to release any residual steam. Remove the lid from the pot and, using a slotted spoon, transfer the beef and onion to a bowl.

To serve, spoon an equal amount of the beef mixture into each pita and top with lettuce, tomato, and onion. Sprinkle with chopped dill and finish with a dollop of tzatziki.

Gnocchi Bolognese

This meaty Bolognese gets extra oomph from umami-rich dried porcini mushrooms, but they're optional if your family doesn't care for fungi. Shelf-stable gnocchi need only a quick heat-up right in the sauce. Look for them in Cryovac packages where dried pasta is sold.

SERVES 4

- **2 tablespoons olive oil**
- **¾ lb (340 g) 90% lean ground beef**
- **1 yellow onion, finely chopped**
- **1 large carrot, peeled and finely chopped**
- **1 rib celery, finely chopped**
- **2 teaspoons dried Italian seasoning**
- **2 tablespoons tomato paste**
- **3 cloves garlic, chopped**
- **½ cup (120 ml) beef or chicken stock (pages 272 and 270 or store-bought)**
- **2 cups (500 g) canned crushed tomatoes with basil**
- **½ oz (15 g) dried porcini mushrooms (optional)**
- **Kosher salt and black pepper**
- **1 package (16 oz/453 g) shelf-stable potato gnocchi**
- **½ cup (60 g) grated Parmesan cheese**

Put the oil in the Instant Pot®, select Sauté, and adjust to More/High heat. When the oil is hot, add the ground beef and cook, breaking up the meat into 2-inch (5-cm) chunks with a spatula, until browned, about 4 minutes. Add the onion, carrot, celery, and Italian seasoning and cook, stirring occasionally, until the onions are tender, about 4 minutes. Add the tomato paste and garlic and cook until fragrant, about 45 seconds. Press the Cancel button.

Add the stock to the pot, stirring with a wooden spoon to scrape up any browned bits. Add the tomatoes and mushrooms (if using) and stir to combine.

Lock the lid in place and turn the valve to Sealing. Press the Pressure Cook button and set the cook time for 15 minutes at high pressure.

When the cooking time is up, turn the valve to Venting to quick-release the steam. Carefully remove the lid. Season the sauce to taste with salt and pepper. Add the gnocchi, breaking up any clumped gnocchi with your fingers, and stir gently to combine. Select Sauté, adjust to Less/Low heat, and cook, stirring only once, until the sauce is bubbly and the gnocchi are heated through, about 5 minutes. Sprinkle with the cheese and serve.

TIP *If you'd prefer a lower-carb version (and an extra serving of vegetables), replace the potato gnocchi with frozen cauliflower-based gnocchi and simmer for 3 minutes longer at the end.*

One-Pot Pasta with Bolognese

Save hours at the stove by pressure cooking the sauce and then simply adding in the pasta at the end. The Instant Pot® comes up to pressure more quickly the second time around, so the second step takes no time at all.

SERVES 4

- **5 oz (150 g) bacon, diced**
- **3 tablespoons unsalted butter**
- **1 yellow onion, chopped**
- **1 carrot, peeled and finely chopped**
- **1 rib celery, finely chopped**
- **2 cloves garlic, minced**
- **¾ lb (340 g) ground beef**
- **¾ lb (340 g) ground pork**
- **1 tablespoon chopped fresh sage**
- **⅓ cup (75 ml) red wine**
- **1 tablespoon tomato paste**
- **1 can (28 oz/800 g) crushed tomatoes**
- **Kosher salt and freshly ground black pepper**
- **1 lb (450 g) dried pasta (such as penne)**
- **1 cup (240 ml) water**
- **1 cup (115 g) grated Parmesan cheese, plus more for serving**
- **Whole or chopped fresh sage or flat-leaf parsley leaves, for serving**

Select Sauté on the Instant Pot® and add the bacon. Cook until the bacon is crispy and almost all the fat has rendered, about 5 minutes. Add the butter, onion, carrot, and celery and cook until softened, about 5 minutes. Add the garlic and cook until fragrant, about 1 minute. Add the beef, pork, and sage and cook, breaking up the meat with a wooden spoon, for 5 minutes. Add the wine and cook until combined. Add the tomato paste, tomatoes, 3 teaspoons salt, and 3 teaspoons pepper and stir to combine. Press the Cancel button to reset the program.

Lock the lid in place and turn the valve to Sealing. Press the Pressure Cook button and set the cook time for 8 minutes at high pressure. Turn the valve to Venting to quick-release the steam. Carefully remove the lid. Taste the sauce and adjust the seasoning as needed. Press the Cancel button to reset the program.

Add the pasta and water. Lock the lid in place and turn the valve to Sealing. Press the Pressure Cook button and set the cook time for 6 minutes at high pressure. Let the steam release naturally for 15 minutes, then turn the valve to Venting to quick-release any residual steam. Carefully remove the lid and stir in the 1 cup (115 g) cheese. Taste and adjust the seasoning as needed.

Serve in individual bowls topped with cheese and fresh herbs.

Use a firm, hearty dried pasta shape for this dish, such as penne, rigatoni, or gemelli, which can stand up to pressure.

For more greenery, add a handful or two of fresh spinach to the pot with the broccoli and toss with tongs.

Thai Basil Noodles with Beef

Put down that to-go menu and make your own pad Thai with this super-quick one-pot recipe. Look for rice noodles that are about the width of fettuccine noodles where Asian ingredients are sold. Thinner "pad Thai" noodles tend to overcook under pressure.

SERVES 4

1 tablespoon canola oil

¾ lb (340 g) sirloin steak, sliced across the grain into strips ¼ inch (6 mm) thick

Freshly ground black pepper

1 large carrot, peeled and thinly sliced

3 cloves garlic, chopped

1 cup (240 ml) plus 2 tablespoons cold water

1 cup (240 ml) chicken stock (page 270 or store-bought)

4 Thai lime leaves (optional)

3 tablespoons firmly packed light brown sugar

3 tablespoons fish sauce or low-sodium soy sauce

2 teaspoons tamarind paste

1 teaspoon–1 tablespoon sambal oelek (Indonesian red chile paste), to taste

½ lb (225 g) wide dried Thai rice noodles

1 red bell pepper, seeded and sliced

4 oz (115 g) broccoli crowns, cut into florets

½ cup (90 g) roughly chopped roasted peanuts

½ cup (15 g) fresh basil leaves

Put the oil in the Instant Pot®, select Sauté, and adjust to More/High heat. Season the beef all over with pepper. When the oil is hot, add half of the beef and cook, stirring frequently, until just browned, about 1 minute. Add the remaining beef, the carrot, and garlic and cook, stirring frequently, for 1 minute. Press the Cancel button.

Add the 1 cup (240 ml) cold water, the stock, and lime leaves (if using), stirring with a wooden spoon to scrape up any browned bits. In a small bowl, stir together the brown sugar, fish sauce, tamarind paste, and sambal oelek and pour over the beef mixture. Place the noodles on top of the beef mixture, pushing them down a bit so they are partially submerged. Place the bell pepper on top but don't stir.

Lock the lid in place and turn the valve to Sealing. Press the Pressure Cook button and set the cook time for 2 minutes at high pressure.

Meanwhile, in a microwave-safe bowl, combine the broccoli and the remaining 2 tablespoons cold water. Cover and microwave on High until crisp-tender, about 3 minutes. Drain and set aside, uncovered.

When the cooking time is up, turn the valve to Venting to quick-release the steam. Carefully remove the lid. Add the broccoli to the pot and toss with tongs. Cover with the lid and let the noodles stand with the Instant Pot® off for 3 minutes to allow them to absorb the sauce and finish cooking. Remove the lime leaves and discard. Serve, garnished with the peanuts and basil.

Cherry Cola Short Ribs

These fall-apart ribs, which cook alongside plenty of tender carrots, have a crowd-pleasing sauce that's not overtly cherry cola flavored, just a nice balance of sweet and tart thanks to cola + balsamic vinegar. Serve with mashed potatoes, whipped cauliflower, or polenta to catch all of the lovely sauce.

SERVES 4–6

2 tablespoons olive oil

4 lb (1.8 kg) bone-in beef short ribs

Kosher salt and black pepper

1 yellow onion, chopped

3 tablespoons tomato paste

1¼ cups (300 ml) cherry cola

1 tablespoon balsamic vinegar

1 bay leaf

4 large carrots, peeled and cut into large chunks

Put the oil in the Instant Pot®, select Sauté, and adjust to More/High heat. Season the short ribs all over with salt and pepper. When the oil is hot, working in batches, brown the ribs, meaty side down, about 6 minutes per batch. Transfer to a plate. Remove the inner pot, pour off all but 1 tablespoon of the oil, and return the pot to the appliance.

Add the onion to the pot and cook, stirring frequently, until tender, about 4 minutes. Add the tomato paste and cook until fragrant, about 30 seconds. Press the Cancel button. Add the cherry cola and vinegar, stirring with a wooden spoon to scrape up any browned bits. Return the short ribs to the pot and add the bay leaf. Place the carrots on top but don't stir.

Lock the lid in place and turn the valve to Sealing. Press the Pressure Cook button and set the cook time for 40 minutes at high pressure.

When the cooking time is up, let the steam release naturally for 15 minutes, then turn the valve to Venting to quick-release any residual steam. Carefully remove the lid and remove the bay leaf and discard. Transfer the ribs and carrots to a serving platter. They'll be very tender, so handle them gently or they'll fall apart. Tent with aluminum foil.

Pour the cooking liquid into a fat separator and pour off the fat. Alternatively, pour the cooking liquid into a large glass measuring cup, spoon off the fat, and discard. (There will be as much as ½ cup–2 cups/120–475 ml fat.)

Return the defatted cooking liquid to the pot, select Sauté, and adjust to More/High heat. Simmer until the liquid is reduced by half, about 8 minutes. Pour the sauce over the ribs and carrots and serve.

Beef Tips & Gravy with Chive Whipped Potatoes

Petite sirloin steaks, or tip steaks, are a great value, have tons of beefy flavor, and become fork-tender after just 10 minutes in the Instant Pot®. Don't use a tougher cut like stew meat or chuck roast, or the timing will be off. The whipped potatoes are cooked at the same time using the pot-in-pot method (see page 10).

SERVES 4

2 tablespoons olive oil

2 lb (1 kg) petite sirloin steaks, cut into 1-inch (2.5-cm) pieces

Kosher salt and black pepper

1 yellow onion, sliced through root end

½ cup (120 ml) chicken stock (page 270 or store-bought)

2 tablespoons Worcestershire sauce

2 tablespoons ketchup

1 teaspoon garlic powder

½ teaspoon ground ginger

1 bay leaf

5 large carrots, peeled and cut into 1-inch (2.5-cm) pieces

2 russet potatoes (about ¾ lb/340 g each), cut into 1-inch (2.5-cm) pieces

½ cup (120 ml) plus 2 tablespoons cold water

3 tablespoons unsalted butter, at room temperature

¼–½ cup (60–120 ml) heavy cream or whole milk, warmed

2 tablespoons minced fresh chives

2 tablespoons cornstarch

Put the oil in the Instant Pot®, select Sauté, and adjust to More/High heat. Season the beef with salt and pepper. When the oil is hot, add one handful of the beef and cook without stirring until well browned, about 4 minutes, then stir and continue to cook for 3 minutes longer. Using a slotted spoon, transfer to a plate. Add the onion to the pot and cook, stirring frequently, until beginning to brown, about 6 minutes. Press the Cancel button. Add the stock, Worcestershire sauce, ketchup, garlic powder, ginger, and bay leaf, stirring with a wooden spoon to scrape up any browned bits. Add all of the beef and stir to combine. Place the carrots on top but don't stir.

Place a trivet with tall (2-inch/5-cm) feet in the pot over the beef mixture. In a 7-inch (18-cm) round metal pan with a 6-cup (1.4-L) capacity, combine the potatoes and ½ cup (120 ml) of the cold water and season with salt. Cover tightly with aluminum foil and place on the trivet.

Lock the lid in place and turn the valve to Sealing. Press the Pressure Cook button and set the cook time for 10 minutes at high pressure.

When the cooking time is up, turn the valve to Venting to quick-release the steam. Carefully remove the lid and remove the pan and trivet. Drain the potatoes and transfer to a bowl. Add the butter and whip with a hand-held mixer or mash with a potato masher until smooth. Stir in the cream and chives, and season to taste with salt and pepper. Cover to keep warm.

Using a slotted spoon, transfer the beef and carrots to a large serving bowl and cover to keep warm. In a small bowl, stir together the cornstarch and 2 tablespoons cold water. Add to the pot, select Sauté, and adjust to More/High heat. Simmer until the gravy has thickened, about 1 minute. Pour the gravy over the beef and carrots and serve with the whipped potatoes.

Pizza-Stuffed Bell Peppers

This recipe features all the awesomeness of pizza, stuffed into a bell pepper, for a weeknight meal that's ready in no time. The raw ground beef is cooked directly in the pepper without being browned first, so use very lean ground beef (5% fat or less) or the peppers will be too greasy.

SERVES 4

1 cup (240 ml) canned tomato sauce

½ cup (120 ml) chicken stock (page 270 or store-bought)

1½ teaspoons dried Italian seasoning

1 teaspoon garlic powder

Kosher salt and black pepper

1 lb (450 g) 95% lean ground beef

1 cup (120 g) shredded mozzarella cheese

½ cup (1¾ oz/50 g) Italian-style dried bread crumbs

1 can (2.25 oz/64 g) sliced black olives, drained

1 teaspoon fennel seeds

4 bell peppers of different colors

2 oz (60 g) sliced pepperoni

In a large bowl, stir together the tomato sauce, stock, Italian seasoning, and garlic powder, and season with salt and pepper. Pour 1 cup (240 ml) plus 2 tablespoons of this mixture into the pot. Place a steam rack/trivet with handles in the pot.

Add the ground beef, ½ cup (60 g) of the cheese, the bread crumbs, olives, fennel seeds, and ½ teaspoon each salt and pepper to the remaining tomato sauce in the large bowl.

Cut ½ inch (12 mm) off the top of each bell pepper; reserve the tops. Scoop out the seeds and inner membranes. Finely chop the tops, discarding the stems, and add to the meat and sauce mixture in the large bowl. Add the pepperoni slices and stir until everything is thoroughly combined. Spoon the mixture into the peppers and place them upright on the trivet. Gently press the remaining ½ cup (60 g) cheese onto the filling.

Lock the lid in place and turn the valve to Sealing. Press the Pressure Cook button and set the cook time for 10 minutes at high pressure.

When the cooking time is up, turn the valve to Venting to quick-release the steam. Carefully remove the lid. Using tongs and a large spoon, gently remove the peppers from the pot; they will be very tender. Remove the trivet and stir the sauce in the pot. Spoon the sauce over the peppers and serve right away.

Be careful when topping the peppers with the mozzarella cheese; any that falls off may burn on the bottom of the pot. It's best to gently press the cheese onto the meat filling.

Barbecue Brisket with Carrots & Parsnips

Brisket needs to braise in the oven for at least 3 hours to become irresistibly succulent, but in the Instant Pot®, it's ready in 1½ hours, with buttery carrots and parsnips cooked in a foil packet at the same time. Be sure to cut the veggies into thick sticks and wrap them tightly in the foil so they don't overcook.

SERVES 4–6

1 tablespoon olive oil, plus more as needed

1 flat-cut beef brisket (2½–3 lb/1.1–1.4 kg), cut crosswise into 2 pieces

1 tablespoon chili powder

Kosher salt and black pepper

¼ cup (60 ml) lager beer

1 cup (115 g) chopped yellow onion

¾ cup (175 g) ketchup, at room temperature

3 cloves garlic, chopped

3 large carrots, peeled and cut into pieces 3 inches (7.5 cm) long and ½ inch (12 mm) thick

2 parsnips, peeled and cut into pieces 3 inches (7.5 cm) long and ½ inch (12 mm) thick

2 tablespoons unsalted butter

1 teaspoon chopped fresh thyme or ¼ teaspoon dried thyme

¼ cup (90 g) honey

2 tablespoons Worcestershire sauce

1 tablespoon toasted sesame oil

1 tablespoon Dijon mustard

Put the 1 tablespoon olive oil in the Instant Pot®, select Sauté, and adjust to More/High heat. Rub the beef all over with the chili powder and season with salt and pepper. When the oil is hot, working in batches if needed, brown the beef on two flat sides, about 3 minutes per side; add more oil between batches if needed. Transfer to a plate. Add the beer to the pot, stirring with a wooden spoon to scrape up any browned bits. Press the Cancel button. Add the onion, ¼ cup (60 g) of the ketchup, and the garlic to the pot and stir to combine. Add the beef in a single layer.

Put the carrots, parsnips, butter, and thyme in the center of a 12-inch (30-cm) length of foil, and season with salt and pepper. Fold up the sides and seal to form a tight packet. Place the packet directly on top of the brisket.

Lock the lid in place and turn the valve to Sealing. Press the Pressure Cook button and set the cook time for 1 hour and 30 minutes at high pressure.

When the cooking time is up, let the steam release naturally for 20 minutes, then turn the valve to Venting to quick-release any residual steam. Remove the lid and transfer the foil packet to a serving bowl but keep it sealed. Transfer the brisket to a cutting board and tent with foil.

Pour 1 cup (240 ml) of the cooking liquid into a fat separator and pour off the fat. Alternatively, pour the 1 cup (240 ml) liquid into a large glass measuring cup, spoon off the fat, and discard. In a bowl, whisk together ½ cup (120 ml) of the defatted cooking liquid, the remaining ketchup, the honey, Worcestershire sauce, sesame oil, and mustard. Thinly slice the brisket across the grain, transfer to a platter, and top with the sauce. Remove the vegetables from the foil and serve alongside.

Cheese-Stuffed Beef Burgers

The Midwest is famous for its messy burgers with cheesy centers. For this version, sharp Cheddar balances the richness of the meat. Be sure to make an indentation with your thumb in the center of the patty to keep it from puffing as it cooks. Toppings like Spicy Mayo (page 121), sliced avocado, and crispy bacon take this sandwich to the next level.

SERVES 2

¾ lb (340 g) 85% lean ground beef

½ teaspoon garlic powder

½ teaspoon onion powder

Kosher salt and freshly ground black pepper

2 oz (60 g) Cheddar cheese, preferably sharp, shredded

2 brioche buns (Jam-Filled Brioche Doughnuts, page 38 or store-bought)

FOR SERVING

Lettuce, tomato slices, pickle slices, mayonnaise or Spicy Mayo (Crispy Fried Chicken Sandwiches, page 121), mustard, ketchup

In a bowl, combine the beef, garlic powder, onion powder, ½ teaspoon salt, and a few grindings of pepper and mix gently with your hands or a wooden spoon until just combined (be careful not to overmix or the meat will become tough). Divide the meat mixture into 2 patties, each about 5 inches (13 cm) in diameter and 1 inch (2.5 cm) thick.

Place half of the cheese in the center of each patty and shape the meat into a ball to enclose the cheese, then reshape into 5-by-1-inch (13-by-2.5-cm) patties. Use your thumb to make an indentation in the center of each patty (this will prevent them from puffing up during cooking).

Coat the Instant Pot® air fryer basket with canola oil spray. Arrange the patties in a single layer in the basket, making sure they don't touch. Insert the basket into the pot and attach the air fryer lid. Press the Air Fry button and set the cook time for 8 minutes (for medium) or 9 minutes (for medium-well) at 400°F (200°C), then press Start. Flip the burgers when prompted.

When the cooking time is up, use a nonstick spatula to carefully transfer the burgers to a plate.

Place 1 bun, cut-sides down, on the dehydrating tray, insert the tray into the basket, and attach the air fryer lid. Press the Air Fry button and set the cook time for 2 minutes at 400°F (200°C), then press Start. Use tongs to transfer the bun to a plate. Repeat to toast the remaining bun.

Place the burgers on the buns, add the desired toppings, and serve.

Provolone is a classic cheese pairing for this juicy sandwich, but white Cheddar, pepper jack, or Swiss would also be delicious.

French Dip Sandwiches

This easy one-pot way to cook a crowd-pleasing sandwich is made even simpler by slicing the beef before it is cooked so that everything is ready to go at the end. The cooking liquid becomes a flavorful jus, or thin gravy, for dipping. Onion lovers can add some cooked onion slices on top of the beef.

SERVES 4

2 lb (1 kg) boneless beef chuck, sliced about ¼ inch (6 mm) thick (by a butcher)

Kosher salt and freshly ground black pepper

1 tablespoon olive oil

1 yellow onion, sliced

3 cloves garlic, minced

2 tablespoons Worcestershire sauce

1 teaspoon oregano

1 teaspoon garlic powder

1½ cups (350 ml) beef stock (page 272 or store-bought)

1 bay leaf

4 French rolls, split (and toasted, if desired)

4 slices provolone cheese

Pat the beef slices dry with a paper towel and season generously with salt and pepper. Set aside.

Select Sauté on the Instant Pot® and heat the oil. Add the onion and cook, stirring occasionally, until it starts to soften, about 3 minutes. Add the garlic and cook for 1 minute. Add the Worcestershire sauce, oregano, and garlic powder and stir to combine. Press the Cancel button to reset the program.

Add the stock, bay leaf, beef slices, ½ teaspoon salt, and ¼ teaspoon pepper. Lock the lid in place and turn the valve to Sealing. Press the Pressure Cook button and set the cook time for 30 minutes at high pressure.

Let the steam release naturally for 15 minutes, then turn the valve to Venting to quick-release any residual steam. Carefully remove the lid and use tongs to remove the beef slices from the jus and transfer them to a plate. (They will be very soft.) Pour the jus through a fine-mesh sieve. Taste and adjust the seasoning as needed. Let the jus cool slightly and skim the fat off the top. Transfer to a small bowl or serving pitcher.

To serve, place an equal amount of beef slices onto each roll, pour some jus over the beef, and top with a slice of provolone. Serve the remaining jus in individual bowls for dipping.

BBQ Brisket Sandwiches

Brisket usually takes about three hours to cook, but it comes out of the Instant Pot® tender and full of flavor in one-third of the time. Classic pickles and peperoncini make great toppings on these sandwiches, but you could add some homemade pickled red onions (see page 274), as well.

SERVES 4

1 flat-cut beef brisket (about 2½ lb/1.2 kg)

Kosher salt and freshly ground black pepper

3 cloves garlic, minced

1 tablespoon Worcestershire sauce

1 tablespoon vegetable oil

½ cup (120 ml) red wine

1 yellow onion, thinly sliced

2 cups (475 ml) chicken or beef stock (pages 270 and 272 or store-bought)

½ cup (120 ml) barbecue sauce

1 tablespoon firmly packed light brown sugar

1 tablespoon Dijon mustard

2 fresh thyme sprigs

2 tablespoons all-purpose flour

4 brioche buns (Jam-Filled Brioche Doughnuts, page 38) or soft hamburger buns, toasted toasted

Pickles and/or pickled peperoncini, for serving (optional)

Let the brisket stand at room temperature for 30 minutes. Pat dry with a paper towel and season generously with salt and pepper. In a small bowl, whisk together the garlic and Worcestershire sauce. Brush the fat side of the brisket with the mixture.

Select Sauté on the Instant Pot® and heat the oil. Add the brisket, fat side up, and cook until browned, about 3 minutes. Transfer to a plate as browned. Add the wine to the pot and bring to a simmer, stirring occasionally with a wooden spoon to scrape up any browned bits. Add the onion, stock, barbecue sauce, brown sugar, mustard, and thyme and stir to combine. Press the Cancel button to reset the program.

Return the brisket to the pot, fat side up. Lock the lid in place and turn the valve to Sealing. Press the Pressure Cook button and set the cook time for 1 hour at high pressure.

Let the steam release naturally. Carefully remove the lid and transfer the brisket to a cutting board, tent with aluminum foil, and let rest for 5 minutes before thinly slicing against the grain. Press the Cancel button to reset the program.

Press the Sauté button and heat the cooking juices until they begin to simmer. Whisk in the flour and simmer until the gravy has thickened, about 10 minutes. Remove and discard the thyme sprigs.

To assemble each sandwich, add a few slices of brisket to the bottom half of each bun and spoon some gravy over the meat. Top with pickles, if using. Cover with the top of the bun and serve.

Korean BBQ Flank Steak

A Korean fermented chile paste, gochujang is combined here with garlic, ginger, soy sauce, rice vinegar, and brown sugar, taking this simple marinade for flank steak to the next level. The meat turns lusciously salty-sweet with a crispy crust when broiled. Leftovers are wonderful with eggs for breakfast or atop a rice bowl for lunch.

SERVES 2–4

- **3 tablespoons soy sauce**
- **1 tablespoon rice vinegar**
- **¼ cup (60 g) firmly packed light brown sugar**
- **1 tablespoon gochujang (Korean chile paste)**
- **2 cloves garlic, grated**
- **1 teaspoon peeled and grated fresh ginger**
- **1 flank steak (¾–1½ lb/ 340–680 g and about 1 inch/2.5 cm thick)**

In a glass measuring cup or small bowl, whisk together the soy sauce, vinegar, brown sugar, gochujang, garlic, and ginger. Place the steak in a large lock-top plastic bag or a shallow baking dish just large enough to hold it and pour the marinade over the meat. Seal the bag or cover the dish with plastic wrap and let stand at room temperature for 30 minutes or refrigerate up to overnight, turning occasionally. If refrigerated, let stand at room temperature for about 30 minutes before cooking.

Coat the Instant Pot® air fryer basket with canola oil spray. Working in batches if needed, remove the steak from the marinade, letting the excess drip off, and place in the basket. If the steak is too big to fit in the basket in 1 piece, cut it in half crosswise, making sure the pieces don't touch. Insert the basket into the pot and attach the air fryer lid. Press the Broil button and set the cook time for 10 minutes at 400°F (200°C), then press Start. Flip the steak halfway through the cooking time.

When the cooking time is up, insert an instant-read thermometer into the thickest part of the meat; it should register 130°–135°F (54°–57°C) for medium-rare and 135°–145°F (57°–63°C) for medium. If the steak is not cooked to the desired doneness, add more cooking time in 2-minute intervals until the steak is cooked as desired. Use tongs to carefully transfer the steak to a cutting board and let rest for 5–10 minutes, then cut across the grain into slices. If cooking in batches, repeat to cook the remaining piece, then serve.

NOTE *Flank steak is sold in a range of sizes and weights. The marinade in this recipe will cover up to 1½ lb (680 g) of meat, so if your piece is large, cut it in half to fit in the basket and cook the meat in 2 batches.*

PORK

Can't find boneless country-style ribs? Use a pork butt roast instead and cut it into 1½-by-1-inch (4-by-2.5-cm) strips, then cut them crosswise into chunks.

Pork Verde & Pinto Bean Tostadas

This easy tomatillo pork dish becomes fork-tender in just 20 minutes under high pressure, thanks to convenient boneless country-style pork ribs. It's wonderful on tostadas, but you can also serve it as a stew with steamed rice (page 266), or tuck the meat and beans into tortillas for delicious tacos.

SERVES 6

1 tablespoon olive oil

1 tablespoon ground cumin

1 tablespoon ground coriander

Kosher salt and black pepper

3 lb (1.4 kg) boneless country-style pork ribs, cut into 1½-inch (4-cm) pieces

1 cup (240 ml) thin, mild green salsa, such as Herdez

1 yellow onion, sliced through root end

4 cloves garlic, chopped

2 teaspoons dried Mexican oregano

¼ cup (15 g) chopped fresh cilantro

Zest and juice of 1 lime

1 can (15 oz/425 g) refried pinto beans, warmed

12 tostada shells

1½ cups (170 g) grated Cheddar cheese

4 cups (140 g) shredded romaine lettuce

¾ cup (170 g) sour cream

Put the oil in the Instant Pot®, select Sauté, and adjust to More/High heat. In a large bowl, stir together the cumin, coriander, 1 teaspoon salt, and ½ teaspoon pepper. Add the pork and toss to coat. When the oil is hot, add one handful of the pork and cook, stirring occasionally, until well browned, about 5 minutes. Press the Cancel button.

Add the salsa to the pot, stirring with a wooden spoon to scrape up any browned bits. Add the remaining pork, the onion, garlic, and oregano and stir to combine.

Lock the lid in place and turn the valve to Sealing. Press the Pressure Cook button and set the cook time for 20 minutes at high pressure.

When the cooking time is up, let the steam release naturally for 10 minutes, then turn the valve to Venting to quick-release any residual steam. Carefully remove the lid. Using a slotted spoon, transfer the pork to a medium bowl and spoon ½ cup (120 ml) of the solids and cooking liquid over the pork. (Save the remaining cooking liquid for a base for chili, if desired.) Add the cilantro, lime zest, and lime juice to the bowl and stir to combine.

Spread the refried beans on the tostada shells. Top with the pork, cheese, lettuce, and a dollop of sour cream. Serve right away.

Sausage & Fennel Penne

Fennel is a bulb vegetable with a sweet flavor that pairs well with Italian sausage. Never fear if you have picky eaters; the vegetable melts into the sauce beautifully under pressure. If your fennel still has the feathery fronds attached, chop them and sprinkle over the finished pasta for a lovely green garnish.

SERVES 4

2 tablespoons olive oil

1 lb (450 g) sweet Italian sausages, casings removed

1 yellow onion, chopped

1 small fennel bulb, trimmed, cored, and thinly sliced, fronds reserved for garnish (optional)

1½ tablespoons minced fresh sage or 1½ teaspoons dried sage

1 teaspoon fennel seeds

4 cloves garlic, minced

2 cups (475 ml) chicken stock (page 270 or store-bought)

1 cup (240 ml) water

2 tablespoons tomato paste

Kosher salt and black pepper

Pinch of red pepper flakes

¾ lb (340 g) penne pasta

½ cup (60 g) grated pecorino romano cheese

Put the oil in the Instant Pot®, select Sauté, and adjust to More/High heat. Form the sausage meat into rustic little dabs, about 1 tablespoon each. (No need to roll them into perfect balls.) When the oil is hot, add the sausage and cook without stirring for 2 minutes. Using a spatula, carefully flip the sausage over and cook until golden brown on the second side, about 3 minutes. Transfer to a plate.

Add the onion, sliced fennel, sage, and fennel seeds to the pot and cook, stirring frequently, until the onion and fennel are tender, about 4 minutes. Add the garlic and cook until fragrant, about 30 seconds. Press the Cancel button.

Add the stock, water, and tomato paste, stirring to scrape up any browned bits. Return the sausage to the pot. Add ½ teaspoon each salt and black pepper and the red pepper flakes and stir to combine. Add the pasta and gently press down on the noodles to partially submerge them.

Lock the lid in place and turn the valve to Sealing. Press the Pressure Cook button and set the cook time for 6 minutes at low pressure.

When the cooking time is up, turn the valve to Venting to quick-release the steam. Carefully remove the lid, stir gently, and let stand uncovered for 1–2 minutes to allow the pasta to absorb more of the stock mixture. Season to taste with salt and black pepper. Sprinkle with the cheese and fennel fronds (if using) and serve.

TIP *To remove the hard core from the fennel bulb, cut it in half lengthwise, then use a paring knife to cut the solid white core out of the bottom center of the bulb. Save for stock or discard.*

Pork Lo Mein

These are just like takeout noodles but faster and healthier. The vegetables and pork will cook along with the dry noodles in just 2 minutes under high pressure. Look for thin wheat noodles, called lo mein (not fried noodles), in Asian markets or online.

SERVES 4

½ cup (120 ml) plus 2 tablespoons chicken stock (page 270 or store-bought)

3 tablespoons low-sodium soy sauce

2 tablespoons rice cooking wine or dry sherry

2 tablespoons canola oil

1 pork tenderloin (about 1 lb/450 g)

1 teaspoon Chinese five-spice powder

Kosher salt and black pepper

1 small red bell pepper, seeded and sliced

½ yellow onion, thinly sliced

5 shiitake mushrooms, stemmed and brushed clean, caps thickly sliced

1 can (15 oz/425 g) baby corn, drained and cut into bite-size pieces

4 cloves garlic, thinly sliced

6 oz (170 g) dried lo mein or chow mein noodles

2 tablespoons hoisin sauce

3 green onions, thinly sliced

In a small bowl, stir together the stock, soy sauce, and rice cooking wine; set aside.

Put the oil in the Instant Pot®, select Sauté, and adjust to More/High heat. Cut the pork crosswise into 2 pieces then rub all over with the five-spice powder and season with salt and pepper. When the oil is hot, brown the pork all over for about 5 minutes total. Transfer to a cutting board and cut crosswise into ½-inch (12-mm) slices, and then into 1-1½-inch (2.5–4-cm) pieces; set aside.

Add the bell pepper, onion, mushrooms, and baby corn to the pot and cook, stirring frequently, until the onion begins to brown, about 5 minutes. Add the garlic and cook until fragrant, about 30 seconds. Press the Cancel button.

Add the stock mixture, stirring with a wooden spoon to scrape up any browned bits. Return the pork to the pot and stir to combine. Break the noodles into 3-inch (7.5-cm) lengths and scatter over the pork and vegetables. Gently press down on the noodles to partially submerge them but don't stir.

Lock the lid in place and turn the valve to Sealing. Press the Pressure Cook button and set the cook time for 2 minutes at high pressure.

When the cooking time is up, turn the valve to Venting to quick-release the steam. Carefully remove the lid. Add the hoisin sauce and green onions, stir gently (some noodles may not be completely cooked), and cover with the lid. Let stand for 2–3 minutes to finish cooking the noodles. Serve right away.

Maple-Mustard Pork Chops with Sweet Potatoes

Look for thick bone-in chops cut from the center portion of the loin. The best ones will have a "T-bone" with a bit of the lighter loin meat and a section of the tenderloin on them. The side of sweet potatoes cooks at the same time in a steamer basket.

SERVES 4

- **2 tablespoons olive oil**
- **3 slices bacon, coarsely chopped**
- **4 center-cut, bone-in pork chops (each about ½ lb/225 g and 1½ inches/4 cm thick)**
- **Kosher salt and black pepper**
- **1 small yellow onion, chopped**
- **2 tablespoons chopped fresh sage or 2 teaspoons dried sage**
- **2 cloves garlic, chopped**
- **½ cup (120 ml) chicken stock (page 270 or store-bought)**
- **3 tablespoons maple syrup**
- **2 tablespoons whole-grain mustard**
- **2 lb (1 kg) orange-fleshed sweet potatoes, peeled and cut into 2-inch (5-cm) chunks**
- **¼ cup (30 g) toasted chopped pecans**
- **2 tablespoons cornstarch**
- **2 tablespoons cold water**

Put the oil in the Instant Pot®, select Sauté, and adjust to Normal/Medium heat. When the oil is hot, add the bacon and cook, stirring occasionally, until crisp and browned, 4–5 minutes. Transfer to a plate.

Season the chops with salt and pepper. Working in batches, brown until golden on one side, 3 minutes per batch. Transfer to a plate. Remove the inner pot, pour off all but 1 tablespoon of the fat, and return the pot to the appliance. Add the onion and cook, stirring, until tender, 4 minutes. Add the sage and garlic and cook until fragrant, 30 seconds. Press the Cancel button.

Add the stock, maple syrup, and mustard, stirring to scrape up any browned bits. Add the chops and bacon to the pot. Place a steamer basket in the pot over the pork. Put the sweet potatoes in the basket.

Lock the lid in place and turn the valve to Sealing. Press the Pressure Cook button and set the cook time for 10 minutes at high pressure.

When the cooking time is up, let the steam release naturally for 10 minutes, then turn the valve to Venting to quick-release any residual steam. Carefully remove the lid. Transfer the sweet potatoes to a serving bowl, season with salt and pepper, and sprinkle with the pecans. Cover to keep warm. Remove the steamer basket from the pot.

Check the pork for doneness; an instant-read thermometer inserted near (but not touching) the bone should register 140°F (60°C). If not done, cover with a regular pan lid, select Sauté, and adjust to Normal/Medium heat. Simmer, turning, until done, 1–5 minutes longer. Transfer to a platter and tent with foil. In a bowl, stir together the cornstarch and cold water. Add to the pot, select Sauté, and adjust to More/High heat. Simmer, stirring, until the sauce is thickened, 2 minutes. Season to taste. Serve the chops with the sweet potatoes and top with the sauce.

You can substitute another hard vegetable, such as potatoes, carrots, parsnips, or butternut squash, for the sweet potatoes, if you like.

Bruise then slice the lemongrass stalks before adding them to the marinade to release their full flavor.

Lemongrass & Garlic Pork Chops

Thick-cut pork chops benefit from a light, lemongrass-infused marinade. A handful of fresh spinach added to the warm pot just before serving adds bright flavor, or you can sub in bok choy, shredded kale, or another leafy green.

SERVES 4

FOR THE MARINADE

2 stalks lemongrass, tough outer leaves removed

3 tablespoons tamari, soy sauce, or coconut aminos

3 tablespoons fish sauce

¼ cup (60 g) firmly packed brown sugar

6 cloves garlic, minced or grated

2 large shallots, minced

½ teaspoon freshly ground black pepper

4 bone-in, thick-cut pork chops (about 3 lb/1.4 kg)

1 tablespoon canola oil

1 cup (240 ml) chicken or beef stock (pages 270 and 272 or store-bought)

5 oz (150 g) baby spinach

Steamed white rice (page 266), for serving

Use the flat side of your knife to firmly push down on each stalk of lemongrass until it splits. Then thinly slice the stalks.

To make the marinade, in a small bowl or measuring cup, whisk together the tamari, fish sauce, brown sugar, garlic, shallots, pepper, and lemongrass. Place the pork chops in a shallow pan or baking dish and pour the marinade over the top. Cover with plastic wrap and marinate in the refrigerator for at least 30 minutes and up to 2 hours, turning occasionally to coat.

Select Sauté on the Instant Pot® and heat the oil. Working in batches, add the pork chops, reserving the marinade, and brown evenly on both sides, 2–3 minutes per side. Transfer to a plate. Add the stock and use a wooden spoon to scrape up any browned bits. Add the reserved marinade and stir to combine. Return the pork and its juices to the pot. Press the Cancel button to reset the program.

Lock the lid in place and turn the valve to Sealing. Press the Pressure Cook button and set the cook time for 10 minutes at high pressure.

Let the steam release naturally, or for at least 10 minutes, before turning the valve to Venting to quick-release any residual steam.

Carefully remove the lid and use tongs to transfer the pork chops to a serving platter. Drain all but two tablespoons of cooking liquid from the pot. Press the Cancel button to reset the program.

Press the Sauté button and add the spinach. Cook until the spinach has wilted, 3–5 minutes. Transfer to the platter with the pork chops. Serve with rice alongside.

Apricot-Ginger Glazed Pork Chops

Brushing meat with a jam-based glaze is a genius way to contribute color and flavor to a dish. A second coating of glaze after cooking adds extra zing and a shiny finish. Round out the meal with Spicy Sweet Potato Wedges (page 72) or Spiced Green Beans (page 75).

SERVES 2

2 bone-in pork chops (each ½–¾ lb/225–340 g and about 1 inch/2.5 cm) thick

Kosher salt and freshly ground black pepper

3 tablespoons apricot jam

3 teaspoons peeled and grated fresh ginger

Pat the pork chops dry with paper towels. Season generously with salt and pepper. In a small bowl, stir together the jam and ginger; if desired, reserve some of the glaze for serving. Brush the chops on both sides with the glaze.

Coat the Instant Pot® air fryer basket with canola oil spray. Place the pork chops in the basket, making sure they don't touch. Insert the basket into the pot and attach the air fryer lid. Press the Air Fry button and set the cook time for 18 minutes at 350°F (180°C), then press Start. Flip the pork chops when prompted, brushing with more glaze when flipping.

When the cooking time is up, insert an instant-read thermometer into the thickest part of the pork, away from the bone; it should register 140°F (60°C). If the pork is not fully cooked, add more cooking time in 2-minute intervals until the pork is fully cooked. Use tongs to carefully transfer the pork to a plate. Brush with more glaze, if desired, and serve.

Pork Schnitzel

Super-thin, breaded pork chops cook in under 10 minutes in the air fryer, making this a fast weeknight dinner for one or many. If preparing 4 chops, increase the breading quantities to ½ cup (2 oz/60 g) flour, 3 eggs mixed with 3 tablespoons water, and 2 cups (7 oz/200 g) panko.

SERVES 2

2 boneless pork chops (each about ¼ lb/115 g)

⅓ cup (1½ oz/40 g) all-purpose flour

Kosher salt and freshly ground black pepper

¼ teaspoon cayenne pepper (optional)

2 large eggs

1 tablespoon water

1 cup (3½ oz/100 g) panko bread crumbs

Place a piece of plastic wrap on a cutting board and set the pork chops on top. Cover the pork with another piece of plastic wrap. Using a meat pounder, rolling pin, or hammer, gently pound the pork flat, working from the center outward and stretching the pork chops as you pound, so they are just slightly thicker than ¼ inch (6 mm). Transfer to a plate.

In a medium bowl, whisk together the flour, 1 teaspoon salt, ¼ teaspoon black pepper, and cayenne (if using). In a large, shallow bowl, whisk together the eggs and water. Place the bread crumbs in another medium bowl or on a large plate.

Line a rimmed baking sheet with parchment paper. Pat the pork chops dry with paper towels. Working with 1 chop at a time, coat the pork in the flour mixture, shaking off the excess. Dip in the egg mixture, letting the excess drip off, then dredge in the bread crumbs, turning to coat well and pressing gently to adhere. Place the coated chops on the prepared baking sheet as you go.

Coat the Instant Pot® air fryer basket with canola oil spray. Coat 1 chop generously with olive oil spray and place in the basket. Insert the basket into the pot and attach the air fryer lid. Press the Air Fry button and set the cook time for 9 minutes at 400°F (200°C), then press Start. Flip the chop when prompted.

When the cooking time is up, insert an instant-read thermometer into the thickest part of the chop; it should register 140°F (60°C) and the chop should be golden and crispy. If it is not, add more cooking time in 2-minute intervals until the pork is fully cooked. Use tongs to carefully transfer the pork to a plate. Repeat to cook the remaining chop, then serve.

Sweet & Spicy Mexican Chile Carnitas

This dish is perfect for big gatherings. Set out a large platter of pork along with bowls of toppings, and let guests assemble their own tacos. The sweet and spicy caramelized meat is balanced by a bright salsa verde and a tangy chile crema.

SERVES 6–8

4 dried ancho chiles

4 dried pasilla chiles

2 cups (475 ml) boiling water

3 lb (1.5 kg) boneless pork shoulder, cut into 4 pieces

Kosher salt

1 tablespoon canola oil

FOR SERVING

Warmed corn or flour tortillas, Salsa Verde (page 274), Chile Crema (page 274), fresh cilantro leaves, Quick-Pickled Red Onion (page 274), and lime wedges

Place all of the chiles in a medium heatproof bowl. Pour the boiling water over them and soak for 30 minutes. (Use a smaller bowl or plate to weight the chiles down.) Drain the chiles, reserving the soaking liquid, and remove the stems and seeds. (They will be soft enough to pull apart with your hands.)

Season the pork generously with salt. Select Sauté on the Instant Pot® and heat the oil. Working in batches, brown the pork pieces on all sides, about 12 minutes total. Transfer to a plate as browned. Press the Cancel button to reset the program. Carefully remove the inner pot to pour off the fat, then return the inner pot to the Instant Pot® housing.

Add 1 cup (240 ml) chile-soaking liquid, the chiles, and the pork, nestling the pieces snugly into the pot. Lock the lid in place and turn the valve to Sealing. Press the Pressure Cook button and set the cook time for 45 minutes at high pressure.

Line a rimmed baking sheet with aluminum foil.

Let the steam release naturally, or for at least 30 minutes, before turning the valve to Venting to quick-release any residual steam. Carefully remove the lid and use tongs to transfer the pork to the prepared baking sheet. Preheat the broiler. Using two forks, shred the pork. Pour the cooking liquid from the inner pot into a bowl or measuring cup through a fine-mesh sieve to strain out the chiles, then pour about half of the strained liquid over the pork. (Reserve the chiles and remaining cooking liquid for the chile crema.) Broil until the edges of the pork are crispy, 7–10 minutes.

Serve the carnitas in warmed tortillas, topped with salsa verde, chile crema, cilantro, pickled onion, and lime wedges alongside.

Beer-Braised Sausage & Pepper Sandwiches

An adult spin on a ballpark staple, these hearty sandwiches are updated with sautéed leeks in place of onions, which are then cooked in beer for a richer flavor. You can play around with craft lagers for a deeper flavor profile, or replace the ale with the same amount of apple cider, if you like.

SERVES 6

1 tablespoon olive oil

6 Italian sweet or hot pork sausages (about 1½ lb/ 680 g), pricked with a fork

2 large leeks, white and pale green tops, halved lengthwise and sliced crosswise

1 cup (240 ml) brown ale or lager

1 teaspoon red wine vinegar

3 bay leaves

Kosher salt and freshly ground black pepper

2 red bell peppers, seeded and sliced

6 Italian rolls, split and toasted, for serving

Select Sauté on the Instant Pot® and heat the oil. Cook the sausages until evenly browned on both sides, about 6 minutes. Use tongs to transfer the sausages to a plate. Using tongs to hold a paper towel, wipe out all but 1–2 tablespoons of fat from the pot. Add the leeks and cook, stirring occasionally, until they just begin to soften, about 3 minutes. Add 1 tablespoon of the ale to the pot and stir with a wooden spoon to scrape up any browned bits. Press the Cancel button to reset the program.

Add the remaining ale, the vinegar, bay leaves, ½ teaspoon salt, and ½ teaspoon pepper and stir to combine. Return the sausage to the pot and layer the red pepper slices on top. Lock the lid in place and turn the valve to Sealing. Press the Pressure Cook button and set the cook time for 15 minutes at high pressure.

Let the steam release naturally for 10 minutes, then turn the valve to Venting to quick-release any residual steam. Carefully remove the lid, discard the bay leaves, and use tongs to transfer one sausage to the bottom half of each roll. Top with leeks and slices of peppers and the top half of the roll. Serve warm.

Korean Pork Sliders with Asian Pear Slaw

These succulent sliders feature a zingy, gingery barbecue sauce made with gochujang, the addictive Korean miso-red chile paste. Look for it online and where Asian ingredients are sold. The crunchy slaw boasts a touch of sweetness thanks to an Asian pear, although a medium-firm Bartlett pear makes a fine substitute.

SERVES 6–12

FOR THE PORK

2 tablespoons canola oil

1 boneless pork butt (4–5 lb/1.8–2.3 kg)

Kosher salt and black pepper

1 yellow onion, sliced

6 cloves garlic, chopped

3 tablespoons plus 1 teaspoon peeled and chopped fresh ginger

½ cup (120 ml) low-sodium soy sauce

½ cup (115 g) gochujang (Korean chile paste)

½ cup (115 g) ketchup

⅓ cup (80 g) firmly packed light brown sugar

2 tablespoons rice vinegar

2 tablespoons toasted sesame oil

2 teaspoons Chinese five-spice powder

To make the pork, put the canola oil in the Instant Pot®, select Sauté, and adjust to More/High heat. Season the pork all over with salt and pepper. When the oil is hot, brown the pork all over, about 3 minutes per side. Transfer to a plate. Add the onion to the pot and cook, stirring frequently, until tender, about 4 minutes. Add the garlic and ginger and cook until fragrant, about 30 seconds. Add ½ cup (120 ml) water and the soy sauce, stirring with a wooden spoon to scrape up any browned bits. Return the pork to the pot. Press the Cancel button.

In a small bowl, stir together the gochujang, ketchup, brown sugar, vinegar, sesame oil, and five-spice powder. Spoon ¼ cup (60 ml) of the mixture over the pork, spreading it evenly on the top of the meat but limiting the amount that drips into the liquid below. Set the remaining gochujang mixture aside.

Lock the lid in place and turn the valve to Sealing. Press the Pressure Cook button and set the cook time for 1 hour and 15 minutes at high pressure for a 4-lb (1.8-kg) roast and 1 hour and 30 minutes for a 5-lb (2.3-kg) roast.

When the cooking time is up, let the steam release naturally for 15 minutes, then turn the valve to Venting to quick-release any residual steam. Carefully remove the lid, transfer the pork to a cutting board, and tent with aluminum foil.

continued on page 183

These flavor-rich and hearty sliders are also terrific for easy entertaining or any game-day menu; pair them with onion rings (page 66) and cold beer.

continued from page 181

Pour the cooking liquid into a fat separator and pour off the fat. Alternatively, pour the cooking liquid into a large glass measuring cup, spoon off the fat, and discard. Return 1 cup (240 ml) of the defatted cooking liquid to the pot. Whisk in the reserved gochujang mixture, select Sauté, and adjust to Normal/Medium heat. Cook, stirring frequently, until the sauce is thickened and bubbly, about 5 minutes. Meanwhile, cut the pork into thin slices or shred with 2 forks, discarding most of the fat. (A little fat is okay; it adds flavor.) Return the meat to the pot and stir to combine with the sauce. (The meat can be kept warm, covered, using the Keep Warm function, for up to 3 hours.)

To make the slaw, in a large bowl, toss the cabbage with 1 teaspoon salt, then add the pear, carrot, and green onions. In a small bowl, whisk together the vinegar, canola oil, granulated sugar, ginger, and sesame oil. Add the dressing to the cabbage mixture and toss to combine.

Divide the pork among the slider buns, top with the slaw, and serve.

TIP *Despite its name, pork butt comes from the front shoulder area of the pig. It's a fatty cut of meat, so you may wish to trim some of the fat on the outside of the roast before searing it. The fat that runs within the roast adds flavor and will dissolve as it cooks, yielding very tender meat.*

FOR THE SLAW

5 cups (425 g) finely shredded green cabbage

Kosher salt

1 firm Asian pear, cored and cut into matchsticks

1 large carrot, peeled and grated

2 green onions, thinly sliced

¼ cup (60 ml) rice vinegar

3 tablespoons canola oil

1 tablespoon granulated sugar

1 teaspoon peeled and finely grated fresh ginger

1 teaspoon toasted sesame oil

20–25 slider buns

Five-Spice Pork Ribs

Barbecuing ribs is often an all-day affair, but it doesn't have to be! This method cuts cooking to a fraction of the time, but combined with the quick broiling step at the end, yields the same results—falling-off-the-bone meat with a finger-licking coating flavored with an aromatic blend of spices.

SERVES 6

3 lb (1.5 kg) baby back pork ribs

Kosher salt

½ cup (120 ml) freshly squeezed orange juice (from 1 large orange)

2 tablespoons soy sauce

2 tablespoons fish sauce

1 tablespoon Chinese five-spice powder

2 teaspoons sambal oelek (Indonesian red chile paste) or Sriracha

1 teaspoon sugar

1 tablespoon canola oil

2 shallots, diced

3 cloves garlic, minced

2-inch (5-cm) piece fresh ginger, peeled and minced

Cut rib racks into slabs of about 3 ribs each. Place in a large bowl, season lightly with salt, and set aside.

In a small bowl or measuring cup, whisk together the orange juice, soy sauce, fish sauce, five-spice powder, sambal oelek, and sugar. Set aside.

Select Sauté on the Instant Pot® and heat the oil. Cook the shallots, stirring occasionally, until soft and slightly browned, about 4 minutes. Add the garlic and ginger and cook until fragrant, about 1 minute. Add the juice mixture and bring to a simmer. Press the Cancel button to reset the program.

Pour the five-spice sauce over the ribs and let sit for 5 minutes. Stack the ribs upright in the pot and pour the sauce over the ribs. Lock the lid in place and turn the valve to Sealing. Press the Pressure Cook button and set the cook time for 25 minutes at high pressure.

Line a rimmed baking sheet with aluminum foil.

Let the steam release naturally. Carefully remove the lid and use tongs to transfer the ribs to the prepared baking sheet. Preheat the broiler.

Select Sauté on the Instant Pot® and simmer the sauce until thickened, 10–12 minutes. Brush the top side of the ribs with the sauce, place in the broiler, and broil for 3 minutes. Carefully remove the baking sheet from the broiler. Using tongs, turn the ribs over and brush them with the remaining sauce. Return the ribs to the broiler and broil for 3 minutes.

Transfer to a platter and serve.

Cajun-Rubbed Pork Tenderloin

When served with creamy polenta (page 273) and a side salad, this recipe yields an impressive weeknight dinner. Cut a long tenderloin in half crosswise and place the pieces side by side in the air fryer basket. Then transform leftovers into a Cubano sandwich the next day (see note below).

SERVES 4

1 lb (450 g) pork tenderloin, cut crosswise into 2 pieces

2 teaspoons canola oil

1 tablespoon Cajun seasoning

1 tablespoon firmly packed light brown sugar

Kosher salt and freshly ground black pepper

Polenta (page 273), for serving (optional)

Pat the pork tenderloin dry with paper towels. Rub each piece with 1 teaspoon of the oil.

In a small bowl, whisk together the Cajun seasoning, brown sugar, ½ teaspoon salt, and ¼ teaspoon pepper. Sprinkle the pork evenly on all sides with the rub.

Coat the Instant Pot® air fryer basket with canola oil spray. Place the pork pieces in the basket, making sure they don't touch. Insert the basket into the pot and attach the air fryer lid. Press the Air Fry button and set the cook time for 20 minutes at 350°F (180°C), then press Start. Rotate the pork pieces when prompted.

When the cooking time is up, insert an instant-read thermometer into the thickest part of the pork; it should register 140°F (60°C). If the pork is not fully cooked, add more cooking time in 2-minute intervals until the pork is fully cooked. Use tongs to carefully transfer the pork to a cutting board and let rest for 5–10 minutes, then cut into slices. Serve over a bowl of polenta, if desired.

IF YOU HAVE LEFTOVERS

Sliced pork tenderloin makes an excellent filling for Cuban sandwiches. Layer the pork with slices of Swiss cheese, pickles, ham, and mustard on long sandwich rolls. Cut the sandwich in half, spread the tops of each half with softened butter, and place in the air fryer basket. (Use a piece of aluminum foil underneath to prevent a cheesy mess.) Press the Air Fry button and set the cook time for 5 minutes at 375°F (190°C) (or until the cheese is melted), then press Start.

Sticky Hoisin Baby Back Ribs

These tender ribs get a quick dry rub and a delicious Asian-inspired hoisin glaze before being cooked for just 25 minutes. For a get-ahead dinner, cook the ribs in the Instant Pot® in advance and refrigerate them for up to 3 days and then reheat them on the grill or under the broiler before serving (see Tip).

SERVES 4

2 racks baby back pork ribs (about 3 lb/1.4 kg each)

1 tablespoon garlic powder

1 tablespoon firmly packed light brown sugar

2 teaspoons dry mustard

2 teaspoons ground ginger

Kosher salt

½ cup (120 g) hoisin sauce

½ cup (115 g) ketchup

1 teaspoon toasted sesame oil

½ cup (120 ml) water

4 green onions, finely chopped

2 tablespoons toasted sesame seeds

Place the ribs on a baking sheet. In a small bowl, stir together the garlic powder, brown sugar, mustard, ginger, and 2 teaspoons salt. Rub the mixture all over the ribs, particularly the meaty sides. Let stand at room temperature for 1 hour, or cover and refrigerate for up to 24 hours.

In a small bowl, stir together the hoisin sauce, ketchup, and sesame oil. Brush the ribs with a few tablespoons of the sauce, just to lightly coat them; set the remaining sauce aside. Place the ribs in the Instant Pot®, standing them upright against the sides. (You may need to cut the racks into smaller portions to fit them in the pot.) Pour the water into the pot.

Lock the lid in place and turn the valve to Sealing. Press the Pressure Cook button and set the cook time for 25 minutes at high pressure.

Meanwhile, in a small saucepan over medium heat, bring the remaining sauce to a simmer. Remove from the heat.

When the cooking time is up, turn the valve to Venting to quick-release the steam. Carefully remove the lid. Transfer the ribs to a large platter, spoon the warm sauce over them, and sprinkle with the green onions and sesame seeds. Cut into individual ribs and serve.

TIP *To grill the cooked ribs, brush them with some of the remaining sauce and grill over direct, medium-high heat until charred on the edges, 4 minutes if just out of the pot, 10 minutes if made ahead and refrigerated. Alternatively, broil the ribs on a foil-lined baking sheet about 4 inches (10 cm) from the broiler element until the edges are charred, 2 minutes if just out of the pot, or 6 inches (15 cm) away from the broiler element until heated through, about 10 minutes, if cold. Brush again with the sauce and serve.*

SEAFOOD

Studded with thick slices of chorizo and liberally seasoned with two types of paprika and loads of garlic, this Spanish favorite begs for a cold beer or glass of sangria.

Chorizo & Seafood Paella

In Spain, paella is classically prepared in a wide, shallow metal pan over an open fire and must be tended nearly constantly as it cooks. The Instant Pot® simplifies the process, cooking quickly and with little effort from the chef.

SERVES 6–8

- **4 tablespoons olive oil**
- **1 lb (450 g) cured Spanish chorizo, cut into slices 1 inch (2.5 cm) thick**
- **1 yellow onion, diced**
- **3 cloves garlic, minced**
- **Salt and freshly ground pepper**
- **2 teaspoons smoked paprika**
- **1 teaspoon sweet paprika**
- **½ teaspoon granulated garlic**
- **½ teaspoon saffron threads**
- **½ cup (120 ml) dry white wine**
- **1 can (14 oz) crushed tomatoes with juice**
- **2 cups (400 g) basmati rice**
- **4½ cups (1 L) chicken broth**
- **1 lb (450 g) littleneck or other small clams**
- **¾ lb (340 g) large shrimp, peeled and deveined with tails intact**
- **1½ cups (210 g) frozen peas**
- **Chopped fresh flat-leaf parsley and lemon wedges, for serving**

Select Sauté on the Instant Pot® and warm 2 tablespoons of the oil. Add the chorizo and cook, stirring occasionally, until lightly browned and warmed through, about 4 minutes. Transfer the chorizo to a plate.

Warm the remaining 2 tablespoons oil in the pot. Add the onion and minced garlic and cook, stirring occasionally, until the onion is tender and translucent, about 3 minutes. Season with salt and pepper, then add the smoked paprika, sweet paprika, granulated garlic, and saffron. Cook, stirring often, until the onion is well coated with the spices, about 3 minutes. Pour in the wine and, using a wooden spoon, scrape up any browned bits from the pot bottom. Add the tomatoes, rice, 4 cups of the broth, and the clams, discarding any clams that fail to close to the touch.

Lock the lid in place and turn the valve to Sealing. Press the Keep Warm/Cancel button to reset the program, then press the Manual/Pressure Cook button and set the cook time for 8 minutes at high pressure.

Turn the valve to Venting to manually release the steam. When the steam stops, carefully remove the lid, press the Keep Warm/Cancel button to reset the program, then select Sauté. Add the remaining ½ cup broth, the shrimp, and the peas and cook, stirring occasionally, until the shrimp are opaque throughout, about 5 minutes.

Divide the paella among individual bowls, discarding any clams that failed to open. Top with parsley and a squeeze of lemon juice and serve.

Creamy Tuna Noodle Casserole

Just like the creamy casserole of your childhood but lighter, faster, and tastier! The dried noodles and vegetables cook under pressure first, and then soft whipped cream cheese and solid albacore tuna are stirred into the mixture to make a delicious sauce. The "casserole" is finished with a crisp topping of pan-toasted bread crumbs and Parmesan cheese.

SERVES 4

3 tablespoons unsalted butter

2 large shallots, finely chopped

2 ribs celery, sliced

¼ lb (115 g) shiitake mushrooms, stemmed and brushed clean, caps sliced

Kosher salt and black pepper

1 clove garlic, chopped

¼ cup (60 ml) dry white wine

1½ cups (350 ml) vegetable or chicken stock (pages 270–271 or store-bought)

½ lb (225 g) dried wide egg noodles

1 bread slice, finely ground in a food processor

½ cup (60 g) grated Parmesan cheese

½ cup (80 g) whipped cream cheese

¼ cup (60 ml) whole milk, warmed

2 cans (5 oz/142 g each) solid albacore tuna, drained and flaked with a fork

1 tablespoon fresh lemon juice

Put 1½ tablespoons of the butter in the Instant Pot®, select Sauté, and adjust to More/High heat. When the butter is hot, add the shallots, celery, mushrooms, and a pinch of salt and cook, stirring frequently, until the vegetables are tender, about 4 minutes. Add the garlic and cook until fragrant, about 30 seconds. Add the wine and simmer until nearly evaporated, about 2 minutes. Press the Cancel button. Stir in the stock. Add the noodles but don't stir.

Lock the lid in place and turn the valve to Sealing. Press the Pressure Cook button and set the cook time for 5 minutes at low pressure.

Meanwhile, in a small nonstick saucepan over medium heat, melt the remaining 1½ tablespoons butter. Add the bread crumbs and cook, stirring occasionally, until golden brown, 3–4 minutes. Sprinkle ¼ cup (30 g) of the Parmesan over the crumbs and cook, stirring constantly, until the cheese is crisp and begins to brown, about 1 minute. Remove from the heat.

Turn the valve to Venting to quick-release the steam. Carefully remove the lid, add the remaining ¼ cup (30 g) Parmesan, the cream cheese, and milk and stir until the cream cheese has melted, about 5 stirs. Fold in the tuna and lemon juice. Season to taste with salt and pepper. Sprinkle with the bread crumbs and serve.

For the best flavor and texture, use solid albacore tuna instead of chunk light tuna, which tends to be mushy.

Lemon Risotto with Crab & Fennel

Craving a luxurious crab dish but don't want to spend a mint to feed the family? This easy recipe is the answer—it's elegant and super quick, and a 1-lb (450-g) container of picked crabmeat feeds four when served alongside creamy, filling risotto.

SERVES 4

2 tablespoons unsalted butter

1 yellow onion, chopped

1 small fennel bulb, trimmed, cored, and chopped

1 carrot, peeled and finely chopped

1 cup (200 g) Arborio rice

¼ cup (60 ml) dry white wine

2¾ cups (650 ml) clam juice or seafood broth, or chicken stock (page 270 or store-bought)

Kosher salt

1 lb (450 g) fresh crabmeat, picked over

2 tablespoons chopped fresh dill

Finely grated zest and juice of ½ lemon

Freshly ground black pepper

Pinch of cayenne pepper

Put the butter the Instant Pot®, select Sauté, and adjust to More/High heat. When the butter is hot, add the onion, fennel, and carrot and cook, stirring frequently, until the onion is tender, about 5 minutes. Add the rice and cook, stirring frequently, for 1 minute. Add the wine and simmer until nearly evaporated, about 2 minutes. Press the Cancel button.

Add the clam juice and ¾ teaspoon salt, stirring with a wooden spoon to scrape up any browned bits.

Lock the lid in place and turn the valve to Sealing. Press the Pressure Cook button and set the cook time for 8 minutes at high pressure.

Meanwhile, in a bowl, stir together the crabmeat and 1 tablespoon of the dill and half of the lemon zest and juice. Season to taste with salt and black pepper. Set aside at room temperature.

When the cooking time is up, turn the valve to Venting to quick-release the steam. Carefully remove the lid. The risotto will look brothy at first but will thicken as it stands. Add the cayenne and the remaining 1 tablespoon dill and lemon zest and juice. Season to taste with salt and black pepper.

Divide the risotto among 4 bowls. Mound the crabmeat evenly in the center of each bowl and serve.

TIP *Look for picked crabmeat in plastic tubs in the seafood department of grocery stores. Drain off any liquid in the container before using.*

Creamy Shrimp Pasta

Jumbo-size frozen shrimp cook perfectly in 5 minutes under low pressure, which also happens to be the perfect timing for dried linguine in a yummy garlic sauce. Don't skip the herbs, as they add a spark of vibrant flavor to this rich dish.

SERVES 4–6

3 tablespoons olive oil

¾ cup (90 g) chopped shallot

6 cloves garlic, thinly sliced

¼ cup (60 ml) dry white wine

1 lb (450 g) linguine or spaghetti, broken in half

3½ cups (825 ml) chicken stock (page 270 or store-bought)

Kosher salt and black pepper

1 lb (450 g) frozen jumbo or extra-jumbo peeled and deveined shrimp

½ cup (80 g) whipped cream cheese

2 tablespoons chopped fresh tarragon or dill

Finely grated zest and juice of ½ lemon

Put the oil in the Instant Pot®, select Sauté, and adjust to Normal/Medium heat. When the oil is hot, add the shallot and cook, stirring frequently, until tender, about 4 minutes. Add the garlic and cook until fragrant, about 30 seconds. Add the wine and simmer until nearly evaporated, about 1 minute. Press the Cancel button.

Add the pasta, fanning it out at different angles to reduce clumping. Add the stock, ½ teaspoon salt, and several grinds of pepper. Place the frozen shrimp on top but don't stir.

Lock the lid in place and turn the valve to Sealing. Press the Pressure Cook button and set the cook time for 5 minutes at low pressure.

When the cooking time is up, turn the valve to Venting to quick-release the steam. Carefully remove the lid and add the cream cheese, tarragon, and lemon zest and juice. Quickly stir with tongs, breaking up any clumps of pasta. Cover with the lid and let stand with the Instant Pot® off for 2–5 minutes to allow the ingredients to finish cooking and absorb some of the liquid. Serve right away.

TIP *For the best texture, buy extra-jumbo or jumbo shrimp, also labeled "16/20" and "21/25," respectively. (The numbers indicate how many shrimp are in a pound; the lower the numbers, the larger the shrimp.)*

Shrimp & Cheesy Grits

In this quick weeknight supper, the cheese grits cook at the same time as the zippy Cajun sauce, thanks to a tall trivet and the "pot-in-pot" method (see page 10). Simmering the shrimp briefly in the sauce right before serving keeps them from overcooking. Cajun seasoning blends vary in spiciness, so taste yours before adding it to the pot to gauge how spicy you'd like this dish to be.

SERVES 4

FOR THE CAJUN SAUCE

1 tablespoon olive oil

2 slices bacon, coarsely chopped

1 yellow onion, chopped

1 green or red bell pepper, seeded and chopped

2 ribs celery, chopped

2 teaspoons mild Cajun seasoning blend

½ cup (100 g) chopped tomatoes (fresh or canned)

¼ cup (60 ml) chicken stock (page 270 or store-bought)

FOR THE GRITS

2⅔ cups (630 ml) chicken stock (page 270) or warm water

¾ cup (120 g) grits or polenta (not quick-cooking)

½ cup (60 g) grated Cheddar cheese

1 tablespoon unsalted butter

Kosher salt and black pepper

1½ lb (680 g) large shrimp, peeled and deveined

1 lemon, quartered

To make the Cajun sauce, put the oil in the Instant Pot®, select Sauté, and adjust to More/High heat. When the oil is hot, add the bacon and cook, stirring occasionally, until crisp and browned, 4–5 minutes. Add the onion, bell pepper, celery, and Cajun seasoning and cook, stirring frequently, until the onions are tender, about 4 minutes. Press the Cancel button. Add the tomatoes and stock, stirring with a wooden spoon to scrape up any browned bits.

To make the grits, place a trivet with tall (2-inch/5-cm) feet in the pot over the Cajun mixture. Pour the warm stock into a 7-inch (18-cm) round metal pan with a 6-cup (1.4-L) capacity. Gradually whisk in the grits. Cover tightly with aluminum foil and place on the trivet.

Lock the lid in place and turn the valve to Sealing. Press the Pressure Cook button and set the cook time for 8 minutes at high pressure.

When the cooking time is up, turn the valve to Venting to quick-release the steam. Carefully remove the lid and remove the pan and trivet. Uncover the grits and whisk in the cheese and butter. Season to taste with salt and pepper. Cover and set aside. The grits will thicken as the pan stands.

Select Sauté and adjust to Normal/Medium heat. Add the shrimp to the pot and cook, stirring occasionally, until they are pink and opaque, about 2 minutes. Season the sauce to taste with salt and pepper.

Serve the shrimp and sauce over the grits, with lemon on the side.

Coconut Shrimp

Unsweetened shredded coconut adds an amazing taste and texture to this healthier version of the popular fried seafood dish. Serve by itself as an appetizer or with white rice (page 266) and veggies as a main meal. Sweet chili sauce or duck sauce pairs well with the crunchy coating on the shrimp.

SERVES 4

½ cup (2 oz/60 g) all-purpose flour

Kosher salt and freshly ground black pepper

2 large eggs

2 teaspoons water

⅔ cup (2½ oz/70 g) unsweetened shredded coconut

⅔ cup (2¼ oz/65 g) panko bread crumbs

1 lb (450 g) jumbo shrimp, peeled and deveined

Thai sweet chili sauce or duck sauce, for serving (optional)

In a bowl, whisk together the flour, 2 teaspoons salt, and ½ teaspoon pepper. In another bowl, whisk together the eggs and water. In a third bowl, stir together the coconut and bread crumbs.

Line a rimmed baking sheet with parchment paper. Pat the shrimp dry with paper towels. Working with a few shrimp at a time, toss them in the flour mixture, shaking off the excess. Dip in the egg mixture, letting the excess drip off, then dredge in the coconut mixture, pressing firmly to adhere. Place the coated shrimp on the prepared baking sheet as you go.

Coat the Instant Pot® air fryer basket with canola oil spray. Working in batches, arrange a single layer of shrimp in the basket, making sure they don't touch. Insert the basket into the pot and attach the air fryer lid. Press the Air Fry button and set the cook time for 8 minutes at 400°F (200°), then press Start. Flip the shrimp when prompted.

When the cooking time is up, use tongs to carefully transfer the shrimp to a plate. Repeat to cook the remaining batches. Serve with chili sauce or duck sauce alongside for dipping, if desired.

White Fish Tacos with Mango Salsa & Lime Crema

Wahoo is a mild, firm-textured fish that pairs beautifully with a fruity salsa and zesty lime mayo in this Baja-inspired recipe. The frozen fish turns out moist and tender when cooked at high pressure for just 4 minutes, so there's no need to plan ahead. If using fresh fish, reduce the cook time to 2 minutes.

SERVES 4

FOR THE LIME CREMA & MANGO SALSA

½ cup (120 ml) mayonnaise

Zest and juice of 1 lime (lime halves reserved)

1 large mango, pitted, peeled, and diced

1 shallot, finely chopped (trimmings reserved)

1 tablespoon chopped fresh cilantro (stems reserved)

Kosher salt

FOR THE FISH TACOS

1 lb (450 g) frozen wahoo or other firm white fish fillets (at least ¾ inch/2 cm thick)

1 tablespoon mayonnaise

1½ teaspoons lemon pepper

1 teaspoon sweet paprika

Pinch of cayenne pepper (optional)

Kosher salt

8 small (6-inch/15-cm) corn tortillas

2 cups (170 g) finely shredded red cabbage, or coleslaw mix

To prepare the lime crema, in a small bowl, stir together the mayonnaise and lime zest and juice; set aside. To prepare the mango salsa, in a medium bowl, stir together the mango, shallot, and cilantro. Season to taste with salt; set aside.

To prepare the fish tacos, pour 1 cup (240 ml) water into the Instant Pot®. Add the reserved lime halves, shallot trimmings, and cilantro stems to impart flavor to the steam. Place a steamer basket in the pot and lightly spray with nonstick cooking spray. Spread the top of the frozen fish fillets with the 1 tablespoon mayonnaise. In a small bowl, stir together the lemon pepper, paprika, cayenne (if using), and ½ teaspoon salt. Sprinkle the seasoning all over the fish and place the fillets on the steamer basket in a single layer.

Lock the lid in place and turn the valve to Sealing. Press the Pressure Cook button and set the cook time for 4 minutes at high pressure.

Meanwhile, wrap the tortillas in damp paper towels and microwave on high until hot, about 2 minutes. Wrap in a cloth napkin or aluminum foil and set aside.

When the cooking time is up, let the steam release naturally for 1 minute, then turn the valve to Venting to quick-release any residual steam. Carefully remove the lid, transfer the fish to a cutting board, and cut into strips. Divide the fish among the tortillas and top with the lime crema, mango salsa, and cabbage. Serve right away.

Baja Fish Tacos

Lots of fresh toppings—lime crema, homemade pico de gallo, shredded cabbage, and cilantro—brighten up beer-battered fish fillets in these Mexican-inspired tacos. Warm the corn tortillas over an open flame on the stove for a few seconds for a charred effect.

SERVES 4

¾ cup (3 oz/90 g) all-purpose flour

¾ cup (3 oz/90 g) cornstarch

Kosher salt and freshly ground black pepper

1 teaspoon granulated garlic

¼ teaspoon cayenne pepper

1 large egg

⅔ cup (150 ml) light beer

1 lb (450 g) firm, skinless white fish, such as cod

FOR THE LIME CREMA

1 cup (225 g) sour cream

Juice of 1 lime

Pico de Gallo (Veggie Tacos, page 220)

Corn tortillas, shredded cabbage, cilantro, and lime wedges, for serving

In a medium bowl, stir together the flour, cornstarch, 2 teaspoons salt, 1 teaspoon black pepper, granulated garlic, and cayenne. In another medium bowl, whisk together the egg and beer.

Set a wire rack on a rimmed baking sheet. Pat the fish dry with a paper towel. Cut into strips about 3 inches (7.5 cm) long and 1 inch (2.5 cm) wide. Working with a few strips at a time, coat the fish in the flour mixture, shaking off the excess. Dip in the egg mixture, letting the excess drip off. Return the fish to the flour mixture and coat well, shaking off the excess. Place the coated fish on the wire rack as you go.

Coat the Instant Pot® air fryer basket with canola oil spray. Working in batches, coat the fish strips generously with canola oil and arrange a single layer of strips in the basket, making sure they don't touch. Insert the basket into the pot and attach the air fryer lid. Press the Air Fry button and set the cook time for 15 minutes at 375°F (190°C), then press Start. Flip the fish strips when prompted, coating again with oil.

Meanwhile, make the lime crema: In a small bowl, stir together the sour cream, half the lime juice, ¼ teaspoon salt, and a few grindings of black pepper. Taste and adjust the seasoning as needed.

Make the pico de gallo. When the cooking time is up, use tongs to carefully transfer the fish to a plate and season to taste with salt and black pepper. Repeat to cook the remaining batches.

Spread some lime crema on the tortillas and top with the fish, cabbage, pico de gallo, and cilantro. Serve with lime wedges alongside.

Steamed Halibut & Veggies in Parchment

Steaming fish inside a parchment packet does double duty, infusing the fillets with flavor and making cleanup easy. You can swap the halibut for any other white, meaty fish such as striped bass, haddock, or cod.

SERVES 4

2 tablespoons olive oil

1 teaspoon freshly grated lemon zest

2 tablespoons fresh lemon juice (about 1 lemon)

1 tablespoon minced shallot

1 teaspoon minced fresh thyme leaves

Kosher salt and freshly ground black pepper

4 halibut fillets (about 6 oz/180 g each)

1 bulb fennel, halved and thinly sliced, fronds reserved for serving

1 red bell pepper, seeded and thinly sliced

2 cups (475 ml) water

FOR SERVING

Steamed white or brown rice (page 266), fennel fronds

In a small bowl, mix the olive oil, lemon zest and juice, shallot, thyme, ½ teaspoon salt, and ¼ teaspoon pepper. Place the halibut fillets on one side of a large piece of parchment paper and drizzle the sauce evenly over the fish. Top each piece with sliced fennel and bell pepper and seal the parchment around the fish (see note below).

Pour the water into the Instant Pot® and place the fish in its parchment packet on the steam rack. Using the handles, lower the packet and steam rack into the pot. Lock the lid in place and turn the valve to Sealing. Press the Steam button and set the cook time for 3 minutes.

Let the steam release naturally for 5 minutes before turning the valve to Venting to quick-release any residual steam.

Carefully remove the lid and, using the steam rack handles, lift out the packet. Open the steam-filled parchment packet carefully and use tongs to transfer the fish, fennel, and peppers to a serving platter. Sprinkle with reserved fennel fronds and black pepper. Serve right away with rice alongside.

NOTE *To seal the fish in parchment paper, fold a large piece of parchment paper in half and cut it into a heart shape. Arrange the fish and vegetables on one side of the heart. Fold the uncovered half of the parchment over the fish. Starting at the top of the heart, begin to tightly fold the edges together. When you have reached the bottom of the heart, twist the paper to seal.*

Parmesan-Crusted Halibut

Here, Parmesan cheese in the bread crumb mixture lends a sharp, nutty, savory flavor along with a little crunch—a wonderful complement to a silky fillet of fresh halibut. Spritzing a bit of olive oil on the breading mixture before coating the fish will help it to stick.

SERVES 2

¼ cup (1 oz/30 g) all-purpose flour

1 large egg

1 teaspoon water

½ cup (1¾ oz/50 g) panko bread crumbs

½ cup (60 g) freshly grated Parmesan cheese

½ teaspoon dried oregano

Kosher salt and freshly ground black pepper

2 halibut fillets (each 6–8 oz/ 170–225 g and 1–1½ inches/ 2.5–4 cm thick), skin removed

Lemon wedges, for serving

Place the flour in a medium bowl. In a large, shallow bowl, whisk together the egg and water. In another medium bowl or on a large plate, stir together the bread crumbs, cheese, oregano, ½ teaspoon salt, and ¼ teaspoon pepper.

Line a rimmed baking sheet with parchment paper. Pat the halibut fillets dry with paper towels. Season generously with salt and pepper. Working with 1 fillet at a time, coat the fish in flour, shaking off the excess. Dip in the egg mixture, letting the excess drip off, then dredge in the bread crumb mixture, turning to coat well on all sides and pressing gently to adhere. Place the coated fillets on the prepared baking sheet as you go.

Make a foil sling for the Instant Pot® air fryer basket by folding a sheet of aluminum foil into a strip about 4 inches (10 cm) wide by 20 inches (50 cm) long. Lay the strip of foil across the center of the basket, pressing it into and up the sides. Fold any excess foil over the top edges of the basket. Coat the basket and foil with canola oil spray.

Coat the fillets with olive oil spray and arrange them in a single layer on the sling, making sure they don't touch. (The ends of the fillets will hang over the foil and touch the basket.) Insert the basket into the pot and attach the air fryer lid. Press the Air Fry button and set the cook time for 8 minutes at 400°F (200°C), then press Start. Cook undisturbed.

When the cooking time is up, insert an instant-read thermometer into the thickest part of a fillet; it should register 130°–135°F (54°–57°C) for medium. If the halibut is not cooked to the desired doneness, add more cooking time in 1-minute intervals until the halibut is cooked as desired. Use a nonstick spatula to carefully transfer the halibut to a plate. Serve with lemon wedges alongside.

Crispy Crab Cakes with Tartar Sauce

Fresh cooked lump crabmeat will yield the best flavor and texture, which is well balanced by a crisp coating of panko bread crumbs. Serve these crab cakes with tartar sauce by themselves, atop a bed of mixed greens, or nestled in a brioche bun (Jam-Filled Brioche Doughnuts, page 38) for a fantastic sandwich.

SERVES 4

½ lb (225 g) cooked crabmeat, preferably lump

Kosher salt and freshly ground black pepper

2 large eggs, lightly beaten

1 tablespoon Dijon mustard

1 tablespoon Worcestershire sauce

2 cloves garlic, minced

¼ cup (15 g) chopped fresh dill

1 cup (3½ oz/100 g) crushed saltine crackers (about 16 crackers)

FOR THE TARTAR SAUCE

1 cup (240 ml) mayonnaise

2 tablespoons chopped cornichons

1 tablespoon minced fresh tarragon

1 tablespoon fresh lemon juice

1 teaspoon Dijon mustard

Kosher salt and freshly ground black pepper

1 cup (3½ oz/100 g) panko bread crumbs

Lemon wedges, for serving

Line a rimmed baking sheet with parchment paper. Place the crabmeat in a medium bowl and season generously with salt and pepper. Add the eggs, mustard, Worcestershire sauce, garlic, and dill and mix with a rubber spatula until just combined. Add the crushed crackers and mix gently to combine. Divide the mixture into 4 equal portions, then shape into patties, each about 3 inches (7.5 cm) in diameter and 1 inch (2.5 cm) thick. Place on the prepared baking sheet, cover with plastic wrap, and refrigerate for 30 minutes.

Meanwhile, make the tartar sauce: In a small bowl, stir together the mayonnaise, cornichons, tarragon, lemon juice, and mustard. Season to taste with salt and pepper. Stir in water 1 teaspoon at a time to reach the desired consistency. Cover and refrigerate until ready to use.

Place the bread crumbs on a large plate and spritz lightly with olive oil spray. (This will help the crumbs stick to the crab cakes.) Working with 1 crab cake at a time, dredge in the crumbs, coating all sides, and return to the baking sheet.

Coat the Instant Pot® air fryer basket with canola oil spray. Working with 2 at a time, coat the crab cakes with olive oil spray and arrange a single layer of crab cakes in the basket, making sure they don't touch. Insert the basket into the pot and attach the air fryer lid. Press the Air Fry button and set the cook time for 16 minutes at 350°F (180°C), then press Start. Carefully flip the crab cakes when prompted.

When the cooking time is up, use a nonstick spatula to carefully transfer the crab cakes to a plate. Repeat to cook the remaining batches. Serve with the tartar sauce and lemon wedges alongside.

Soy-Glazed Salmon with Ginger

Healthy and light, salmon fillets are a breeze to cook in an Instant Pot—and won't leave a fishy smell in your kitchen. Marinating them in a zesty mix of soy sauce, ginger, and lime both tenderizes and flavors the fish, and a sprinkling of toasted sesame seeds imparts a crunchy nuttiness to the finished dish.

SERVES 4

¼ cup (60 ml) soy sauce

Finely grated zest of 1 lime

Juice of 2 limes

2 tablespoons peeled and grated fresh ginger

2 tablespoons firmly packed brown sugar

4 salmon fillets with skin, about 6 oz (180 g) each

FOR SERVING

Toasted sesame seeds, steamed white or brown rice (page 266)

In a small bowl or measuring cup, whisk together the soy sauce, lime zest and juice, ginger, and brown sugar. Place the salmon fillets in a shallow pan or baking dish and pour the marinade over the top. Cover with plastic wrap and marinate in the refrigerator for at least 30 minutes and up to 2 hours.

Transfer the salmon to the Instant Pot®, skin side up, and pour the remaining marinade over the fish. Lock the lid in place and turn the valve to Sealing. Press the Pressure Cook button and set the cook time for 1 minute (for rare salmon) or 2 minutes (for medium salmon) at low pressure.

Let the steam release naturally for 5 minutes, then turn the valve to Venting to quick-release any residual steam. Carefully remove the lid and use tongs to transfer the salmon to a serving platter. Press the Cancel button to reset the program.

Press the Sauté button and simmer the cooking liquid until it has thickened, 3–4 minutes. To serve, spoon over the salmon and top with sesame seeds. Serve rice alongside.

BONUS STEP *To make this dish into a meal, add 1 tablespoon olive oil, 2 cups (150 g) sliced bok choy or other firm green vegetable, and a splash of water to the hot pot after the sauce is spooned over the salmon and cook in Sauté mode until tender, about 3 minutes.*

Sesame Salmon & Soba Noodles

Marinated with honey and sesame and quickly cooked under pressure, salmon adds distinctive flavor, color, and nutrition to this Asian-inspired dish. To make it gluten-free, look for buckwheat soba noodles and swap in tamari for soy sauce.

SERVES 4

FOR THE MARINADE

¼ cup (60 ml) rice vinegar

2 tablespoons tamari or coconut aminos

1 tablespoon honey

2 tablespoons toasted sesame oil

1 clove garlic, minced or grated

2-inch (5-cm) piece of ginger, peeled and grated (about 1 tablespoon)

1 lb (500 g) salmon, skin on, cut into 4 fillets

1 package (9½ oz/270 g) soba noodles

1 tablespoon avocado or canola oil

2 cups (150 g) sliced bok choy or other firm, green vegetable

FOR SERVING

Toasted sesame seeds, chopped green onions

To make the marinade, in a small bowl or measuring cup, whisk together the vinegar, tamari, honey, sesame oil, garlic, and ginger. Place the salmon fillets in a shallow pan or baking dish and pour the marinade over the top. Cover with plastic wrap and marinate in the refrigerator for at least 30 minutes and up to 2 hours, turning occasionally to coat.

Transfer the salmon to the Instant Pot®, skin-side up, and pour the remaining marinade over the fish. Lock the lid in place and turn the valve to Sealing. Press the Pressure Cook button and set the cook time for 2 minutes at low pressure.

Meanwhile, bring a pot of water to a boil and cook the noodles according to the package directions. Drain well in a colander set in the sink, rinse with cold water, and drain again. Set aside.

When the fillets have finished cooking, let the steam release naturally for 5 minutes, then turn the valve to Venting to quick-release any residual steam. Remove the lid and use tongs to transfer the salmon to a serving platter. Press the Cancel button to reset the program.

Press the Sauté button and simmer the cooking liquid until it has thickened, 3–4 minutes. Transfer the sauce to a small bowl; set aside.

Add the oil, sliced bok choy, and a splash of water to the hot pot and cook until tender, about 3 minutes.

Transfer the noodles, vegetables, and salmon to a serving platter. To serve, spoon the sauce over the salmon, and top with sesame seeds and green onions.

Dijon Salmon & Vegetable Packets

Cooking fish fillets and thinly cut vegetables together in foil packets in the Instant Pot® seals in the steam and juices without overcooking anything. Serve with steamed rice (page 266), orzo, or crusty sourdough bread to mop up the buttery sauce.

SERVES 4

4 tablespoons (½ stick/60 g) unsalted butter, at room temperature

4 teaspoons Dijon mustard

1 tablespoon mixed minced fresh herbs (dill, flat-leaf parsley, and/or tarragon)

1 clove garlic, minced and smashed with side of knife

Finely grated zest of ½ lemon

Kosher salt

4 skin-on salmon or steelhead fillets (5–6 oz/140–170 g each), pin bones removed

1 carrot, peeled and julienned

1 small red bell pepper, seeded and julienned

1 small zucchini, julienned

Freshly ground black pepper

In a small bowl, using a fork, mash together the butter, mustard, herbs, garlic, and lemon zest until blended. Season with a few pinches of salt.

Have ready 4 pieces of aluminum foil, each 10 inches (25 cm) long. Place a salmon fillet, skin-side down, in the center of each piece of foil. Mound the carrot, bell pepper, and zucchini on the top and sides of the fish, and season with salt and pepper. Spoon big blobs of the butter mixture evenly over the fish and vegetables. Fold up the sides of the foil and seal to form tight packets.

Pour 1 cup (240 ml) water into the pot and place a steam rack/trivet with handles in the pot. Place the packets on the trivet, arranging them in 2 layers.

Lock the lid in place and turn the valve to Sealing. Press the Pressure Cook button and set the cook time for 5 minutes at high pressure.

When the cooking time is up, turn the valve to Venting to quick-release the steam. Carefully remove the lid and transfer the packets to plates. Cut them open at the table (be careful, the escaping steam will be hot!). You can also slide the fish, vegetables, and buttery sauce out of the foil onto plates, if desired.

TIP *To prevent overcooking, be sure to use fillets that are about ½ inch (12 mm) thick. These are usually pieces cut from the collar end, as opposed to the thin tail end, of the fish.*

Shave brussels sprouts using a cheese shredder—an unexpected yet easy tool for cutting the small sprouts into thin shreds.

Salmon Tacos with Crispy Slaw

Salmon develops an irresistible, silky texture when cooked quickly on the steam setting. Topped with a citrusy slaw of nutrient-rich brussels sprouts and cabbage, these will likely become your new favorite tacos.

SERVES 4

¾ teaspoon ancho chile powder

¼ teaspoon ground cumin

¼ teaspoon ground coriander

Kosher salt and freshly ground black pepper

1 lb (500 g) salmon, skin on

1 cup (240 ml) water

FOR THE SLAW

½ lb (250 g) brussels sprouts, shaved

½ cup (50 g) shredded red cabbage

¼ cup (25 g) sliced red onion

¼ cup (7 g) fresh cilantro leaves, chopped

2 tablespoons fresh lime juice

1 serrano chile, minced

FOR THE CREMA

½ cup (120 ml) mayonnaise

½ cup (125 g) Greek yogurt

2 teaspoons grated lime zest

1½ teaspoons fresh lime juice

FOR SERVING

Corn tortillas, fresh cilantro leaves, lime wedges

In a small bowl, mix the chile powder, cumin, coriander, ½ teaspoon salt, and ¼ teaspoon pepper. Place the salmon in a shallow pan or on a plate and rub spice mixture over the non-skin side of the salmon.

Pour the water into the Instant Pot® and place the salmon, skin-side down, on the steam rack. Using the handles, lower the steam rack into the pot. Lock the lid in place and turn the valve to Sealing. Press the Steam button and set the cook time for 3 minutes.

Meanwhile, make the slaw and crema. To make the slaw, combine the brussels sprouts, cabbage, onion, cilantro, lime juice, chile, and ½ teaspoon salt in a medium bowl. Taste and adjust the seasoning. To make the crema, combine the mayonnaise, yogurt, lime zest and juice, and ½ teaspoon salt. Taste and adjust the seasoning. Set both aside.

When the salmon has finished cooking, let the steam release naturally for 5 minutes before turning the valve to Venting to quick-release any residual steam.

Carefully remove the lid and, using the steam rack handles, lift out the steam rack. Use tongs to transfer the salmon to a plate. When cool enough to handle, flake it into pieces with a fork.

To serve, divide the salmon evenly among 8 tortillas, top with the slaw, drizzle with crema, and sprinkle with cilantro. Serve right away with lime wedges alongside.

VEGETARIAN

Black Bean Chili–Stuffed Sweet Potatoes

These veggie chili–stuffed sweet potatoes are perfect for Meatless Monday—they're easy to make and so filling that no one will miss the meat! Be sure to purchase medium orange-fleshed sweet potatoes that are 10–12 oz (285–340 g) each. Any larger and they won't fit in the pot; any smaller and they'll overcook.

SERVES 4

1 tablespoon olive oil

1 yellow onion, chopped

1 red bell pepper, seeded and chopped

1 carrot, peeled and chopped

4 cloves garlic, chopped

2½ tablespoons mild chili powder

1 tablespoon ground cumin

1 cup (200 g) dried black beans, rinsed and picked over

Kosher salt and black pepper

4 medium orange-fleshed sweet potatoes (10–12 oz/285–340 g each)

Juice of ½ lime

1 cup (115 g) grated Cheddar cheese

½ cup (115 g) sour cream

2 green onions, chopped

Put the oil in the Instant Pot®, select Sauté, and adjust to More/High heat. When the oil is hot, add the onion, bell pepper, and carrot and cook, stirring frequently, until the onion is tender, about 5 minutes. Add the garlic, chili powder, and cumin and cook until fragrant, about 30 seconds. Add 2 cups (475 ml) water, stirring with a wooden spoon to scrape up any browned bits. Press the Cancel button. Add the black beans and 1 teaspoon salt and stir to combine.

Place a trivet with tall (2-inch/5-cm) feet in the pot over the bean mixture. Place a piece of aluminum foil on the trivet and poke 2 holes in the foil. Prick the sweet potatoes all over with a fork and place them on the foil-lined trivet.

Lock the lid in place and turn the valve to Sealing. Press the Pressure Cook button and set the cook time for 20 minutes at high pressure.

When the cooking time is up, let the steam release naturally for 10 minutes, then turn the valve to Venting to quick-release any residual steam. Carefully remove the lid, transfer the sweet potatoes to a cutting board, and cut in half lengthwise. Season with salt and pepper, cover with foil, and set aside.

Select Sauté, adjust to More/High heat, and simmer uncovered until the chili has thickened and the beans are done, if they are not completely tender, about 5 minutes. Add the lime juice and season the chili to taste with salt and pepper.

Spoon the chili over the sweet potatoes, sprinkle with the cheese, and top with dollops of sour cream and the green onions.

Veggie Fried Rice with Cashews

This time-saving one-pot recipe cooks the rice and veggies at the same time using the "pot-in-pot" method (page 10). When they're tossed together with the raw eggs, the heat from the rice cooks the eggs perfectly. Put a spin on this blank canvas—add sliced mushrooms, diced ham, or tofu to the pot.

SERVES 4

Put the oil in the Instant Pot®, select Sauté, and adjust to Normal/Medium heat. When the oil is hot, add the carrots, celery, and water chestnuts and cook, stirring frequently, until the vegetables are beginning to brown, about 4 minutes. Add the garlic and ginger and cook until fragrant, 30 seconds. Press the Cancel button.

Add the stock, the 2 tablespoons soy sauce, and vinegar to the pot, stirring with a wooden spoon to scrape up any browned bits. Place a trivet with tall (2-inch/5-cm) feet in the pot over the vegetable mixture. In a 7-inch (18-cm) round metal pan with a 6-cup (1.4-L) capacity, stir together the rice and 1½ cups (355 ml) water. Place the uncovered pan on the trivet.

Lock the lid in place and turn the valve to Sealing. Press the Pressure Cook button and set the cook time for 5 minutes at high pressure.

When the cooking time is up, turn the valve to Venting to quick-release the steam. Carefully remove the lid and remove the pan and trivet. Pour the rice into the pot with the vegetables. Add the eggs, peas, cashews, and green onions and stir well so the eggs coat the rice. Cover with the lid and let stand with the Instant Pot® off for 1 minute to gently cook the eggs.

Season the fried rice to taste with soy sauce and pepper and serve right away.

3 tablespoons toasted sesame oil

2 large carrots, peeled and diced

2 ribs celery, sliced

1 can (8 oz/227 g) sliced water chestnuts, drained

3 cloves garlic, chopped

1 tablespoon peeled and chopped fresh ginger

½ cup (120 ml) vegetable or chicken stock (pages 270–271 or store-bought)

2 tablespoons low-sodium soy sauce, plus more as needed

1 tablespoon rice vinegar

1½ cups (300 g) long-grain white rice, rinsed and drained

2 large eggs, lightly beaten

½ cup (70 g) frozen peas or edamame, thawed

½ cup (70 g) roasted cashews

3 green onions, sliced

Freshly ground black pepper

Red Beans & Rice

There's no need to pre-soak small red beans for this Cajun-inspired dish; they cook in the same amount of time as the brown rice using the pot-in-pot method (page 10). Look for firm, pre-cooked veggie sausages for this dish. The recipe also works well with fully cooked meat sausages if you'd like to use meat.

SERVES 4–6

2 tablespoons unsalted butter

14 oz (400 g) vegetarian andouille or kielbasa sausages, sliced

1 yellow onion, chopped

1 red or green bell pepper, seeded and chopped

3 ribs celery, sliced

4 cloves garlic, chopped

1 tablespoon mild Cajun seasoning blend

1½ cups (300 g) dried small red beans, rinsed and picked over

1 bay leaf

Kosher salt and black pepper

2 cups (400 g) long-grain or short-grain brown rice, rinsed and drained

Hot sauce

3 green onions, chopped

Put the butter in the Instant Pot®, select Sauté, and adjust to More/High heat. When the butter is hot, add the sausages, onion, bell pepper, and celery and cook, stirring frequently, until the onion is tender, about 5 minutes. Add the garlic and Cajun seasoning and cook until fragrant, about 45 seconds. Press the Cancel button.

Add the red beans, 3 cups (700 ml) water, the bay leaf, and ½ teaspoon salt to the pot. Place a trivet with tall (2-inch/5-cm) feet in the pot over the bean mixture. In a 7-inch (18-cm) round metal pan with a 6-cup (1.4-L) capacity, stir together the rice, 2 cups (475 ml) water, and a generous pinch of salt. Cover tightly with aluminum foil and place on the trivet.

Lock the lid in place and turn the valve to Sealing. Press the Pressure Cook button and set the cook time for 30 minutes at high pressure.

When the cooking time is up, let the steam release naturally for 10 minutes, then turn the valve to Venting to quick-release any residual steam. Carefully remove the lid and remove the pan and trivet. Check the beans to make sure they are tender. (If not, select Sauté, adjust to Normal/Medium heat, place a regular pan lid on the pot, and simmer, stirring occasionally, until the beans are done.)

Season the beans to taste with salt, pepper, and hot sauce. Serve the beans with the rice, sprinkled with the green onions, with additional hot sauce on the side.

TIP *Cajun seasoning blends vary in spiciness, so taste yours before adding it to this dish. You can always include more after you feed the kids.*

Lentil & Vegetable Dal

This fully loaded Indian comfort meal boasts a texture trifecta—firm rice, creamy dal, and soft naan. If purple, yellow, or green cauliflower is in the market, use it in place of the common white head for extra color. And don't skip the butter. It adds a rich, creamy finish.

SERVES 6

3 cloves garlic, minced

1-inch (2.5-cm) piece fresh ginger, peeled and grated

1 tablespoon ground coriander

1 teaspoon ground cumin

¼ teaspoon cayenne pepper

¼ teaspoon ground turmeric

3 tablespoons grapeseed or coconut oil

2 cups (200 g) bite-size cauliflower florets

Kosher salt

4 cups (950 ml) plus 2 tablespoons water

1 yellow onion, chopped

1 cup (about 225 g) puréed or finely chopped tomatoes

1 cup (200 g) black lentils, picked over and rinsed

2 tablespoons unsalted butter

FOR SERVING

Steamed rice (page 266), chopped fresh cilantro leaves, warmed naan, plain yogurt (optional)

In a small bowl, combine the garlic, ginger, coriander, cumin, cayenne, and turmeric and stir to mix.

Select Sauté on the Instant Pot® and heat 1 tablespoon of the oil. Add the cauliflower and ½ teaspoon salt, stir to mix, and cook for 1 minute. Add the 2 tablespoons water and cook, stirring occasionally, until the cauliflower begins to soften, about 5 minutes. Transfer the cauliflower to a plate.

Heat the remaining 2 tablespoons oil in the pot, add the onion, and cook, stirring occasionally, until softened, about 3 minutes. Add the garlic mixture, stir to mix, and cook for about 1 minute. Add the tomatoes, stir to mix, and cook for 1 minute. Press the Cancel button to reset the program.

Add the lentils, the 4 cups (950 ml) water, and 1 teaspoon salt to the pot and stir to mix. Lock the lid in place and turn the valve to Sealing. Press the Pressure Cook button and set the cook time for 15 minutes at high pressure.

Let the steam release naturally. Carefully remove the lid, return the cauliflower to the pot, and stir to mix well and warm through. Stir in the butter until melted. Taste and adjust with salt as needed.

Spoon the dal over rice in individual bowls and sprinkle with cilantro. Serve with naan and yogurt alongside, if desired.

Veggie Tacos

Once you get the hang of pressure cooking, you may find your fridge filling up with some of the easy-to-prepare staples in this recipe. Select your own favorite rice, beans, and veggies to tuck into these simple tacos, or use any leftovers and add to them with your choice of ingredients.

SERVES 4

1 cup (160 g) steamed rice (page 266)

1 cup (180 g) cooked beans (page 268)

FOR THE PICO DE GALLO

2 plum tomatoes, seeded and diced

¼ white onion, diced

1 serrano or jalapeño chile, minced

2 tablespoons finely chopped fresh cilantro

Kosher or fine sea salt

Fresh lime juice

4 corn or flour tortillas, warm

1 cup (90 g) shredded red or green cabbage

4 oz (120 g) cotija, crumbled, or Mexican blend shredded cheese

Sour cream and cilantro, for serving

Prepare the rice, beans, and veggies (if desired) as directed, if you don't have any left over from other meals.

To make the pico de gallo, in a small bowl, combine the tomatoes,onion, chile, cilantro, ½ teaspoon salt, and 1 tablespoon lime juice. Stir to mix well, taste, and adjust the salt and lime juice as needed. (Use right away or store in an airtight container in the refrigerator for up to 3 days.)

To assemble the tacos, place a layer of rice on each tortilla, dividing it evenly, followed by layers of beans. Top with cabbage and pico de gallo and sprinkle with cheese. Add a dollop of sour cream to each taco and garnish with cilantro.

Eggplant Parmesan

This simple take on a classic Italian meal makes for a satisfying main dish or as a complement alongside spaghetti squash pasta (page 231). The dehydrating tray melts the cheese on the breaded eggplant rounds in no time. If your eggplant is larger than 1 lb (450 g), you may need to add more crumbs to the breading mixture.

SERVES 4

1 large eggplant (about 1 lb/ 450 g), cut crosswise into slices ½ inch (12 mm) thick

Kosher salt and freshly ground black pepper

2 large eggs

1 teaspoon water

1 cup (3½ oz/100 g) plain dried Italian bread crumbs

3 tablespoons freshly grated Parmesan cheese, plus more for serving

½ lb (225 g) fresh or regular mozzarella cheese, cut into slices ¼ inch (6 mm) thick

1 cup (240 ml) Marinara Sauce (page 265)

Chopped fresh flat-leaf parsley, for serving

Place the eggplant slices in a single layer on a plate or rimmed baking sheet and sprinkle with ¾ teaspoon salt. Let stand for 15 minutes. Using paper towels, gently blot the eggplant to remove excess moisture.

In a bowl, whisk together the eggs and water. In another bowl, stir together the bread crumbs, Parmesan, and a few grindings of pepper.

Working with 1 slice at a time, dip the eggplant in the egg mixture, letting the excess drip off. Dredge in the bread crumb mixture.

Coat the Instant Pot® air fryer basket with canola oil spray. Working in batches, coat the eggplant slices on both sides with olive oil spray and arrange a single layer of slices in the basket, making sure they don't touch. Insert the basket into the pot and attach the air fryer lid. Press the Air Fry button and set the cook time for 7 minutes at 400°F (200°C), then press Start. Flip the eggplant when prompted.

When the cooking time is up, use tongs to carefully transfer the eggplant to a plate. Repeat to cook the remaining batches.

Insert the dehydrating tray into the air fryer basket. Working in batches, arrange a single layer of eggplant slices on the tray. Lay 1 piece of mozzarella cheese on top of each eggplant slice. Attach the air fryer lid. Press the Broil button and set the cook time for 3 minutes at 400°F (200°C), then press Start. (If using fresh mozzarella cheese, set the cook time for 4 minutes.)

When the cooking time is up, use a nonstick spatula or tongs to transfer the eggplant to a plate. Top each eggplant slice with a dollop of marinara sauce, sprinkle with Parmesan and parsley, and serve.

Crispy Tofu with Sesame-Soy-Ginger Sauce

Achieving a crisp exterior on tofu can be a challenge because of its moist texture. By drying the tofu block well before cooking and coating the cubes with canola oil spray, the results are flawless after air frying. This dish is a great match with green beans—try the recipe on page 75, omitting the Old Bay seasoning.

SERVES 4–6

14 oz (400 g) extra-firm tofu

FOR THE SESAME-SOY-GINGER SAUCE

3 tablespoons toasted sesame oil

3 tablespoons soy sauce

2 tablespoons rice vinegar

2 teaspoons peeled and minced or grated fresh ginger

1 clove garlic, minced or grated

2 teaspoons honey

¼ teaspoon red pepper flakes

¼ cup (¾ oz/20 g) thinly sliced green onions, white and pale green parts

Kosher salt

FOR SERVING

Steamed rice (page 266), optional; toasted sesame seeds

Set a wire rack on a rimmed baking sheet. Place the tofu on the rack and cover with several layers of paper towels. Top with a heavy pot to weigh down the tofu and drain the excess water. Let stand for 30 minutes.

Meanwhile, make the sesame-soy-ginger sauce: In a small bowl or glass measuring cup, whisk together the oil, soy sauce, vinegar, ginger, garlic, honey, red pepper flakes, green onions, and ¼ teaspoon salt. Set aside.

Coat the Instant Pot® air fryer basket with canola oil spray. Cut the tofu into 1-inch (2.5-cm) cubes. Working in batches, coat the tofu cubes with canola oil spray and arrange a single layer of cubes in the basket, making sure they don't touch. Insert the basket into the pot and attach the air fryer lid. Press the Air Fry button and set the cook time for 12 minutes at 400°F (200°C), then press Start. Flip the tofu when prompted.

When the cooking time is up, use tongs to carefully transfer the tofu to a plate. Repeat to cook the remaining batches.

Place the rice (if using) in a serving bowl and top with the tofu. Pour the sauce over the tofu, sprinkle with sesame seeds, and serve.

Noodles with Mixed Veggies & Tofu

Loaded with veggies and protein-rich tofu in a savory Chinese-inspired sauce, these noodles tick all the boxes. Feel free to change things up in this pantry put-together—firm-ish vegetables like sliced carrots, baby corn, bamboo shoots, or water chestnuts will all taste great.

SERVES 4

- **2 tablespoons canola oil**
- **3 cloves garlic, minced**
- **2 teaspoons peeled and minced fresh ginger**
- **2 carrots, peeled and thinly sliced**
- **1 red bell pepper, seeded and thinly sliced**
- **¼ lb (115 g) shiitake mushrooms, stemmed and brushed clean, caps sliced**
- **2 cups (475 ml) vegetable stock (page 271 or store-bought) or water**
- **3 tablespoons hoisin sauce**
- **2 tablespoons low-sodium soy sauce**
- **2 teaspoons rice vinegar**
- **1 teaspoon toasted sesame oil**
- **14 oz (400 g) baked savory or teriyaki-flavored tofu, cut into bite-size cubes**
- **½ lb (225 g) linguine, broken in half**
- **3 cups (250 g) finely shredded green cabbage**
- **1 cup (50 g) bean sprouts**
- **2 green onions, chopped**

Put the canola oil in the Instant Pot®, select Sauté, and adjust to More/High heat. When the oil is hot, add the garlic and ginger and cook until fragrant, about 20 seconds. Press the Cancel button.

Add the carrots, bell pepper, and mushrooms to the pot and stir to combine. Add the stock, hoisin sauce, soy sauce, vinegar, and sesame oil, stirring with a wooden spoon to scrape up any browned bits. Gently stir in the tofu. Fan the pasta over the top of the vegetables and tofu. Gently press down on the noodles to partially submerge them.

Lock the lid in place and turn the valve to Sealing. Press the Pressure Cook button and set the cook time for 5 minutes at high pressure (see Tip).

When the cooking time is up, turn the valve to Venting to quick-release the steam. Carefully remove the lid. Add the cabbage, bean sprouts, and green onions and toss everything together with tongs. Cover with the lid for 1 minute to wilt the vegetables and serve.

TIP *Cooking times for linguine vary by brand. To calculate how long yours will take in the Instant Pot®, divide the recommended cooking time on the package by 2 and subtract 1 minute. For instance, if the linguine will take 12 minutes to cook in boiling water, it will require 5 minutes in the Instant Pot®.*

Three-Cheese Mac 'n' Cheese

This is definitely an adult mac 'n' cheese. The aromatic blend of cheeses creates a tangy, gooey, creamy meal. For a milder flavor, use all Cheddar cheese and leave out the dry mustard. The bread crumbs come together quickly while the pasta is cooking, and lend a just-from-the-oven finish.

SERVES 6–8

1 lb (450 g) medium shells or any short dried pasta

2½ cups (600 ml) water

2 cups (475 ml) heavy cream

6 tablespoons (3 oz/90 g) unsalted butter

2 teaspoons dry mustard

Kosher salt and freshly ground black pepper

1 cup (115 g) shredded Gruyère cheese

1 cup (115 g) shredded white Cheddar cheese

1 cup (115 g) shredded Fontina cheese

HERBED BREAD CRUMBS (OPTIONAL)

2 tablespoons olive oil

1 cup (3½ oz/100 g) fresh or fine dried bread crumbs, or panko

2 tablespoons chopped fresh flat-leaf parsley

In the Instant Pot®, combine the shells, water, 1½ cups (350 ml) of the cream, 4 tablespoons (60 g) of the butter, and the mustard. Season with 1 teaspoon salt and ½ teaspoon pepper. Give the mixture a stir, then lock the lid in place and turn the valve to Sealing. Press the Pressure Cook button and set the cook time for 7 minutes at high pressure.

While the pasta cooks, make the bread crumbs, if using. In a frying pan over medium heat, heat the oil. Add the bread crumbs and parsley, season with salt and pepper, and cook, stirring constantly, until the crumbs are well toasted, about 3 minutes. Remove from the heat.

Let the steam release naturally for 10 minutes, then turn the valve to Venting to quick-release any residual steam. Carefully remove the lid, add the cheeses, the remaining ½ cup (120 ml) cream, and the remaining 2 tablespoons (30 g) butter, and stir to mix well. Taste and adjust the seasoning, if needed.

Divide among individual bowls, top with the herbed bread crumbs, if using, and freshly ground black pepper, and serve.

Shells are an iconic pasta for this classic comfort food, but little diners might like smaller shapes like elbow macaroni or ditalini.

Falafel Pita Sandwiches

If you've been reluctant to prepare falafel at home because of all the fuss involved with frying, this recipe is for you. Soak dried chickpeas overnight so they become just soft enough to grind in a food processor,

SERVES 6 (MAKES 12 FALAFEL BALLS)

2 cups (14 oz/400 g) dried chickpeas, rinsed and picked over, soaked overnight, and drained

2 shallots, halved

3 cloves garlic

¼ cup (7 g) fresh flat-leaf parsley leaves

¼ cup (7 g) fresh cilantro leaves

2 teaspoons ground cumin

2 teaspoons ground coriander

2 teaspoons smoked paprika

¼ teaspoon cayenne pepper

3 tablespoons olive oil, plus more for drizzling

Kosher salt and freshly ground black pepper

In a food processor, combine the chickpeas, shallots, garlic, parsley, and cilantro and process until finely chopped. Add the cumin, coriander, paprika, cayenne, 2 tablespoons of the oil, 1½ teaspoons salt, and a few grindings of black pepper and process until blended. (The mixture should have an even consistency but should not be completely smooth.)

Line a rimmed baking sheet with parchment paper. Pour the remaining 1 tablespoon oil into a small bowl. Use a large ice cream scoop about 2 inches (5 cm) in diameter or a tablespoon measure to scoop the chickpea mixture into equal-size balls, each about 3 tablespoons. Place on the prepared baking sheet. Coat your palms and fingertips lightly with the oil. Roll each ball between your palms until smooth and evenly rounded.

Coat the Instant Pot® air fryer basket with canola oil spray. Working in batches, arrange a single layer of chickpea balls in the basket, making sure they don't touch. Insert the basket into the pot and attach the air fryer lid. Press the Air Fry button and set the cook time for 15 minutes at 400°F (200°C), then press Start. Rotate the balls when prompted.

Meanwhile, make the lemon-yogurt sauce: In a small bowl, stir together the yogurt, lemon juice, and dill. Season to taste with salt and black pepper. Set aside.

then blend in a good amount of aromatics, herbs, and spices and a little olive oil and you have falafel batter in minutes. These balls are equally delicious tucked inside a pita sandwich or served over a fresh green salad.

When the cooking time is up, use tongs to carefully transfer the falafel to a plate. Drizzle with oil and sprinkle with a little salt. Repeat to cook the remaining batches.

Warm the pita breads, if desired (see tip), and cut them in half. For each sandwich, cut a falafel in half and place inside a pita half, then add lettuce leaves and tomato slices. Drizzle with the lemon-yogurt sauce and serve.

TIP *You can warm the pita breads on the dehydrating tray set in the air fryer basket. Place 1 or 2 breads at a time on the tray, insert the basket into the pot, and attach the air fryer lid. Press the Air Fry button and set the cook time for 2 minutes at 400°F (200°C), then press Start.*

VARIATION

Falafel Salad: *To make individual falafel salads, assemble and cook the falafel as directed above. Chop the lettuce and place in a bowl. Top each salad with 2 falafel balls, a few tomato slices, and any other vegetables you like, such as thinly sliced cucumbers, carrots, radishes, and celery. Make the lemon-yogurt sauce as directed, adding more lemon juice, if desired, for a thinner consistency. Drizzle the sauce over the salad and sprinkle with chopped dill and a few grindings of pepper.*

FOR THE LEMON-YOGURT SAUCE

½ cup (115 g) plain whole-milk yogurt

1 tablespoon fresh lemon juice

1 teaspoon chopped fresh dill

Kosher salt and freshly ground black pepper

FOR SERVING

Pita breads, lettuce leaves, tomato slices

Farrotto Two Ways

Farro contributes both nutrients and earthy flavor to this riff on classic Italian risotto. Switch up the mix-ins according to the season, layering in peas and asparagus for spring and Parmesan and spinach for autumn.

SERVES 4–6

2 tablespoons olive oil

2 shallots, minced

2 cloves garlic, minced

1½ cups (315 g) farro

½ cup (120 ml) dry white wine

3 cups (700 ml) vegetable or chicken stock (pages 270–271)

3 fresh thyme sprigs

Kosher salt and freshly ground black pepper

FOR PARMESAN & SPINACH

¼ cup (30 g) freshly grated Parmesan cheese, plus more for serving

5 oz (150 g) spinach or kale

2 tablespoons chopped fresh tarragon

FOR ASPARAGUS & PEA

½ lb (250 g) asparagus

1 cup (150 g) English peas

¼ cup (30 g) freshly grated Asiago cheese, plus more for serving

1 tablespoon chopped fresh flat-leaf parsley, plus more for serving

Fresh lemon zest, for serving

Select Sauté on the Instant Pot® and heat the oil. Add the shallots and garlic and cook, stirring occasionally, until softened, about 3 minutes. Add the farro and cook, stirring occasionally, until it smells nutty and starts to pop, about 3 minutes. Add the wine and cook, stirring occasionally with a wooden spoon to scrape up any browned bits. Cook until the wine is absorbed, then stir in the stock, thyme, and 1 teaspoon salt. Press the Cancel button to reset the program.

Lock the lid in place and turn the valve to Sealing. Press the Pressure Cook button and set the cook time for 10 minutes at high pressure. Let the steam release naturally for about 10 minutes, then turn the valve to Venting to quick-release any residual steam and carefully remove the lid. Remove and discard the thyme sprigs.

For Parmesan & Spinach Farrotto, stir the Parmesan, spinach, and 1 tablespoon of the tarragon into the farrotto until the spinach is wilted, and season with salt and pepper. Transfer to a serving bowl. Sprinkle with Parmesan and the remaining 1 tablespoon tarragon and serve right away.

For Asparagus & Pea Farrotto, press the Cancel button to reset the program. Trim the cut ends from the asparagus and cut the spears into ½-inch (12-mm) pieces. Select Sauté and stir in the peas and asparagus. Cook until the vegetables begin to soften and are warmed through, about 3 minutes. Stir in the cheese and parsley and season with salt and pepper. Transfer to a serving platter. Sprinkle with parsley and lemon zest and serve right away.

Risotto with Miso & Shiitake "Bacon"

This savory spin on risotto gets its umami from miso soup—available where Asian ingredients are sold and in the soup section of most grocery stores. The baked shiitake mushroom "bacon" topping adds the perfect counterpoint to the creamy rice. Garnish with nori flakes or vegetarian furikake, if you like.

SERVES 4

FOR THE SHIITAKE "BACON"

½ lb (225 g) shiitake mushrooms, stemmed and brushed clean, caps thinly sliced

4 teaspoons toasted sesame oil

1 tablespoon maple syrup

½ teaspoon garlic powder

¼ teaspoon smoked paprika

Freshly ground black pepper

FOR THE RISOTTO

2 tablespoons unsalted butter

1 cup (115 g) chopped sweet onion

1 cup (200 g) Arborio rice

½ cup (120 ml) dry sake or white wine

3 cups (700 ml) vegetarian miso soup broth or prepared miso soup mix

2 cups (60 g) loosely packed baby spinach leaves

1 tablespoon fresh lemon juice

Kosher salt and black pepper

To make the shiitake "bacon," preheat the oven to 375°F (190°C). Line a baking sheet with parchment paper or aluminum foil and spray with nonstick cooking spray. In a bowl, toss together the mushrooms, oil, maple syrup, garlic powder, paprika, and ⅛ teaspoon pepper. Transfer to the prepared baking sheet and spread in a single layer. Bake, stirring occasionally, until browned and crisp, 20–30 minutes. Set aside.

Meanwhile, make the risotto: Put the butter in the Instant Pot®, select Sauté, and adjust to More/High heat. When the butter is hot, add the onion and cook, stirring frequently, until tender, about 4 minutes. Add the rice and cook, stirring frequently, for 1 minute. Add the sake and simmer for 1 minute until nearly evaporated. Press the Cancel button.

Add the miso soup broth, stirring with a wooden spoon to scrape up any browned bits.

Lock the lid in place and turn the valve to Sealing. Press the Pressure Cook button and set the cook time for 8 minutes at high pressure.

When the cooking time is up, turn the valve to Venting to quick-release the steam. Carefully remove the lid. Add the spinach and lemon juice and stir until the spinach is wilted. Season the risotto to taste with salt and pepper and let stand uncovered for 2 minutes. (The rice will absorb more liquid as it stands.)

Divide the risotto among 4 bowls, sprinkle with the shiitake "bacon," and serve.

Spaghetti Squash

This hard-shelled yellow squash is harvested in the fall and is readily available throughout winter and spring. As the name indicates, its flesh falls away from the shell after cooking in strands like spaghetti. A healthful alternative to pasta, it pairs perfectly with Eggplant Parmesan (page 221).

SERVES 4–6

3 cups (700 ml) water

1 medium spaghetti squash (2–3 lb/1–1.5 kg), halved crosswise and seeded

Olive oil, for drizzling

Kosher salt and freshly ground black pepper

Pour the water into the Instant Pot® and insert the steam rack. Place the squash halves, cut side down, in a steamer basket and set it on the steam rack. Lock the lid in place and turn the valve to Sealing. Press the Pressure Cook button and set the cook time for 4–6 minutes at high pressure (about 2 minutes per pound/500 g).

Let the steam release naturally for 5 minutes, then turn the valve to Venting to quick-release any residual steam. Carefully remove the lid and transfer the squash to a cutting board. Gently run a fork along the inside of the squash to scrape the flesh free from the skin, and transfer the strands to a bowl. Drizzle the squash with oil and season with salt and pepper. Serve warm with your favorite sauce.

TIP *Alternatively, skip the olive oil and serve the spaghetti squash simply with butter and grated Parmesan cheese, seasoned with a little salt and few grinds of pepper.*

DESSERTS

Carrot Cake with Cream Cheese Frosting

A perennial birthday favorite, carrot cake turns out wonderfully dense and moist when cooked in the Instant Pot®. If you're pressed for time, skip the frosting and serve the cake as a single layer, dusting the top with confectioners' sugar.

SERVES 6

FOR THE CAKE

1¼ cups (295 g) all-purpose flour

1 teaspoon ground cinnamon

½ teaspoon ground nutmeg

¼ teaspoon ground allspice

1 teaspoon kosher salt

½ teaspoon baking soda

½ teaspoon baking powder

2 large eggs

¾ cup (170 g) granulated sugar

¼ cup (60 g) firmly packed dark brown sugar

¾ cup (180 ml) canola oil

1 teaspoon vanilla extract

1½ cups (6 oz) peeled and grated carrots

¼ cup (475 ml) dried currants

FOR THE FROSTING

1 package (8 oz) cream cheese, at room temperature

4 tablespoons (2 oz/60 g) unsalted butter, at room temperature

2 tablespoons sour cream

1 teaspoon vanilla extract

¼ teaspoon kosher salt

¾ cup (90 g) confectioners' sugar

To make the cake, lightly spray a 7-inch (18-cm) springform pan with nonstick cooking spray. In a bowl, whisk together the flour, cinnamon, nutmeg, allspice, salt, baking soda, and baking powder. In another bowl, whisk together the eggs, both sugars, oil, and vanilla until smooth. Fold half of the flour mixture into the egg mixture until well mixed, then fold in the remaining flour mixture just until no dry streaks remain. Finally, fold in the carrots and currants. Transfer to the prepared pan and smooth the top. Cover the pan with aluminum foil, crimping the edges.

Pour 2 cups (475 ml) water into the Instant Pot®. Place the springform pan on the steam rack and lower the pan into the pot. Lock the lid in place and turn the valve to Sealing. Press the Pressure Cook button and set the cook time for 65 minutes at high pressure.

Let the steam release naturally for 15 minutes, then turn the valve to Venting to quick-release any residual steam. Carefully remove the lid and transfer the springform pan to a cooling rack. Remove the foil and let the cake cool in the pan for 15 minutes, then remove the pan sides and let cool completely.

Meanwhile, make the frosting. In a bowl, using an electric mixer, beat together the cream cheese and butter on medium-high speed until smooth, about 45 seconds. Beat in the sour cream, vanilla, and salt until well mixed. On low speed, beat in the confectioners' sugar until combined, then increase the speed to medium-high and beat until smooth and fluffy, about 1 minute.

Split the cake into 2 layers. Spread a thin layer of frosting on the bottom layer, top with the second layer, and then frost the top and sides. Cut into wedges to serve.

For an embellishment at serving time, stir vanilla extract, honey, and grated lemon zest into a small bowl of Greek yogurt for adding at the table, if you like.

Apple Cranberry Yogurt Cake

Yogurt adds a wonderfully light texture to this pretty cake. Select a good baking apple to arrange on top or substitute the apples with firm-fleshed pears, such as Bosc or Anjou. If cranberries are unavailable, use blueberries instead.

SERVES 6–8

4 tablespoons (2 oz/60 g) butter, melted, plus more for greasing

1½ cups (6½ oz/185 g) all-purpose flour

2½ teaspoons baking powder

¼ teaspoon kosher salt

2 large eggs, at room temperature

1 cup (200 g) sugar

1 cup (250 g) Greek or plain whole-milk yogurt

1 teaspoon vanilla extract

1 cup (100 g) fresh or thawed frozen cranberries, roughly chopped

1 Braeburn, Jonagold, Honeycrisp, Crispin, or Pink Lady apple, cored and cut into thin slices

1½ cups (350 ml) water

Lightly grease a 7-inch (18-cm) springform pan or 6-cup (1.5-L) Bundt pan with butter.

In a small bowl, whisk together the flour, baking powder, and salt. In a large bowl, whisk the eggs and sugar until combined. Whisk in the yogurt and vanilla, then whisk in the 4 tablespoons melted butter. Fold the flour mixture into the egg mixture with a rubber spatula, then fold in the cranberries. Pour into the prepared pan and place the apples in a single layer on the top of the batter. Cover with aluminum foil.

Pour the water into the Instant Pot® and place the pan on the steam rack. Using the handles, lower the pan and steam rack into the pot. Lock the lid in place and turn the valve to Sealing. Press the Pressure Cook button and set the cook time for 40 minutes at high pressure.

Let the steam release naturally for 10 minutes, then turn the valve to Venting to quick-release any residual steam. Carefully remove the lid and, using the steam rack handles, lift out the springform pan. Let the cake cool slightly before removing it from the pan.

Cut into wedges and serve.

Wild Blueberry Crisp

A long-awaited summer fruit in Maine, wild blueberries taste absolutely amazing. And thanks to frozen wild blueberries, you can prepare this dessert year-round wherever you live. The crisp is versatile, so feel free to swap in other frozen or fresh berries; if they are very ripe and juicy, add another tablespoon of flour to the fruit mixture.

SERVES 6

Unsalted butter, for greasing

3 cups (425 g) frozen wild blueberries

3 tablespoons granulated sugar

1 tablespoon all-purpose flour

1 tablespoon fresh lemon juice

FOR THE TOPPING

⅔ cup (2½ oz/70 g) rolled oats (not quick cooking)

⅓ cup (1½ oz/40 g) all-purpose flour

⅓ cup (80 g) firmly packed light brown sugar

¼ cup (¾ oz/20 g) oat bran

1 teaspoon baking powder

½ teaspoon ground cinnamon

½ teaspoon ground ginger

¼ teaspoon kosher salt

4 tablespoons (2 oz/60 g) cold unsalted butter, cut into small pieces

Vanilla ice cream, for serving

Grease a 1½-qt (1.4-L) round ceramic baking dish with butter or coat with canola oil spray.

In a bowl, gently stir together the blueberries, granulated sugar, flour, and lemon juice. Transfer to the prepared baking dish.

To make the topping, in another bowl, stir together the oats, flour, brown sugar, oat bran, baking powder, cinnamon, ginger, and salt. Add the butter and rub into the flour mixture with your fingertips until the mixture is crumbly. Sprinkle evenly over the fruit.

Place the baking dish on the steam rack. Using the handles, lower the baking dish and the steam rack into the Instant Pot® and attach the air fryer lid. Press the Bake button and set the cook time for 30 minutes at 350°F (180°C), then press Start. Bake undisturbed.

When the cooking time is up, check to see if the crisp topping is golden and the fruit has started to bubble around the edges. If not, add more cooking time in 2-minute intervals until the crisp is cooked as desired. Using the steam rack handles, lift out the baking dish and transfer it to a wire rack until cool enough to handle. Use a large spoon to scoop heaping servings onto individual bowls. Serve warm with a scoop of vanilla ice cream alongside.

Bosc or Asian pear slices would work well in place of the apples, since they are crisp varieties and can stand up to the pressure.

Spiced Apple & Raisin Bread Pudding

The next time you have a loaf of bread lying around going stale, transform it into a luscious, custardy bread pudding layered with spiced apples and sweet raisins. Wonderful on its own, this dessert also welcomes a scoop of vanilla ice cream or a dollop of freshly whipped cream on top.

SERVES 6–8

Butter, for greasing

½ cup (100 g) sugar

1 teaspoon cinnamon

2 teaspoons ground cardamom

2 apples (such as Honeycrisp, Gala, Pink Lady, or other crisp varieties), peeled and thinly sliced

2 large eggs

1½ cups (350 ml) whole milk

1 teaspoon pure vanilla extract

Kosher salt

8 oz (225 g) day-old baquette or country bread, cut into 1-inch (2.5-cm) cubes

¼ cup (45 g) raisins

2 cups (475 ml) water

Grease a 1½-qt (1.5-L) round ceramic baking dish with butter.

In a medium bowl, combine the sugar, cinnamon, and cardamom. Add the apples and toss to coat. In another medium bowl, whisk together the eggs, milk, vanilla, and a pinch of salt.

Arrange one-third of the bread cubes in a single layer in the prepared baking dish. Layer half the apple mixture on top, followed by half the raisins. Place another third of the bread cubes in another layer on top, followed by the remaining apples and raisins, along with any extra sugar-spice mixture. Layer the remaining bread cubes on top and pour the egg mixture over all, pressing down gently so that the bread absorbs the liquid. Cover with aluminum foil and refrigerate for at least 1 hour or up to overnight.

Pour the water into the Instant Pot® and place the baking dish on the steam rack. Using the handles, lower the dish into the pot. Lock the lid in place and turn the valve to Sealing. Press the Pressure Cook button and set the cook time for 30 minutes at high pressure.

Let the steam release naturally for 15 minutes, then turn the valve to Venting to quick-release any residual steam. Carefully remove the lid and, using the steam rack handles, lift out the pan. Transfer to a cooling rack, remove the foil, and let cool slightly. Cut into wedges and serve.

Key Lime Pie

For the best flavor and the most juice, look for plump, firm Key limes with smooth, greenish-yellow skin and a floral citrusy aroma. In a pinch, bottled Key lime juice and zest from conventional limes can be substituted.

SERVES 8

FOR THE CRUST

1 cup fine graham cracker crumbs (about 9 whole crackers)

2 tablespoons granulated sugar

3 tablespoons unsalted butter, melted

FOR THE FILLING

4 large egg yolks

1 can (14 oz) sweetened condensed milk

½ cup (65 ml) fresh Key lime juice

⅓ cup (80 g) sour cream

2 tablespoons grated Key lime zest

1½ cups (350 ml) water

FOR THE TOPPING

1 cup (240 ml) heavy cream

¼ cup (30 g) confectioners' sugar

1 teaspoon vanilla extract

Grated Key lime zest, for sprinkling

To make the crust, lightly spray a 7-inch (18-cm) springform pan with nonstick cooking spray. In a bowl, stir together the graham cracker crumbs, sugar, and butter until a crumbly, evenly moistened mixture forms. Press the mixture evenly onto the bottom of the prepared pan, packing it tightly. Place the pan in the freezer while you make the filling, at least 15 minutes.

To make the filling, in a bowl, whisk together the egg yolks and condensed milk, mixing well. Whisk in the lime juice, sour cream, and lime zest until incorporated. Pour into the prepared pan. Cover the pan with a paper towel and then with aluminum foil, crimping the edges.

Pour the water into the Instant Pot®. Place the springform pan on the steam rack. Using the rack handles, lower the pan into the pot. Lock the lid in place and turn the valve to Sealing. Press the Pressure Cook button and set the cook time for 20 minutes at high pressure.

Let the steam release naturally for 10 minutes, then turn the valve to Venting to quick-release any residual steam. Remove the lid and transfer the springform pan to a cooling rack. Remove the foil and paper towel, let the pie cool in the pan for about 5 minutes, then remove the pan sides and let cool to room temperature. Wrap with plastic wrap and refrigerate for at least 1 hour or up to overnight before serving.

Just before serving, in a bowl, using a handheld mixer, beat together the cream, confectioners' sugar, and vanilla on medium speed until soft peaks form. Spread the whipped cream on top of the pie, then garnish with the lime zest. Cut into wedges and serve chilled.

Mini Ricotta Cheesecakes with Fresh Berries

A blend of ricotta cheese and Greek yogurt offers a lighter option than cream cheese in these single-serving cheesecakes. Garnish them with fresh fruit—berries, pitted and sliced stone fruit, or any in-season produce pair wonderfully—or make a quick sauce of sweetened fresh berries warmed over medium heat.

SERVES 6

FOR THE CRUST

4 tablespoons (2 oz/60 g) unsalted butter, plus more for greasing

1 cup (100 g) ground almonds

¼ cup (50 g) sugar

2 teaspoons lemon zest

FOR THE FILLING

1 lb (500 g) whole-milk ricotta cheese

⅓ cup (75 g) Greek yogurt

⅓ cup (70 g) sugar

3 teaspoons vanilla extract

2 eggs, at room temperature

2 cups (475 ml) water

FOR SERVING

Fresh raspberries, blueberries, or blackberries, or a mix

To make the crust, lightly grease the sides of six 3-inch (7.5-cm) cake pans with removable bottoms or a 7-inch (18-cm) springform pan with butter. In a medium bowl, mix the ground almonds, sugar, lemon zest, and the 4 tablespoons butter until combined. Divide evenly among the prepared pan(s), press the crust into the pan(s), and set aside.

To make the filing, in a food processor, mix the ricotta, yogurt, the ⅓ cup (70 g) sugar, and vanilla until blended. Add the eggs, one at a time, and beat just until incorporated. (Do not overmix.) Pour over the crust in the pan(s) and cover each with aluminum foil.

Pour the water into the Instant Pot® and place 3 of the small pans or the single large pan on the steam rack. Using the handles, lower the pan(s) and steam rack into the pot. Lock the lid in place and turn the valve to Sealing. Press the Pressure Cook button and set the cook time for 20 minutes at high pressure (for 3-inch/7.5-cm pans) or 35 minutes (for a 7-inch/18-cm pan).

Let the steam release naturally. Carefully remove the lid and, using the steam rack handles, lift out the pans. Transfer to a cooling rack, remove the foil, and let cool completely. Repeat with the remaining 3 pans, if using small pans. Cover each with plastic wrap and refrigerate for at least 2 hours or up to overnight.

To serve, remove the pan bottoms (or sides of the springform) and carefully remove the cheesecakes from the pans. Top with fresh berries and serve.

Giant Chocolate Chip Cookie

This confection combines the best of both worlds: a crispy skillet chocolate chip cookie and a tray of thick, gooey blondies. While the outside cooks up crunchy and golden, the inside stays melt-in-your-mouth soft. Bake it in a 7-inch (18-cm) round cake pan and cut into wedges to serve.

SERVES 6

- **1 cup (4 oz/115 g) all-purpose flour, plus more for dusting**
- **1 teaspoon baking powder**
- **½ teaspoon kosher salt**
- **6 tablespoons (3 oz/90 g) unsalted butter, at room temperature, plus more for greasing (optional)**
- **⅓ cup (70 g) granulated sugar**
- **⅓ cup (80 g) firmly packed light brown sugar**
- **2 large eggs, at room temperature**
- **1 teaspoon pure vanilla extract**
- **1 cup (6 oz/170 g) semisweet chocolate chips**
- **Flaky sea salt (optional)**

Grease a 7-inch (18-cm) round cake pan with butter and dust with flour. Alternatively, coat it with canola oil spray and dust with flour.

In a bowl, whisk together the flour, baking powder, and salt. Set aside.

In the bowl of a stand mixer fitted with the paddle attachment, beat together the butter and both sugars on medium-high speed until light and fluffy, 3–5 minutes. Add the eggs one at a time, beating well on medium speed after each addition. Add the vanilla and beat well until combined, about 1 minute. Add the flour mixture and beat on low speed until just combined, about 1 minute. Fold in the chocolate chips with a rubber spatula or wooden spoon. Pour the batter into the prepared pan. Sprinkle with flaky sea salt (if using).

Place the cake pan on the steam rack. Using the handles, lower the pan and the steam rack into the Instant Pot® and attach the air fryer lid. Press the Bake button and set the cook time for 20 minutes at 325°F (165°C), then press Start. Bake undisturbed.

When the cooking time is up, use a toothpick to check if the cookie is cooked all the way through; it should come out clean or with a few loose crumbs attached. If not, add more cooking time in 2-minute intervals until the cookie is light golden brown and cooked through. Using the steam rack handles, lift out the pan and transfer it to a wire rack until cool enough to handle. Remove the cookie from the pan by sliding a butter knife around the edges to loosen it. Place a plate on top of the pan, invert it, and shake gently to loosen the cookie onto the plate. Using a spatula, flip the cookie right-side-up onto the plate. Cut into wedges and serve.

Omit the flaky salt and scatter a small handful of broken pretzels on top for both crunch and some extra malty-salty flavor.

Salted Caramel Cheesecake with Pretzel Crumb Crust

Use your favorite salted caramel sauce—homemade or store-bought—for this easy cheesecake that pairs a salty-malty pretzel crumb crust with a sweet, creamy filling. If the sauce has hardened, warm just until fluid in the microwave.

SERVES 8

FOR THE CRUST

1 cup fine pretzel crumbs (about 4 oz whole pretzels)

2 tablespoons firmly packed light brown sugar

4 tablespoons (2 oz/60 g) unsalted butter, melted

FOR THE FILLING

2 packages (8 oz each) cream cheese, at room temperature

½ cup (100 g) granulated sugar

¼ cup (60 g) sour cream

2 large eggs, at room temperature

2 teaspoons vanilla extract

¼ cup salted caramel sauce

2 cups (475 ml) water

Salted caramel sauce, for drizzling

Flaky sea salt, for sprinkling

To make the crust, lightly spray a 7-inch (18-cm) springform pan with nonstick cooking spray. In a small bowl, stir together the pretzel crumbs, brown sugar, and butter until a crumbly, evenly moistened mixture forms. Press the mixture evenly onto the bottom of the prepared pan, packing it tightly. Place the pan in the freezer while you make the filling, at least 15 minutes.

To make the filling, in a stand mixer fitted with the paddle attachment, beat the cream cheese on medium speed until smooth. Add the granulated sugar and beat until combined, stopping to scrape down the sides of the bowl. Add the sour cream, eggs, vanilla, and caramel sauce and continue to beat on medium speed until smooth and creamy, about 1 minute. Pour into the prepared pan and smooth the top. Cover the pan with a paper towel and then with aluminum foil, crimping the edges.

Pour the water into the Instant Pot®. Place the springform pan on the steam rack. Using the rack handles, lower the pan into the pot. Lock the lid in place and turn the valve to Sealing. Press the Pressure Cook button and set the cook time for 36 minutes at high pressure.

Let the steam release naturally for 15 minutes, then turn the valve to Venting to quick-release any residual steam. Remove the lid and transfer the springform pan to a cooling rack. Remove the foil and paper towel and let cool for 30 minutes. Cover with plastic wrap and refrigerate for at least 3 hours.

To serve, remove the pan sides and cut into wedges. Serve chilled, topped with a drizzle of sauce and a sprinkle of salt.

Cappuccino Crème Brûlée

The combination of espresso and heavy cream creates a luscious cappuccino flavor for this classic French dessert. Steeping the cream with a vanilla bean and its seeds infuses the custard with extra vanilla intensity.

SERVES 6

2 cups (475 ml) heavy cream

1 vanilla bean, split and scraped, or 2 teaspoons pure vanilla extract

1 espresso (or 2 tablespoons boiling water mixed with 1 tablespoon instant espresso powder)

5 large egg yolks

⅓ cup (70 g) granulated sugar

Kosher salt

2 cups (475 ml) water

4 tablespoons turbinado sugar

In a saucepan over medium heat, combine the cream, the vanilla bean and its seeds and bring to a simmer. Turn off the heat, cover, and let steep for 15 minutes. Remove the vanilla bean. Add the espresso (and vanilla extract if using it instead of the vanilla bean) and stir to combine.

Meanwhile, in a large bowl, whisk together the egg yolks, granulated sugar, and a pinch of salt. Quickly whisk about ¼ cup (60 ml) of the warm cream mixture into the egg yolk mixture, then whisk in the remaining cream mixture. Pour the mixture through a fine-mesh sieve placed over a large measuring cup or pitcher. Divide evenly among six 4-oz (120-ml) ramekins. Cover each ramekin with aluminum foil.

Pour the water into the Instant Pot® and insert the steam rack. Place 3 ramekins on the steam rack in a single layer. Lock the lid in place and turn the valve to Sealing. Press the Pressure Cook button and set the cook time for 8 minutes at high pressure.

Let the steam release naturally for 5 minutes, then turn the valve to Venting to quick-release any residual steam. Carefully remove the lid and remove the ramekins from the pot. Repeat to cook the remaining 3 ramekins. (To cook all 6 custards at once, place a plate on top of the first 3 ramekins and place the remaining 3 ramekins on top of the plate.)

When all are cooked, let cool to room temperature, cover with plastic wrap, and refrigerate until set, for at least 2 hours or up to 3 days.

Remove the ramekins from the refrigerator about 30 minutes before you are ready to serve them. Preheat the broiler. Place the ramekins on a rimmed baking sheet and sprinkle each with 2 teaspoons turbinado sugar. Broil until the sugar has darkened, 3–5 minutes. Serve right away.

Chocolate-Hazelnut Pots de Crème

You can serve these luscious French-inspired custards just as they are, but a dollop of whipped cream or crème fraîche and a few berries or a dusting of grated chocolate dresses them up nicely for company.

SERVES 6

2 cups (480 ml) whole milk

⅓ cup (70 g) sugar

1 teaspoon kosher salt

5 large egg yolks

⅔ cup (4 oz/110 g) semisweet chocolate chips

1 cup Nutella or hazelnut butter

1½ cups (350 ml) water

In a saucepan over low heat, combine the milk, sugar, and salt and bring to a simmer, stirring to dissolve the sugar. Meanwhile, in a heatproof bowl, whisk the egg yolks until blended.

When the milk mixture is at a simmer, remove from the heat and whisk in the chocolate chips and Nutella until melted and smooth. Slowly pour about ¼ cup of the hot milk mixture into the egg yolks while whisking constantly. Then slowly pour the egg yolk–milk mixture back into the saucepan, again whisking constantly.

Pour the custard through a fine-mesh sieve set over a large pitcher. Divide the custard evenly among six 4-oz (120-ml) ramekins. Cover each ramekin with aluminum foil, crimping the edges.

Pour the water into the Instant Pot® and put the steam rack into the pot with the handles up. Place 3 ramekins on the rack, making sure they are level. Lock the lid in place and turn the valve to Sealing. Press the Pressure Cook button and set the cook time for 6 minutes at high pressure.

Let the steam release naturally for 15 minutes, then turn the valve to Venting to quick-release any residual steam. Carefully remove the lid and transfer the ramekins to a cooling rack. Let cool for about 5 minutes before removing the foil. Repeat to cook the remaining 3 ramekins.

Let the ramekins cool to room temperature, cover with plastic wrap, and refrigerate for at least 4 hours or up to overnight before serving. Serve chilled.

Sticky Toffee Pudding

Cooks in Britain and Canada argue over which country originated this rich, gooey, crowd-pleasing dessert. Forgot to soak the dates overnight? No problem. Bring them to a boil in water to cover, let stand for 15 minutes, then drain.

SERVES 8–10

¾ cup (3 oz/80 g) all-purpose flour

1¼ teaspoons baking powder

½ teaspoon baking soda

1 teaspoon kosher salt

½ teaspoon ground cinnamon

¼ teaspoon ground cloves

⅛ teaspoon ground nutmeg

1½ cups pitted dates (6 oz), soaked overnight in water to cover and drained

4 tablespoons (2 oz/60 g) unsalted butter, at room temperature

¾ cup (155 g) firmly packed dark brown sugar

1 large egg

1 teaspoon vanilla extract

1½ cups (350 ml) water

FOR THE CARAMEL SAUCE

6 tablespoons (3 oz/90 g) unsalted butter

¾ cup (155 g) firmly packed dark brown sugar

½ cup (120 ml) heavy cream

1 tablespoon vanilla extract

½ teaspoon kosher salt

Spray a 7-inch (18-cm) springform pan with nonstick cooking spray. In a bowl, whisk together the flour, baking powder, baking soda, salt, cinnamon, cloves, and nutmeg. In a food processor, process the dates to a smooth paste, about 2 minutes.

In a stand mixer fitted with the paddle attachment, beat the butter on medium speed until smooth and creamy, then add the sugar and beat until light and fluffy, about 2 minutes. Add the egg and vanilla and beat until thoroughly mixed, then beat in the puréed dates. On low speed, add the flour mixture and beat just until combined. Pour into the prepared pan and smooth the top. Cover with aluminum foil, crimping the edges.

Pour the water into the Instant Pot®. Place the springform pan on the steam rack. Using the rack handles, lower the pan into the pot. Lock the lid in place and turn the valve to Sealing. Press the Pressure Cook button and set the cook time for 50 minutes at high pressure.

Let the steam release naturally for 10 minutes, then turn the valve to Venting to quick-release any residual steam. Carefully remove the lid, transfer the springform pan to a cooling rack, and let cool for 5 minutes.

Meanwhile, make the caramel sauce. In a small saucepan over medium heat, melt the butter. Whisk in the sugar, cream, vanilla, and salt and bring to a simmer. Cook, whisking constantly, until slightly thickened and the color darkens, about 5 minutes. When the sauce is ready, uncover the cake and, using a fork, pierce it about eight times to create tiny holes all over the top. Pour the caramel sauce evenly over the cake and let stand for 10 minutes. Remove the pan sides, cut into wedges, and serve warm.

Chocolate Lava Cake with Raspberry Sauce

If you prefer a less sweet, more intense chocolate flavor for these irresistible cakes, look for chocolate with 60 to 70 percent cacao. For a tangier topping, swap out the whipped cream for whipped crème fraîche.

SERVES 4

FOR THE CAKE

½ cup (4 oz/120 g) unsalted butter, plus more for ramekins

1 cup (200 g) sugar, plus 1 tablespoon for the ramekins

6 oz (45 g) semisweet chocolate, roughly chopped

2 large whole eggs plus 2 large egg yolks

1 teaspoon instant espresso powder

1½ teaspoons vanilla extract

6 tablespoons all-purpose flour

¼ teaspoon salt

1 cup (240 ml) water

FOR THE SAUCE

1 package (10 oz) frozen raspberries, or 2 pints fresh raspberries

½ cup granulated sugar

1 tablespoon fresh lemon juice

Whipped cream, for serving

To make the cake, lightly butter four 4-oz (120-ml) ramekins, then dust each with about ¾ teaspoon of the sugar. Fill a saucepan about one-fourth full with water and bring to a steady simmer. Combine the butter and chocolate in a heatproof bowl, place over (not touching) the simmering water, and heat, stirring occasionally, until the butter and chocolate melt and are smooth. Remove from the heat, whisk in the sugar, and then whisk in the whole eggs, egg yolks, espresso powder, and vanilla until blended. Sift the flour and salt into the chocolate mixture. Using a rubber spatula, fold in the flour just until no streaks remain. Divide the batter evenly among the prepared ramekins.

Pour the water into the Instant Pot® and insert the steam rack. Place the ramekins on the rack. Lock the lid in place and turn the valve to Sealing. Press the Manual/Pressure Cook button. Set the cook time for 9 minutes at high pressure.

Meanwhile, make the raspberry sauce: In a saucepan over medium-high heat, combine the raspberries and sugar and cook, stirring, until the raspberries begin to break down, about 6 minutes. Add the lemon juice, reduce the heat to low, and simmer until saucelike, about 5 minutes. Strain the mixture through a fine-mesh sieve into a bowl.

When the cakes are ready, turn the valve to Venting to manually release the steam. Carefully remove the lid and let cool slightly, then remove the cakes from the pot. Serve the cakes warm, topped with the whipped cream and the sauce.

Dark Chocolate Fudge Brownies

Brownies are a cinch to make in the air fryer. The batter comes together quickly in one saucepan, then is poured into a 7-inch (18-cm) cake pan (or any round, heatproof baking dish that fits in the pot) and bakes for less than 30 minutes.

SERVES 6

3 oz (90 g) unsweetened chocolate, chopped

6 tablespoons (3 oz/90 g) unsalted butter, plus more for greasing (optional)

1 cup (200 g) sugar

½ teaspoon pure vanilla extract

¼ teaspoon kosher salt

2 large eggs

½ cup (2 oz/60 g) all-purpose flour, plus more for dusting

Ice cream, for serving (optional)

Grease a 7-inch (18-cm) round cake pan with butter and dust with flour. Alternatively, coat it with canola oil spray and dust with flour, or use baking spray.

In a large saucepan over low heat, combine the chocolate and butter and heat, stirring occasionally, until melted and smooth, about 5 minutes. Remove from the heat and let cool slightly, then whisk in the sugar, vanilla, and salt. Whisk in the eggs one at a time, mixing well after each addition, then continue to whisk until the chocolate mixture is velvety and smooth, about 2 minutes. Add the flour and whisk until just blended. Pour the batter into the prepared pan.

Place the cake pan on the steam rack. Using the handles, lower the pan and the steam rack into the Instant Pot® and attach the air fryer lid. Press the Bake button and set the cook time for 28 minutes at 325°F (165°C), then press Start. Bake undisturbed.

When the cooking time is up, use a toothpick to check if the brownies are cooked all the way through; it should come out clean or with a few loose crumbs attached. If not, add more cooking time in 2-minute intervals until the brownies are springy to the touch and cooked through. Using the steam rack handles, lift out the pan and transfer it to a wire rack until cool enough to handle. Cut into wedges and serve with ice cream alongside, if desired.

Mini Berry Hand Pies

Fresh blueberries are the ideal filling for these tiny treats since they're firm enough to hold up to intense heat but tender enough to cook quickly. Homemade pastry using your favorite recipe is a wonderful upgrade here, but store-bought refrigerated pie dough makes this a go-to dessert any night of the week.

MAKES 12 HAND PIES

All-purpose flour, for dusting

2 store-bought refrigerated pie dough rounds (each about 7 oz/200 g and 11 inches/28 cm in diameter)

½ cups (210 g) fresh or thawed frozen blueberries

3 tablespoons sugar, plus more for sprinkling

2 tablespoons cornstarch

1 tablespoon fresh lemon juice

½ teaspoon ground cinnamon

Pinch of kosher salt

1 large egg beaten with 1 tablespoon cold water

Line a rimmed baking sheet with parchment paper. Dust a work surface with flour. Place 1 pie dough round on the work surface and use a 4½-inch (11.5-cm) round cutter to cut 4 circles out of the dough. (Alternatively, use a small, sharp knife to trace around the top of a glass and cut circles out of the dough.) Transfer the circles to the prepared baking sheet. Gather up the scraps and roll out the dough twice more, to cut out 2 more circles. Transfer to the baking sheet. Repeat to cut out circles from the remaining dough round.

In a medium bowl, stir together the blueberries, sugar, cornstarch, lemon juice, cinnamon, and salt.

Place 1 tablespoon of the berry mixture on the top half of each circle, leaving a ½-inch (12-mm) border at the top. Brush the top edge of the dough with some of the egg mixture. Gently fold the bottom half of the dough over the berries, tucking them inside. Press the top edge gently with your fingers to seal the dough into a half-moon shape. Use the tines of a fork to crimp (or seal) the edge closed. Repeat to fill the remaining circles. Refrigerate until the dough is cold and firm, 15–20 minutes.

Coat the Instant Pot® air fryer basket with canola oil spray. Working in batches, brush the hand pies on both sides with the egg mixture and sprinkle with sugar. Arrange a single layer of hand pies in the basket, making sure they don't touch. Insert the basket into the pot and attach the air fryer lid. Press the Air Fry button and set the cook time for 15 minutes at 350°F (180°C), then press Start. Bake undisturbed.

When the cooking time is up, use tongs to transfer the hand pies to a plate. Repeat to bake the remaining batches.

Coconut-Cinnamon Rice Pudding with Toasted Pistachios

Here, a classic, comforting dessert gets an update with fresh flavors and a hands-off cooking method. It's an ideal dish to make ahead and store in the fridge in pretty jars or bowls to have ready for when guests arrive—or for when the urge for a late night snack comes on.

SERVES 6–8

1½ cups (300 g) Arborio rice

1 cup (200 g) sugar

3 teaspoons ground cinnamon, plus more for garnish

Kosher salt

5 cups (1.2 L) whole milk

2 large eggs

¾ cup (180 ml) half-and-half

1½ teaspoons pure vanilla extract

2 teaspoons coconut extract

½ cup (45 g) unsweetened shredded coconut, plus more for garnish

1 cup (115 g) toasted pistachios, chopped

Select Sauté on the Instant Pot® and add the rice, sugar, 3 teaspoons cinnamon, 1 teaspoon salt, and milk. Bring to a boil, stirring constantly to dissolve the sugar. Press Cancel to reset the program.

Lock the lid in place and turn the valve to Sealing. Press the Pressure Cook button and set the cook time for 18 minutes at low pressure.

Meanwhile, in a small bowl, whisk together the eggs, half-and-half, and vanilla and coconut extracts. Set aside.

Let the steam release naturally for 10 minutes, then turn the valve to Venting to quick-release any residual steam. Press Cancel to reset the program. Carefully remove the lid, add the egg mixture, and stir to combine. Select the Sauté button and cook, stirring occasionally, until the mixture just begins to boil. Press Cancel to reset the program. Stir in the ½ cup (45 g) shredded coconut.

Serve the pudding warm in individual bowls, sprinkled with cinnamon, additional shredded coconut, and pistachios. Or, divide the pudding among individual bowls or jars and let cool completely, then cover and refrigerate for up to 3 days. Just before serving, sprinkle with the toppings.

Experiment with other crunchy toppings, such as toasted sliced almonds, dark chocolate shavings, and candied pecans.

Egg roll wrappers made with real eggs work best; the vegan alternatives don't cook as well in the air fryer.

Fried Banana Egg Rolls

These dessert egg rolls are an amazing combo of sweet and crunchy. Look for egg roll wrappers in the refrigerated section of Asian markets or large grocery stores. Be sure to secure the banana tightly when wrapping so the filling doesn't ooze out during cooking.

SERVES 8

¼ cup (60 g) firmly packed light brown sugar

2 tablespoons toasted sesame seeds

2 bananas (just underripe)

8 egg roll wrappers

1 large egg, beaten

2 tablespoons toasted sesame oil

Confectioners' sugar, for dusting

In a small bowl, stir together the brown sugar and sesame seeds. Cut each banana in half lengthwise, then cut each half in half crosswise.

Working with 1 wrapper at a time, position a wrapper in a diamond shape on a work surface. (Cover the other wrappers with a damp cloth so they won't dry out). Place 1 banana piece, flat side down, horizontally on the lower third of the wrapper. Lightly brush the edges of the wrapper with some of the beaten egg. Sprinkle 2 teaspoons of the brown sugar mixture on top of the banana. Fold the bottom corner over the banana, encasing it. Fold in the left and right corners toward the center and roll the wrapper away from you into a tight cylinder. Brush the seam with the beaten egg and press the edges firmly to seal. Transfer to a plate. Repeat with the remaining wrappers and banana pieces.

Working in batches, brush the egg rolls generously with the sesame oil and arrange a single layer of rolls in the Instant Pot® air fryer basket, making sure they don't touch. Insert the basket into the pot and attach the air fryer lid. Press the Air Fry button and set the cook time for 9 minutes at 390°F (199°C), then press Start. Cook undisturbed.

When the cooking time is up, the egg rolls should be light golden brown and slightly darker golden brown on the ends. If a darker color is desired, cook for 2 minutes longer. Use tongs to carefully transfer the egg rolls to a plate. Repeat to cook the remaining batches. Dust the egg rolls with confectioners' sugar and serve.

BASICS

MAKES ABOUT 4 CUPS

STEEL-CUT OATS

Combine the oats, milk, and water in the Instant Pot® and stir to mix well. Lock the lid in place and turn the valve to Sealing. Press the Manual/Pressure button and set the cook time for 10 minutes at high pressure. Let the steam release naturally for about 12 minutes, then turn the valve to Venting to release any residual steam. Carefully remove the lid and serve.

1 cup steel-cut oats

1 cup (125 ml) milk, any kind (dairy, nut, coconut)

2 cups (475 ml) water

MAKES 12 BISCUITS

BUTTERMILK BISCUITS

In a large bowl, whisk together the flour, sugar, baking powder, baking soda, and salt until blended. Add the buttermilk and butter and combine gently with a rubber spatula or fork just until the ingredients are blended. Using an ice cream scoop, drop 12 equal-size rounds of dough onto a baking sheet lined with parchment paper. Bake in a 400°F (200°C) degree oven until the biscuits are puffed up and lightly golden brown, 15–18 minutes. Transfer to a wire rack to cool slightly before serving.

2 cups (9 oz/240 g) all-purpose flour

1 teaspoon sugar

2 teaspoons baking powder

½ teaspoon baking soda

½ teaspoon kosher salt

1 cup (240 ml) buttermilk

½ cup (4 oz/120 g) unsalted butter, melted and cooled

SERVES 6

ROASTED PEACHES

Preheat the oven to 350°F (180°C). Butter a 9-inch (23-cm) square baking dish. Arrange the peaches, cut side up, in the prepared dish. In a small bowl, stir together oats, butter, brown sugar, and cardamom, mixing well. Sprinkle the oat mixture evenly over the peaches. Roast in the oven until the peaches are juicy and tender and the topping is browned, 30–35 minutes.

6 peaches, halved and pitted

6 tablespoons old-fashioned rolled oats

3 tablespoons unsalted butter, melted

2 tablespoons firmly packed brown sugar

¼ teaspoon ground cardamom

Hard & Soft-Boiled Eggs

Although cooking eggs in a pressure cooker takes about the same amount of time as it does to cook them on the stove, with this method they will be much easier to peel—and you don't have to watch a pot of boiling water. Adjust the cooking time for how soft or hard you'd like the yolk: 5 to 6 minutes will yield a bright, slightly runny yolk, while 7 to 8 minutes will produce a firm center.

SERVES 1–12

2 cups (475 ml) water

Up to 12 large eggs

Pour the water into the Instant Pot® and insert the steam rack. Carefully arrange the eggs on the rack, stacking them on top of one another if necessary. Lock the lid in place and turn the valve to Sealing. Press the Pressure Cook button and set the cook time for 5–6 minutes at low pressure for soft-boiled eggs and 7–8 minutes at low pressure for hard boiled.

While the eggs are cooking, prepare an ice bath. When the eggs are ready, let the steam release naturally for 5 minutes, then turn the valve to Venting to quick-release any residual steam. Carefully remove the lid and transfer the eggs to the ice bath. When the eggs are cool enough to handle, lift them from the water. Crack the egg shells and peel the eggs. Use as desired.

SERVES 4

PITA CHIPS

4 pita breads, split in half horizontally along the seam

¼ cup (60 ml) olive oil

Kosher salt

Brush the pita halves on both sides with the oil and sprinkle lightly with salt. Cut each half into 8 wedges.

Working in batches, arrange a single layer of pita wedges in the Instant Pot® air fryer basket, making sure they don't touch. Insert the basket into the pot and attach the air fryer lid. Press the Air Fry button and set the cook time for 10 minutes at 350°F (180°C), then press Start. Turn the chips when prompted.

When the cooking time is up, the wedges should be crisp and golden. If not, add more cooking time in 2-minute intervals until the wedges are cooked to the desired crispness. Use tongs to carefully transfer the pita chips to a plate. Repeat to cook the remaining batches.

MAKES ABOUT 1 CUP (40 G)

TOASTED BREAD CRUMBS

1 tablespoon olive oil

1 cup (1½ oz/40 g) fresh bread crumbs (from stale bread)

Kosher salt and freshly ground black pepper

In a small frying pan over medium heat, warm the olive oil. Add the bread crumbs, season with salt and pepper, and toast, tossing occasionally with a wooden spoon, until golden brown, 3–4 minutes. Pour into a bowl and let cool, then use immediately or store in an airtight container at room temperature for up to 2 weeks.

MAKES ABOUT 2 TABLESPOONS

CAJUN SPICE RUB

In a small frying pan over medium heat, toast the fennel seeds, shaking the pan often, until fragrant, 1–2 minutes. Transfer to a spice mill and grind until coarsely ground or crush with a mortar and pestle. In a small bowl, combine the ground fennel, sea salt, black pepper, cayenne, paprika, and dried thyme and stir to mix well. Use right away, or store in an airtight container at room temperature for up to 3 months.

1 teaspoon fennel seeds

1 teaspoon sea salt

1 teaspoon freshly ground black pepper

½ teaspoon cayenne pepper

1 teaspoon paprika

1 teaspoon dried thyme

MAKES 4 CUPS (950 ML)

MARINARA SAUCE

Combine the stock, tomatoes, tomato paste, oil, mustard, basil, oregano, red pepper flakes, ½ teaspoon salt, and ½ teaspoon black pepper in the Instant Pot® and whisk to blend. Attach the pressure-cooking lid and turn the valve to Sealing. Press the Pressure Cook button and set the cook time for 5 minutes at high pressure, then press Start.

When the cooking time is up, let the steam release naturally for 5 minutes, then press the Quick Release Button or turn the valve to Venting to quick-release any residual steam. Carefully remove the lid. Stir, then taste and adjust the seasoning with salt and black pepper. The sauce can be stored in an airtight container in the refrigerator for up to 5 days.

2 cups (475 ml) chicken or vegetable stock (pages 270–271 or store-bought)

1 can (28 oz/800 g) crushed tomatoes

½ cup (115 g) tomato paste

¼ cup (60 ml) olive oil

1 tablespoon Dijon mustard

1 tablespoon chopped fresh basil

2 teaspoons dried oregano

1 teaspoon red pepper flakes, plus more if desired

Kosher salt and freshly ground black pepper

Rice

Cooking rice can be a daunting task, not to mention a long one, when it comes to brown and wild rice varieties. This method is speedy and can be easily adjusted for your texture preference. If you like softer rice, add ¼ cup (60 ml) more water to the pot at the beginning, or let the steam release naturally for a longer period of time.

MAKES ABOUT 4 CUPS (640 G)

WHITE RICE

2 cups (400 g) long-grain white rice, such as jasmine or basmati

½ teaspoon kosher salt

Combine the rice, salt, and 2 cups (475 ml) water in the Instant Pot®. Lock the lid in place and turn the valve to Sealing. Press the Pressure Cook button and set the cook time for 4 minutes at high pressure.

Let the steam release naturally for 10 minutes, then turn the valve to Venting to quick-release any residual steam. Carefully remove the lid and fluff the rice with a fork. If the rice feels too moist, place a dish towel over the pot and let the moisture evaporate for a few minutes longer, until your desired texture is reached.

MAKES ABOUT 4 CUPS (800 G)

BROWN RICE

2 cups (370 g) long-grain brown rice

½ teaspoon kosher salt

Combine the rice, salt, and 2½ cups (600 ml) water in the Instant Pot®. Lock the lid in place and turn the valve to Sealing. Press the Pressure Cook button and set the cook time for 15 minutes at high pressure.

Let the steam release naturally for 10 minutes, then turn the valve to Venting to quick-release any residual steam. Carefully remove the lid and fluff the rice with a fork. If the rice feels too moist, place a dish towel over the pot and let the moisture evaporate for a few minutes longer, until your desired texture is reached.

MAKES ABOUT 3 CUPS (330 G)

QUINOA

1 cup (180 g) quinoa (red, white, or mixed), rinsed

1¼ cups (300 ml) water

½ teaspoon kosher salt

Combine the quinoa, water, and salt in the Instant Pot®. Attach the pressure-cooking lid and turn the valve to Sealing. Press the Pressure Cook button and set the cook time for 1 minute at high pressure, then press Start.

When the cooking time is up, let the steam release naturally for 10 minutes, then press the Quick Release Button or turn the valve to Venting to quick-release any residual steam. Carefully remove the lid and fluff the quinoa with a fork.

MAKES ABOUT 3 CUPS (550 G)

FARRO

1 cup (210 g) farro

1 cup (240 ml) water

½ teaspoon kosher salt

Combine the farro, water, and salt in the Instant Pot®. Attach the pressure-cooking lid and turn the valve to Sealing. Press the Pressure Cook button and set the cook time for 10 minutes at high pressure, then press Start.

When the cooking time is up, let the steam release naturally for 10 minutes, then press the Quick Release Button or turn the valve to Venting to quick-release any residual steam.

MAKES ABOUT 3 CUPS (475 G)

PEARL BARLEY

1 cup (200 g) pearl barley

2½ cups (600 ml) water

½ teaspoon kosher salt

Combine the barley, water, and salt in the Instant Pot®. Attach the pressure-cooking lid and turn the valve to Sealing. Press the Pressure Cook button and set the cook time for 20 minutes at high pressure for a chewier texture and up to 22 minutes for a soft texture, then press Start.

When the cooking time is up, let the steam release naturally for 10 minutes, then press the Quick Release Button or turn the valve to Venting to quick-release any residual steam.

Beans, Chickpeas & Lentils

While canned beans are very convenient, they just don't taste the same as the home-cooked kind. Last-minute cooks, rejoice! The absolute best part about cooking beans this way is that they don't need to be soaked ahead of time. For bigger batches, double the quantities of beans, water, and oil.

MAKES ABOUT 3 CUPS (540 G) COOKED BEANS

BASIC BEANS

1 cup (7 oz/200 g) dried beans, chickpeas, or lentils, picked over and rinsed

4 cups (1 L) water

1 teaspoon canola oil

1–2 teaspoons kosher salt

Combine the beans, water, oil, and salt to taste in the Instant Pot®. Lock the lid in place and turn the valve to Sealing. Press the Beans/Chili button and set the cook time for the cooking time designated in the chart below at high pressure.

Let the steam release naturally, or for at least 15 minutes, before turning the valve to Venting to quick-release any residual steam. When the steam stops, carefully remove the lid. Drain the beans in a colander set in the sink.

TIP *If you would prefer to soak your beans, soak 1 cup of beans in 4 cups (1 L) water for at least 4 hours or up to 12 hours, then cook them in their soaking water. They will cook in about half the time needed for unsoaked beans.*

COOKING TIMES FOR UNSOAKED BEANS

Green, Brown, or Black Lentils	15 minutes
Black Beans	20–25 minutes
Navy Beans	20–25 minutes
Pinto Beans	20–25 minutes
Cannellini Beans	35–40 minutes
Chickpeas	35–40 minutes

SERVES 8–10

MAPLE BAKED BEANS

3 slices bacon, diced

1 yellow onion, chopped

2 cups (400 g) dried navy beans or other small white beans, rinsed and picked over

6 cups (1.5 L) water

Kosher salt

1 tablespoon canola oil

¼ cup (60 ml) cider vinegar

2 tablespoons tomato paste

1 teaspoon dry mustard

⅛ teaspoon cayenne pepper

⅓ cup (75 ml) maple syrup

Select Sauté on the Instant Pot® and cook the bacon until the fat begins to render, 2–3 minutes. Stir in the onion and cook until the bacon and onion are limp, about 3 minutes. Add the beans, water, and a pinch of salt. Drizzle the oil over the liquid; do not stir. Lock the lid in place and turn the valve to Sealing. Press the Beans/Chili button and set the cook time for 25 minutes at high pressure.

In a small bowl, stir together the vinegar, tomato paste, mustard, and cayenne, then stir in the maple syrup. Set aside.

Let the steam release naturally, or for at least 15 minutes, before turning the valve to Venting to quick-release any residual steam. When the steam stops, carefully remove the lid. Press the Cancel button to reset the program.

Press the Sauté button, pour the maple syrup mixture into the pot, and cook, stirring frequently so the beans don't stick, until the beans are tender and the sauce is thickened, 12–15 minutes. Serve right away, or let cool, cover, and refrigerate for up to 4 days (the beans will thicken as they stand). Reheat before serving.

NOTE *Even though using a pressure cooker cuts out the need to cook these beans for hours, they will still have a distinctive smoky-sweet flavor that comes from long cooking. Use real maple syrup for the best flavor.*

Homemade Stock

We can probably all agree that any dish made with homemade stock is better than those made with the store-bought version. While meat stocks used to require the better part of an afternoon to prepare, with this method you can shave hours off that time and eliminate the need to keep an eye on the stockpot. Store extra in the freezer to have on hand for quick weeknight meals.

MAKES ABOUT 3 QT (3 L)

CHICKEN STOCK

3 lb (1.4 kg) chicken parts (drumsticks, backs, necks, and wings)

2 teaspoons kosher salt

1 tablespoon olive oil

1 yellow onion, roughly chopped

2 carrots, cut into 3-inch (7.5-cm) pieces

12 cups (3 L) water

2 cloves garlic, smashed

3 fresh flat-leaf parsley sprigs

3 fresh thyme sprigs

2 bay leaves

¼ teaspoon whole black peppercorns

Season the chicken with the salt. Select Sauté on the Instant Pot®, press Start, and heat the oil. Working in batches, brown the chicken on both sides, about 3 minutes per side. Transfer to a plate as browned. Add the onion and carrots to the pot and cook, stirring occasionally, until browned, about 2 minutes. Add 1 cup (240 ml) of the water and bring to a simmer, stirring occasionally with a wooden spoon to scrape up any browned bits. Press the Cancel button to reset the program.

Return the chicken to the pot and add the garlic, parsley, thyme, bay leaves, peppercorns, and the remaining 11 cups (2.75 L) water, ensuring that the pot is no more than two-thirds full. Attach the pressure-cooking lid and turn the valve to Sealing. Press the Pressure Cook button and set the cook time for 60 minutes at high pressure, then press Start.

When the cooking time is up, let the steam release naturally, or for at least 20 minutes, then press the Quick Release Button or turn the valve to Venting to quick-release any residual steam. Carefully remove the lid and pour the stock through a fine-mesh sieve into a large bowl. Discard the solids. If desired, pour the stock into a fat separator to remove the fat (or chill the stock in the refrigerator until the fat solidifies on top, then remove it with a spoon). Let the stock cool completely, then ladle into airtight storage containers. Refrigerate for up to 4 days or freeze for up to 3 months

TIP *You can skip the browning step and put all of the raw ingredients into the pot instead, but keep in mind that the flavor will be milder.*

MAKES ABOUT 2½ QT (2.5 L)

VEGETABLE STOCK

Combine all the ingredients in the Instant Pot®, ensuring when you add the water that the pot is no more than two-thirds full. Attach the pressure-cooking lid and turn the valve to Sealing. Press the Pressure Cook button and set the cook time for 30 minutes at high pressure, then press Start.

When the cooking time is up, let the steam release naturally, or for at least 20 minutes, then press the Quick Release Button or turn the valve to Venting to quick-release any residual steam. Carefully remove the lid and pour the stock through a fine-mesh sieve into a large bowl. Discard the solids. Let the stock cool completely, then ladle into airtight storage containers. Refrigerate for up to 4 days or freeze for up to 3 months.

2 yellow onions, roughly chopped

2 ribs celery, roughly chopped

2 carrots, roughly chopped

3 oz (90 g) white button or cremini mushrooms, roughly sliced

4 cloves garlic, smashed

4 fresh flat-leaf parsley sprigs

2 bay leaves

1 teaspoon whole black peppercorns

10 cups (2.5 L) water

MAKES ABOUT 2½ QT (2.5 L)

FISH STOCK

Fish stock is best made with the well-cleaned fish frames, or skeletons, as well as at least one fish head from firm white-fleshed, nonoily fish. Parts from oily, fatty fish, such as salmon, mackerel, or tuna, would give the stock a strong flavor. Rinse all fish skeletons well for the best, purest tasting, stock.

Rinse the cleaned fish parts thoroughly under running cold water. With kitchen scissors, break the spine of each frame into at least 2 pieces. Place the head(s) and frames in a large bowl and add the salt and cool water to cover. Refrigerate for 1 hour, covered. Drain, rinse, and repeat the 1-hour soak without the salt.

Drain the fish pieces and transfer to the Instant Pot®. Add all the remaining ingredients, ensuring when you add the water that the pot is not more than two-thirds full. Lock the lid in place and turn the valve to Sealing. Press the Pressure Cook button and set the cook time for 30 minutes at high pressure.

Let the steam release naturally. Carefully remove the lid. Pour the stock through a fine-mesh sieve into a large bowl. Discard the solids. Let the stock cool completely, then ladle into airtight storage containers. Refrigerator for up to 2 days or freeze for up to 2 months.

3 lb (1.5 kg) fish head(s) and frames from nonoily fish such as flounder, cod, sea bass, or snapper, cleaned

3 tablespoons kosher salt

⅓ cup (80 ml) dry white wine

1 small yellow onion, thinly sliced

1 rib celery, thinly sliced

1 fresh flat-leaf parsley sprig

1 fresh thyme sprig

1 small bay leaf

4–5 peppercorns

8 cups (2 L) water

MAKES ABOUT 2 QT (2 L)

BEEF STOCK

- **3 lb (1.4 kg) beef marrow bones, cracked by a butcher**
- **2 thick slices (about 1 lb/ 450 g) meaty beef shin**
- **2 carrots, roughly chopped**
- **2 ribs celery, roughly chopped**
- **1 large yellow onion, roughly chopped**
- **4 fresh flat-leaf parsley sprigs**
- **1 bay leaf**
- **½ teaspoon whole black peppercorns**
- **8 cups (2 L) water**

Combine all the ingredients in the Instant Pot®, ensuring when you add the water that the pot is no more than two-thirds full. Attach the pressure-cooking lid and turn the valve to Sealing. Press the Pressure Cook button and set the cook time for 2 hours at high pressure, then press Start.

When the cooking time is up, let the steam release naturally, or for at least 20 minutes, then press the Quick Release Button or turn the valve to Venting to quick-release any residual steam. Carefully remove the lid and pour the stock through a fine-mesh sieve into a large bowl. Discard the solids. If desired, pour the stock into a fat separator to remove the fat (or chill the stock in the refrigerator until the fat solidifies on top, then remove it with a spoon). Let the stock cool completely, then ladle into airtight storage containers. Refrigerate for up to 4 days or freeze for up to 3 months.

VARIATION

Bone Broth: *Roast the beef marrowbones for 30–40 minutes in a preheated 450°F (230°C) oven. Add 1–2 tablespoons apple cider vinegar to the pot with the other ingredients and cook a thigh pressure for 3 hours.*

Release the steam naturally. (The bone broth has cooked long enough if the bones crumble when touched and the tendons, cartilage, and connective tissue have dissolved.) Strain and store the broth as directed above.

Polenta

Creamy and hearty, polenta is often a forgotten side dish. It provides a wonderful base for Cajun-Rubbed Pork Tenderloin (page 186) but is also a welcome treat by itself mixed with a bit of butter and cheese. The only whisking required is at the beginning, and then the rest of this method is completely hands off.

MAKES 2½ CUPS (600 ML)

4 cups (1 L) liquid, such as water, whole milk, and/or chicken stock (page 270 or store-bought)

Kosher salt and freshly ground black pepper

1 cup (160 g) polenta

2 tablespoons unsalted butter (optional)

½ cup (60 g) grated Parmesan cheese (optional)

Select Sauté on the Instant Pot®. Add the liquid and 2 teaspoons salt and bring to a boil. Slowly stream in the polenta, whisking constantly so it does not clump.

Press the Cancel button to reset the program. Lock the lid in place and turn the valve to Sealing. Press the Pressure Cook button and set the cook time for 8 minutes at high pressure.

Turn the valve to Venting to quick-release the steam. When the steam stops, carefully remove the lid.

Season the polenta to taste with salt and pepper. Stir in the butter and cheese, if using, and serve.

MAKES ABOUT 2 CUPS (500 ML)

SALSA VERDE

Place all of the ingredients along with 1 teaspoon salt in a blender or food processor, and blend until smooth. Taste and add more salt, if desired. If the salsa is too wet, strain out some of the liquid using a fine-mesh sieve set over a measuring cup (this way you can add some liquid back in if it feels too dry). Store in an airtight container in the refrigerator for up to 3 days.

1 bunch cilantro stems (leaves reserved for garnish)

6 tomatillos, husked, rinsed, and quartered

1 small white onion, roughly chopped

1 jalapeño chile, seeded and roughly chopped

Juice of 1 lime

Kosher salt

MAKES ABOUT 1 CUP (250 ML)

CHILE CREMA

Put the reserved chiles and cooking liquid from Sweet & Spicy Mexican Chile Carnitas (page 178) in a blender or food processor, and blend until smooth. Add 3 tablespoons of this chile sauce and ½ teaspoon salt to the sour cream, and stir to combine. Taste and add more sauce and/or salt until the desired flavor is achieved. Store in an airtight container in the refrigerator for up to 3 days.

Reserved chiles and cooking liquid from carnitas (see recipe page 178)

Kosher salt

1 cup (225 g) sour cream

MAKES ABOUT ½ CUP (125 G)

QUICK-PICKLED RED ONION

Put the onions in a medium bowl, add a pinch of salt, and cover with white wine vinegar. The onion will be ready in about 15 minutes. Store in an airtight container in the refrigerator for up to 2 weeks.

1 red onion, thinly sliced

Kosher salt

White wine vinegar

Strawberry Jam

This delicious, kid-friendly jam is made from only two ingredients and does not require any refined sugar. You can sterilize your jars directly in the Instant Pot® first, and then make the jam in a matter of minutes. If you have extra strawberries on hand, double the recipe—or try other berries when they're in season.

MAKES TWO 8-OZ (240-ML) JARS

2 cups (475 ml) water

¾ cup (270 g) regular honey or raw honey

1 lb (450 g) strawberries, hulled and sliced

To sterilize your jam jars, place the steam rack inside the Instant Pot® and add the water. Place two 8-oz (240-ml) jam jars on top of the steam rack. Lock the lid in place and turn the valve to Sealing. Press the Sterilize button at the normal setting. Turn the valve to Venting to quick-release the steam, remove the lid, and, using tongs or oven mitts, carefully transfer the jam jars to a plate or cutting board. Cover with a dish towel to keep them warm. Discard the water. (If your Instant Pot® does not have a Sterilize button, you can also run jam jars through the hottest setting of your dishwasher, or boil them in a large pot of water.)

Remove the steam rack, select the Sauté button, and add the honey. Cook until the honey is soft enough to stir (cook time will vary depending on whether you use regular or raw honey). Add the strawberries, bring to a boil, and cook, stirring occasionally, for about 3 minutes. Press the Cancel button to reset the program.

Lock the lid in place and turn the valve to Sealing. Press the Pressure Cook button and set the cook time for 3 minutes at high pressure.

Let the steam release naturally and carefully remove the lid. Use a fork to mash the strawberries, or blend until smooth (or still somewhat chunky, if desired) either by transferring the mixture to a blender or using an immersion blender in the pot. If you've used a blender to mash the strawberries, return the jam to the pot. Press the Sauté button and simmer to reduce any excess liquid, stirring occasionally, until the jam is thick enough to coat the back of a spoon, about 5 minutes. Transfer to the sterilized jam jars (using a heatproof jam funnel will help), and let cool completely, uncovered, at room temperature. Once the jam is cooled, cover and store it in the refrigerator for up to 2 weeks.

Chicken Marinades

Chicken is a blank canvas for a myriad of flavors, from fragrant five spice to robust tandoori. Try any of these marinades on boneless, skinless chicken thighs or breasts. Cook boneless thighs at high pressure for 10 minutes and breasts for 4 minutes. (If using bone-in chicken, increase the cooking time to 15 minutes for thighs and 7 minutes for breasts.) Then pair with your favorite rice (page 266), grains (page 267), or beans (page 268).

SERVES 4

FIVE SPICE

FOR THE MARINADE

½ cup (120 ml) freshly squeezed orange juice (from 1 large orange)

2 tablespoons soy sauce, tamari, or coconut aminos

2 tablespoons fish sauce

1 tablespoon Chinese five-spice powder

2 teaspoons sambal oelek (Indonesian red chile paste) or Sriracha

1 teaspoon sugar

2 lb (1 kg) boneless, skinless chicken thighs or breasts

Kosher salt

In a small bowl, mix together the marinade ingredients.

Season the chicken lightly with salt. Place in a shallow pan or baking dish and pour the marinade over the top. Cover with plastic wrap and marinate in the refrigerator for at least 30 minutes and up to 2 hours, turning occasionally to coat.

Add the chicken and marinade to the Instant Pot®. Lock the lid in place and turn the valve to Sealing. Press the Pressure Cook button and set the cook time for 10 minutes (for chicken thighs) or 4 minutes (for chicken breasts) at high pressure. Let the steam release naturally for 10 minutes before turning the valve to Venting to quick-release any residual steam. Carefully remove the lid and use tongs to transfer the chicken to a serving plate.

SERVES 3–4

TANDOORI

FOR THE MARINADE

¾ cup (180 ml) plain whole-milk yogurt

1 teaspoon ground cumin

1 teaspoon ground turmeric

½ teaspoon smoked paprika

½ teaspoon saffron threads

½ teaspoon ground cinnamon

½ teaspoon kosher salt

¼ teaspoon black pepper

1½ lb (700 g) boneless, skinless chicken breasts, cut into 1½-inch (4-cm) cubes

½ cup (120 ml) chicken stock (page 270 or store-bought)

In a small bowl, mix together the marinade ingredients.

Place the chicken in a shallow pan or baking dish and pour the marinade over the top. Cover with plastic wrap and marinate in the refrigerator for at least 1 hour and up to 24 hours, turning occasionally to coat.

Add the chicken, marinade, and stock to the Instant Pot®. Lock the lid in place and turn the valve to Sealing. Press the Pressure Cook button and set the cook time for 4 minutes at high pressure. Let the steam release naturally for 10 minutes before turning the valve to Venting to quick-release any residual steam. Carefully remove the lid and use tongs to transfer the chicken to a serving plate.

SERVES 4

LEMON CHIPOTLE

FOR THE MARINADE

1 tablespoon Dijon mustard

1 tablespoon fresh lemon juice

3 tablespoons olive oil

½ shallot, minced

1 teaspoon minced canned chipotle chiles in adobo, with 1 teaspoon sauce

2 lb (1 kg) boneless, skinless chicken breasts or thighs

Kosher salt and freshly ground black pepper

½ cup (120 ml) chicken stock (page 270 or store-bought)

Chopped fresh basil, for serving

In a small bowl, mix together the marinade ingredients.

Season the chicken generously with salt and pepper. Place in a shallow pan or baking dish and pour the marinade over the top. Cover with plastic wrap and marinate in the refrigerator for at least 30 minutes and up to 2 hours, turning occasionally to coat.

Add the chicken, marinade, and stock to the Instant Pot®. Lock the lid in place and turn the valve to Sealing. Press the Pressure Cook button and set the cook time for 10 minutes (for chicken thighs) or 4 minutes (for chicken breasts) at high pressure. Let the steam release naturally for 10 minutes before turning the valve to Venting to quick-release any residual steam. Carefully remove the lid and use tongs to transfer the chicken and sauce to a serving plate. Sprinkle with basil and serve.

Lemon Curd

If you prefer a perfectly smooth lemon curd, after uncovering the jars and stirring the curd, pass it through a fine-mesh sieve. Enjoy this sweet-tart curd with fresh berries, scones or biscuits, or as a filling for layer cakes or tartlets.

MAKES 4 HALF-PINTS

3 large whole eggs

3 large egg yolks

1 cup (200 g) sugar

1 cup (225 ml) fresh lemon juice

1 tablespoon grated lemon zest

3 tablespoons unsalted butter, melted

1 cup (240 ml) water

In a large bowl, whisk together the whole eggs and egg yolks until blended and smooth. Add the sugar, lemon juice and zest, and butter and whisk until the sugar dissolves. Divide the lemon mixture evenly among four ½-pint canning jars. Screw on the lids.

Pour the water into the Instant Pot® and put the trivet into the pot. Put the jars on the trivet. Lock the lid in place and turn the valve to Sealing. Press the Pressure Cook button and set the cook time for 5 minutes at high pressure.

Let the steam release naturally for 10 minutes, then turn the valve to Venting to quick-release any residual steam. Carefully remove the lid, transfer the jars to a cooling rack, and let cool for 5 minutes.

Remove the jar lids and give the curd a stir. It will look chunky at first but will smooth out as you continue to stir. Serve warm or chilled. To store, re-cover the jars and refrigerate for up to 7 days.

Hot Fudge Sauce

With the Instant Pot®, whipping up this thick, shiny, chocolaty sauce is easy and fast—leaving you plenty of time to gather the vanilla ice cream, whipped cream, and cherries you'll need for a round of classic hot fudge sundaes.

MAKES 3 HALF-PINTS

⅓ cup (80 ml) heavy cream

¾ cup light corn syrup

3 tablespoons unsalted butter

1⅔ cups (10 oz/280 g) semisweet chocolate chips

⅓ cup (30 g) Dutch-process cocoa powder

½ cup (100 g) sugar

2 teaspoons vanilla extract

¼ teaspoon kosher salt

1 cup (240 ml) water

In a saucepan over medium-low heat, whisk together the cream, corn syrup, butter, and chocolate chips until the chocolate and butter melt and the mixture is smooth. Add the cocoa powder, sugar, vanilla, and salt and cook, stirring constantly, until the sugar dissolves and the mixture thickens slightly, about 3 minutes. Remove from the heat and divide evenly among three ½-pint canning jars. Screw on the lids.

Pour the water into the Instant Pot® and put the trivet into the pot. Put the jars on the trivet. Lock the lid in place and turn the valve to Sealing. Press the Pressure Cook button and set the cook time for 15 minutes at high pressure.

Let the steam release naturally for 10 minutes, then turn the valve to Venting to quick-release any residual steam. Carefully remove the lid, transfer the jars to a cooling rack, and let cool for 5 minutes.

Remove the lids and serve warm. To store, re-cover the jars and refrigerate for up to 2 weeks. To reheat the sauce, warm gently in a double boiler or microwave.

Dulce de Leche

Boasting a creamy texture and complex flavor, this Latin American caramel sauce is delicious served over ice cream or yogurt, as a filling for sandwich cookies, folded inside crepes, used as a dip for fresh fruit, or stirred into hot coffee or a milk shake.

MAKES 4 HALF-PINTS

3 cans (14 oz each) sweetened condensed milk

1 tablespoon vanilla paste or vanilla extract

2 cups (475 ml) water

In a large bowl (preferably with a spout), combine the condensed milk and vanilla and stir until the vanilla is evenly distributed. Divide evenly among four ½-pint canning jars. Screw on the lids.

Pour the water into the Instant Pot® and put the trivet into the pot. Put the jars on the trivet. Lock the lid in place and turn the valve to Sealing. Press the Pressure Cook button and set the cook time for 40 minutes at high pressure.

Let the steam release naturally for 10 minutes, then turn the valve to Venting to quick-release any residual steam. Carefully remove the lid, transfer the jars to a cooling rack, and let cool for 5 minutes.

Remove the lids and use warm or at room temperature. To store, re-cover the jars and refrigerate for up to 2 weeks. To return the sauce to a pourable consistency, reheat gently in a double boiler or microwave.

Homemade Yogurt

Making yogurt at home allows you to control the quality of the ingredients and the fermentation time, creating a more nutrient-dense result than store-bought varieties. Plus, it's a blank canvas for a suite of delicious toppings. An instant-read thermometer will be useful here, as well as a little patience, since yogurt needs to cook and set for quite a few hours before it's ready to eat.

MAKES 4 CUPS (1 L) • SERVES 6

8 cups (2 L) whole milk

2 tablespoons plain yogurt

FOR SERVING (OPTIONAL)
Honey, toasted sliced almonds, granola, puffed quinoa, sunflower seeds, toasted coconut flakes, chopped dried fruit, and/or fresh fruit

Pour the milk into the Instant Pot®. Lock the lid in place and turn the valve to Sealing. Press the Yogurt button until the screen says "Boil" and cook until the milk reaches 180°F (82°C), about 25 minutes. Have ready an ice-water bath in the sink. Carefully remove the lid and check the milk temperature with an instant-read thermometer. If it is not 180°F (82°C), press the Cancel button to reset the program, then select Sauté and heat until it reaches 180°F (82°C). Transfer the inner pot to the ice-water bath, then stir the milk until it cools to 110°F (43°C), about 10 minutes. Transfer 1 cup of the milk to a small bowl, whisk in the yogurt until smooth, then return the milk-yogurt mixture to the pot. Whisk until blended.

Return the inner pot to the Instant Pot® housing. Lock the lid in place; the valve can be turned to Sealing or Venting. Press the Cancel button to reset the program, then press the Yogurt button and set the cook time for 10 hours. When the yogurt is ready (the screen will read "Yogt"), carefully remove the lid, use pot holders to lift out the inner pot, cover it with plastic wrap, and refrigerate until the yogurt sets, about 4 hours. Do not stir at this point.

When the yogurt is set, line a large fine-mesh sieve with 4 layers of cheesecloth, place the sieve over a bowl, spoon the yogurt into the sieve, and refrigerate for 2 hours to drain.

To serve, spoon the yogurt into individual bowls and top as desired.

INDEX

THE COMPLETE INSTANT POT® COLLECTION

Conceived and produced by Weldon Owen International
in collaboration with Williams Sonoma, Inc.
3250 Van Ness Avenue, San Francisco, CA 94109

A WELDON OWEN PRODUCTION
PO Box 3088
San Rafael, CA 94912
www.weldonowen.com

Printed in Turkey
10 9 8 7 6 5 4 3 2 1

Library of Congress
Cataloging-in-Publication data is available.

ISBN: 978-1-68188-804-0

WELDON OWEN INTERNATIONAL
CEO Roul Goff
Publisher Roger Shaw
Associate Publisher Amy Marr
Editorial Assistant Jourdan Plautz
VP of Creative Chrissy Kwasnik
Design Support Megan Sinead Harris

Managing Editor Katie Killebrew
VP of Manufacturing Alix Nicholaeff
Production Manager Sam Taylor
Imaging Don Hill

Designer Jean Hwang
Photographer Erin Scott
Food Stylist Lillian Kang
Prop Stylist Claire Mack

ACKKNOWLEDGEMENTS

Weldon Owen wishes to thank the following people
for their generous support in producing this book:
Kris Balloun, Lesley Bruynesteyn, Ivy Manning,
Alexis Mersel, and Elizabeth Parson.